Nationalism in the Twent

Nationalism in the Twenty-First Century

Challenges and Responses

Claire Sutherland

First published 2012 by
PALGRAVE MACMILLAN

Palgrave Macmillan in the UK is an imprint of Macmillan Publishers Limited, registered in England, company number 785998, of Houndmills, Basingstoke, Hampshire RG21 6XS.

Palgrave Macmillan in the US is a division of St Martin's Press LLC, 175 Fifth Avenue, New York, NY 10010.

Palgrave Macmillan is the global academic imprint of the above companies and has companies and representatives throughout the world.

Palgrave® and Macmillan® are registered trademarks in the United States, the United Kingdom, Europe and other countries.

ISBN 978–0–230–22082–9   hardback
ISBN 978–0–230–22083–6   paperback

This book is printed on paper suitable for recycling and made from fully managed and sustained forest sources. Logging, pulping and manufacturing processes are expected to conform to the environmental regulations of the country of origin.

A catalogue record for this book is available from the British Library.

A catalog record for this book is available from the Library of Congress.

10   9   8   7   6   5   4   3   2   1
21   20   19   18   17   16   15   14   13   12

Printed and bound in China

From Victoria Park to Viaduct

Contents

Preface

Nationalist ideology continues to shape global politics today, and yet twenty-first-century nationalism is faced with a unique set of challenges. For example, migration and diaspora create cultural, economic and social networks which now bind people across entire continents, let alone countries. The much-discussed onset of globalisation, together with regional integration, has also pushed governments to revise their nation-building rhetoric. Some nation-builders have reacted to globalisation as a potential threat, while others see it as a significant boost to their country's power and influence. This is important because of the implications for nation-state authority and legitimacy; nation-states seek to square national autonomy with deep involvement in regional alliances, trading networks and international organisations. At the same time, sub-state nationalists continue to compete for people's loyalty and support. Today, nationalists must reconsider the meaning of self-determination, independence, autonomy and sovereignty in an increasingly interconnected world.

The close of the twentieth century saw the unfolding of various forms of transnationalism, which led some to predict the end of the nation-state, while a spike in ethnic conflict and secession following Cold War collapse led others to identify a new rise of nationalism. Neither of these characterisations is very helpful in isolation. This text focuses instead on the interrelationship between nationalism and the 'cosmopolitan challenge', used here to denote a set of trends ranging from migration and the creation of diasporas to the even wider phenomena of transnationalism, regionalisation and globalisation. Rather than argue that this challenge is fundamentally antagonistic to supposedly beleaguered nation-states and marginalised nationalists, the text highlights its actual interplay with nationalism and nation-building, and the ways in which nationalist ideologies have attempted to rise to the cosmopolitan challenge. It does not argue that either nationalist ideology or the nation-state are in decline, but looks instead at how they are adapting to the cosmopolitan challenge.

The multidimensional impact of the cosmopolitan challenge on many individuals is what makes our present era qualitatively different from myriad international exchanges, which went on in past centuries. Cosmopolitanism has therefore been deliberately chosen as a concept with global scope, as opposed to the more limited, cross-border links evoked by the terms 'international' and 'transnational'. Evidently, the cosmopolitan challenge by no means affects all individuals directly or uniformly. But this text argues that it definitely has the potential to influence an identity that many hold dear, namely national identity. Population flows, for instance, have an impact on existing nation-states by shaping perceptions of the national community and its members' sense of belonging. In response, nation-builders may reconfigure or entrench official markers of inclusiveness through migration and citizenship policies, as well as political discourse. Sub-state nationalists react to this by putting forward alternative understandings of nationhood and self-determination. In so doing, they are debating and defining what constitutes the nation. This is important because the current challenge to nationalists and nation-builders is to do this in a way that takes account of and even co-opts aspects of globalisation, regionalisation, transnationalism, migration and diaspora. The text looks at how different manifestations of nationalism and nation-building have responded to each of these phenomena in turn. It concludes that nationalism remains an eminently flexible ideology, which enables it to adapt to the demands of twenty-first-century politics. The cosmopolitan challenge is not insurmountable for contemporary nationalism. On the contrary, it forms part of the story of nationalism's continuing development.

Note

Claire Sutherland would like to thank an anonymous reviewer for their valuable comments on earlier drafts of this text.

List of Abbreviations

AU	African Union
ASEAN	Association of Southeast Asian Nations
BJP	Bharatiya Janata Party
CDU	Christlich Demokratische Union Deutschlands
CSU	Christlich-Soziale Union in Bayern
DRV	Democratic Republic of Vietnam
ECOWAS	Economic Community of West African States
EU	European Union
FDP	Freie Demokratische Partei
ICC	International Criminal Court
ILO	International Labour Organisation
LDC	Least Developed Country
NAFTA	North American Free Trade Agreement
NATO	North Atlantic Treaty Organisation
NEPAD	New Partnership for Africa's Development
OAU	Organisation of African Unity
OSCE	Organisation for Security and Co-operation in Europe
PRC	People's Republic of China
RVN	Republic of Vietnam
SADC	Southern African Development Community
SNP	Scottish National Party
SPD	Sozialdemokratische Partei Deutschlands
UK	United Kingdom
UN	United Nations
UNESCO	United Nations Educational, Scientific and Cultural Organisation
US	United States (of America)
USSR	Union of Soviet Socialist Republics
VCP	Vietnamese Communist Party

Introduction

Since the end of the Cold War, all manner of minority, sub-state, terrorist, democratic, irredentist and post-communist nationalisms have been used as evidence of a phenomenon generically termed 'the rise of nationalism'. Some have resulted in violent and bloody conflicts, as in the break-up of Yugoslavia, while others have had an impact on well-established democracies like the United Kingdom, where in 2007 nationalist parties came to power in Scotland (a position spectacularly consolidated in 2011) and in Wales (as junior coalition partner for four years). At the same time, however, the widely anticipated decline of the nation-state in the face of globalisation does not seem to have materialised (Ohmae 1996). Interpreting the principle of national self-determination to mean different degrees of autonomy, or sovereignty, is one pragmatic response to the evolution of globalisation and regional governance, of which the European Union is the most advanced example. Alan Milward (1994, 3) showed the European Community to have been the 'buttress [...] of the nation-state's post-war construction', and nation-states still rely on the returns of region-alisation for nation-building. However, contemporary sub-state national-ists in the likes of Scotland and Catalonia also use the process of regional integration to support demands for greater autonomy from precisely those nation-states. This is just one example of how nation-states and nationalist movements are responding to the current political context, which is differ-ent to that faced by nineteenth and even twentieth-century nationalists. Regionalisation, in turn, is one among a range of contemporary phenomena which can be broadly termed the cosmopolitan challenge, and which exist in creative tension with both sub-state nationalism and nation-building. Building on these trends and concepts, this text sets out to explore various aspects of nationalist ideology in the context of twenty-first-century politics.

What is meant by the cosmopolitan challenge? The cosmopolitan challenge is more than an abstract alternative to national loyalties; cosmo-politanism is not merely a utopian vision for doing away with national allegiances and the existing nation-state system. Instead, the cosmopolitan challenge is used here to denote a range of pressing issues confronting contemporary nation-states and nationalist movements alike, including globalisation, regionalisation, transnationalism, migration and diaspora.

1

These five components of the cosmopolitan challenge are interconnected. To begin with, migration denotes the movement of peoples. This could be for any number of reasons, including work, rejoining family members, claiming asylum or taking refuge abroad. The destination country will consider migrants to be legal or illegal, depending on how they have entered the country and the system of visas, quotas and other legislation in place. Migration is an important aspect of the cosmopolitan challenge for nationalist ideology because the relationship between migrants and the national construct must be managed. Governments will therefore set parameters as to how migrants should 'integrate' into the 'host' society through naturalisation procedures, required language competence, citizenship tests and so on. Nation-builders will decide how inclusive to make their national construct and accordingly erect higher or lower barriers to belonging. Official attitudes towards migrants are thus a good way of gauging the openness or otherwise of a nation-state to new citizens.

Turning to diaspora, this denotes a group of migrants who share a common bond to the homeland they or their forebears left behind. That is, the members of a diaspora will be migrants or their descendants. Not all migrants belong to a diaspora, however, because they might not identify with their country of (ancestral) origin. Neither can we assume that a diaspora represents a homogenous group. On the contrary, we can detect 'the presence of both cosmopolitan anti-nationalists and reactionary ethno-nationalists within diasporas' (Vertovec 2009, 11). Members of a diaspora will feel and express their sense of belonging to the homeland in different ways, be it through upholding its customs and cultural traditions, some form of political activism, or economic solidarity in providing remittances and other types of financial support. They will have other identities, including perhaps several national allegiances. With regard to contemporary nation-building, the growing number of countries that allow dual citizenship testifies to a gradual acceptance of 'divided loyalties', not least in order to ease the flow of remittances and investment. The Philippines, Egypt and the Dominican Republic are just some examples of economies heavily dependent on remittances. Countries like India and Vietnam have also begun courting their respective diaspora communities in recent decades with rights short of citizenship (Barabantseva & Sutherland 2011). Nation-states' developing relationship with their respective diasporas suggests that they are looking beyond their own territorial boundaries to draw those they deem co-nationals into a new sphere of influence. This aspect of the cosmopolitan challenge has resulted in nation-states playing an active role in 'reconfiguring traditional understandings of sovereignty, nation and citizenship' (Levitt & De la Dehesa, cited in Vertovec 2009, 97). On the other hand, possible disadvantages of 'hosting' a diaspora from the point of view of nation-states include uncertainty surrounding military service and readiness to defend the nation in times of crisis, more diffuse concerns about (inter)national security and stability, and worries about diaspora members' willingness to engage fully with their country of residence by actively contributing to its culture and society. As we shall see in Chapter 5, this rests on the problematic assumption that either citizenship or diaspora identities necessarily reflect a clear sense of commitment and solidarity to a single, specific community.

The concept of transnationalism encompasses migration, diaspora and much more, from complex trade routes and capital flows, through a reconceptualisation of place away from a clear territorial frame, to a concomitant growth in alternative social formations, virtual communities, multiple identities and the like. Transnationalism, as distinct from international exchanges between states, refers to the myriad 'sustained linkages and ongoing exchanges among non-state actors based across national borders – businesses, non-government organisations, and individuals sharing the same interests' (Vertovec 2009, 3). Although these linkages have the potential to introduce multiplicity and complexity into national configurations and allegiances, they can also be used to underpin more conventional forms of nation-building and sub-state nationalism. For example, as discussed in Chapter 3, the advocacy, money and influence of some among the Indian diaspora have helped support so-called *Hindutva* nationalism in India, while sections of the Tamil diaspora long supported a Tamil autonomous zone within the majority Sinhalese Sri Lanka. In sum, the concept of transnationalism analyses economic, cultural and political flows between and among networks of non-state actors, thereby seeking to capture social formations which criss-cross nation-state boundaries, including migration and diaspora. In turn, the 'transnational connections between social groups represent a key manifestation of globalization' (Vertovec 2009, 3). As its name suggests, globalisation is an even wider-ranging phenomenon than transnationalism, diaspora or migration.

As we shall see in Chapter 6, there are no clear principles regulating the relationship between globalisation, regionalisation and nationalism. Regionalisation and globalisation have been variously interpreted as beneficial or detrimental, not only to each other, but also to nation-states and nationalism more generally. If we follow the zero-sum analysis epitomised in so-called 'Eurosceptic' discourse, namely that member states 'lose' sovereignty as European integration progresses, then regionalisation appears to work against both the survival of nation-states and the aspirations of sub-state nationalists for autonomy. If, on the other hand, we follow the approach of Alan Milward (1994), and indeed that of sub-state nationalists like the Scottish National Party (SNP), then support for European integration can apparently bolster both nation-states' and sub-state nations' capacity for action in a globalising world. Looking beyond the European Union at other forms of regional integration also suggests that regionalisation does not necessarily entail a loss of sovereignty. For example, organisations like the Association of Southeast Asian Nations (ASEAN) and the North American Free Trade Area (NAFTA) are premised on intergovernmental cooperation, which does not mean ceding sovereignty but rather aims to enhance domestic legitimacy, national prosperity and international clout (Sutherland 2009).

Globalisation denotes an increase in the speed and impact of cultural, technological, economic and financial flows that is qualitatively different in scale to the important global exchanges taking place in centuries past through trade and tribute, colonialism and cultural links. With regard to the interplay between globalisation and nationalism, both phenomena are much too wide-ranging to detect either a positive or negative correlation between the two. Some nationalists will rail against globalisation's alleged dilution of their culture and traditions. Others will point to the way in which globalisation can bring prosperity and thereby support both nation-building and nationalist appeals for greater autonomy. One useful way of approaching specific cases is to distinguish between globalisation as a macro-level phenomenon on the one hand and globalism, understood as an ideological response to that phenomenon, on the other (Gamble 2007, 27). This separates the multifaceted process of globalisation from the political project of globalism, thereby enabling a clearer assessment of their respective relationships to nationalism. Together, then, migration, diaspora, transnationalism, regionalisation and globalisation give a sense of the scale of the cosmopolitan challenge. We now turn to our second key concept, namely nationalist ideology.

Ideology

This text is not primarily about nations, or nationalism studies more generally, but rather about contemporary nationalist ideology and its encounter with the cosmopolitan challenge. According to this reading, the challenge is upon us, and the text examines how nationalists and nation-builders are coping with it. This form of cosmopolitanism challenges nationalism to respond to and even incorporate aspects of current global developments, but it does not strip it of 'local colour' for all that. Indeed, the sheer diversity of nationalist ideology is one of its most striking features. This text focuses on contemporary, or 'neo' nationalism (Nairn 1981, 32), but it does not attempt to find either specific or general causal mechanisms to explain nationalism. Rather, it seeks to interpret nation-building and nationalist movements within their unique, twenty-first-century context. The aim is to supplement existing explanatory theories with an interpretive framework that can be applied to a range of contemporary nationalisms, hence the rather summary treatment of nationalism theory in Chapter 1. The text sets out from the premise that nationalism is an ideology, something that tends to be acknowledged in the literature but rarely provides the focus for research (Guibernau 1999, 7; Keating 2001, 28, but see Malešević 2006). The interpretive framework used here is based on four key propositions. Firstly, that nationalism is ubiquitous but manifests itself in myriad ways, making it an important contemporary phenomenon worthy of study. Secondly, that the concept of ideology can help make sense of this diversity and offer insights into the structure and strategy of nationalisms today. Thirdly, that the notion of 'national identity is as much implicated in "banal nationalism" as in "hot nationalism"' (Reicher & Hopkins 2001, 101), so we should also consider cases that are neither extreme nor violent as expressions of nationalist ideology. Fourthly, that ideology is a useful concept for accessing the meaning, though not the origins, of nationalism. Accordingly, this text is not interested in examining the roots of a nationalist movement, but rather its contemporary construction: 'There is a case for saying that nationalism is, above all, an ideology of the first person plural. The crucial question relating to national identity is how the national "we" is constructed and what is meant by such construction' (Billig 1995, 70).

Ideology can be defined as a set of principles combined with a strategic plan of action for putting them into practice. However, it could be argued that a good number of nationalist variants are so strategic or opportunistic as to have lost sight of their core principles. Michael Freeden (1998, 765) nevertheless answers the central question posed in his article 'Is Nationalism a Distinct Ideology?' with a 'yes', and seeks to confirm that nationalism continues to be a distinct, determinate category of ideology in contemporary politics. His account of 'thick' and 'thin' ideologies is illuminating, since it makes a clear distinction between core and peripheral ideological concepts. Freeden defines a thick ideology as one 'containing particular interpretations and configurations of all the major political concepts attached to a general plan of public policy that a specific society requires' (Freeden 1998, 750). A thick ideology therefore consists of a complete set of principles that can be applied to problem-solving in all policy areas, providing solutions that are recognisably in keeping with the world-view in question. A thin-centred ideology, on the other hand, leaves conceptual vacuums. It does not provide 'chains of ideas [...] stretching from the general to the practical, from the core to the periphery' (Freeden 1998, 750). According to Freeden (1998, 750), nationalism is a thin-centred ideology, as it has few immutable characteristics beyond that of prioritising the nation. Freeden's approach also helps to account for the variety of nationalist forms, because each interprets the core principle of prioritising the nation differently according to a wide range of factors; from the colonial legacy, through cultural norms, to the national status quo and the potential for ethnic conflict.

Ideology is a very useful concept for analysing nationalism because it combines the principles of a coherent world-view with a practical strategy for realising abstract goals. An approach to nationalism based on ideology posits that all nationalists share a core commitment to prioritising national loyalty and legitimacy, but also provides a framework for distinguishing between the principle and practice of different forms of nationalism and nation-building. That is, it helps to categorise the concepts that are core and peripheral to nationalist ideology. Accordingly, Freeden's understanding of ideologies is adopted here;

> [Ideologies] prioritize certain concepts over others, and certain meanings of each concept over other meanings. The external manifestation of this thought practice is a unique conceptual configuration that competes over its legitimacy with other conceptual configurations.
>
> (Freeden 2000, 307)

The notion of conceptual configurations points towards the empirical study of ideology as a construct, and chimes with Michael Billig's definition of nationalism, cited above, as the construction of the national 'we'. It also incorporates a sense of rival ideologies competing to decontest the meaning of core concepts (Norval 2000). Freeden's understanding of a core ideological principle overlaps with Ernesto Laclau and Chantal Mouffe's

(1985, 112) definition of a nodal point of discourse, which they gloss as a privileged discursive point, or a particularly meaningful and enduring concept from which others are derived. This applies well to nationalism; 'Some unusual discursive formations may tend to be organised around a single and relatively stable nodal point – such as a nationalist discourse that has achieved an unusual degree of predominance and stability' (Smith 1998, 98). Prioritising the nation, however defined, is thus the core principle or nodal point of nationalism. It is crucial in bringing together the diverse strands inherent in each manifestation of nationalist ideology to form a more or less coherent world-view. In other words, the nodal point of nationalism is the nation, which corresponds to the core of nationalist ideology in Freeden's terms (Sutherland 2005a). This is what all forms of nationalism have in common, and is a useful way to identify them for purposes of comparison. Positing the nation as nodal to nationalist ideology is also one way of capturing nationalist parties and movements which may not self-identify as such (Sutherland 2001). For instance, the concept of *Heimat*, or homeland, can be understood to be a nodal point of the Bavarian Christlich-Soziale Union's (CSU) ideology equivalent to the nation, as discussed further in Chapter 4 (Sutherland 2001).

Focusing on the core principle of prioritising the nation by achieving a degree of national self-determination or preserving nation-state sovereignty provides a reference point for studying various nationalist ideologies and their evolution. Accordingly, this text also looks in some detail at nation-building, defined here as official, state-led nationalism. Nation-builders and neo-nationalists alike are part of a constant struggle to establish their ideology as dominant. Ironically, they celebrate the moment at which their ideology becomes 'banal' (Billig 1995). This is the point at which it is generally accepted by a given society until successfully challenged by an alternative world-view. The diversity of contemporary nationalist movements can be traced to different definitions of the nation and understandings of how it should best be represented politically. However, all nationalisms are based on the same fundamental principle of politicising a feeling of national belonging. In a world of nation-states, sub-state nationalist movements attempt to mobilise voters behind their alternative ideological interpretation of the nation. They posit the existence of an 'imagined community' (Anderson 1991), justified by means of 'invented tradition' (Hobsbawm & Ranger 1983), and attempt to mobilise this identity in order to achieve some form of national self-determination. Nation-builders, meanwhile, strive to maintain legitimacy and solidarity within the existing nation-state

(Hobsbawm & Ranger 1983, 13). These two, often conflicting, strands of nationalist ideology show that nationalism may be all-pervasive, but is not an analytically useless concept for all that. Ideology and its agents – governments, political parties and movements – can be used to frame the analysis of all nationalist forms.

Nation-builders strive to maintain or reform the existing link between nation and state, while sub-state or irredentist nationalists aspire to redefine the nation or its status. Ultimately, however, both strands aspire to national self-determination of some sort, ranging from full external and internal sovereignty to limited cultural or political autonomy. The concept of ideology thereby lends itself well to theorising both the adaptability and diversity of contemporary nation-building and nationalist movements, and the following empirical chapters set out to show how some contemporary nationalist ideologies combine a flexible, active political strategy with underlying justifying principles. In sum, the first overall contention of this text is that the huge variation in contemporary forms of nationalism can best be understood in terms of ideology, characterised as a combination of core and peripheral principles. The second contention is that, despite their apparent diversity, contemporary nationalists and nation-builders share the core principle of prioritising the nation and its self-determination, and aspire to some form of autonomy or sovereignty in the face of the cosmopolitan challenge. To quote Michael Freeden (2000, 304) once more; 'To analyse an ideology (as distinct from to participate in formulating one) is to categorise, elucidate and decode the ways in which collectivities in fact think about politics'. Chapter 1 will show that the potential of ideology to illuminate and characterise nationalism has been under-exploited in the theoretical literature. First, however, it is necessary to attempt definitions of nation and nationalism.

Nationalism

Though we are all imbued with the language of nation, nationalism is notorious for its multi-faceted nature and the difficulty of defining its central component, the nation. Most of us have a ready answer to the standard question, 'Where are you from?' that identifies us as members of a national community, or as citizens of a nation-state. Classifying everything from Olympic teams, through statistical surveys, to school history books in national terms most often strikes us as common sense. Yet the nation is also a contested concept (Gallie 1962). That is, neither scholars nor ideologues agree on its meaning. Some define the nation as a 'psychological bond' (Connor 1978, 379) uniting members of a community. Others consider it purely a creature of ideology. Still others confuse the nation and the state, a key distinction discussed below. In specific cases, markers like language, religion and descent are also used to set the boundaries of national belonging. Theorists mostly agree that it is pointless to try to identify an objective 'checklist' of nationhood criteria. Instead, contemporary theorising often centres on questions of identity and ethnicity. The present text, by contrast, analyses nationalism first and foremost as an ideology within the twenty-first-century context. From migration to globalisation, current trends are affecting the evolution of nationalist ideology, and this text explores some specific cases of this process.

It is difficult to treat nationalism as a single phenomenon, given the huge range and number of nationalist movements across the world, each one of them unique. We have seen how the concept of ideology can offer a useful framework for analysing nationalism. This is by no means the prevailing view, however. Benedict Anderson (1991, 5), for one, doubts the usefulness of analysing nationalism as an ideology, arguing that it might better be classified 'with "kinship" and "religion", rather than with "liberalism" or "fascism"'. There is also the danger of incorporating value judgements into distinctions between what is ideological and what is not (Kolakowski 1980, 124; Sutherland 2005a). Accordingly, Craig Calhoun (2007, 9) prefers to call nationalism 'a conceptual framework, a discursive formation, a rhetoric, a structure of loyalties and sentiments' rather than an ideology. Yet this only complicates the analysis by introducing a whole range of new concepts, each requiring its own clarification and justification in order to bring us closer to the nature of nationalism. The concept of ideology, on the other hand, encapsulates both the principle and practice of nationalism, thereby offering a simple and solid basis for empirical enquiry.

The concepts of nation and state are so tightly bound together that they are commonly used interchangeably. The term 'nation-state' sums up how closely the nation is identified with the state as a territorial entity and a reservoir of power. Indeed, the adjective 'national' is often used to describe matters pertaining to the state, as in the phrase 'the national interest'. This is because the nation has become the key means for states to legitimate their power over people and place, and exercise both domestically and internationally recognised authority. Nevertheless, it is crucial to distinguish between these two concepts: the nation refers to the cognitive, legitimating basis for authority, whereas the state embodies the territorial and institutional dimensions of authority. As the primary focus of nationalist ideology, the nation is a way of justifying where borders are drawn and a means of contesting those borders. It serves both to underpin the legitimacy of modern states and the conflicting claims of sub-state nationalists. Therefore, a nation need not have a state, but states need some kind of national construct to legitimate their control. The means of achieving this is through nation-building, understood here as state-led nationalism. Nation-building thereby goes beyond nationalist party ideologies in its aim of legitimating the state itself. Governments of whatever stripe are the key actors in nation-building, whereas a whole range of movements may claim to represent sub-state or irredentist nationalism, from inclusive democratic parties to neo-fascist or terrorist organisations.

The link between popular sovereignty, the nation and state legitimacy is now often taken for granted in 'helping people to imagine the world as composed of sovereign nation-states' (Calhoun 2007, 8). This conceptual triad is not a given, however. Feudal and imperial forms of government preceded today's so-called 'Westphalian system', and scholars are also exploring alternative ways of organising the political communities of the future (Archibugi 2003; Kostakopoulou 2008). The increasing use of the term 'post-national' in scholarly discourse also seems to suggest that nations and nationalism are being transcended. Prominent advocates of post-national politics, such as the philosopher Jürgen Habermas (2003, 193), argue for a form of 'constitutional patriotism' whereby national loyalty is replaced by an allegiance to democratic values (although the people, or *demos,* may yet be contained within a state). Others go further in arguing that it is time to move on 'from a nation-state definition of society and politics to a cosmopolitan outlook' (Beck & Sznaider 2010 [2006], 382). Still others wish to see global solidarity derived from shared human rights, or even a world democratic order (Archibugi 2003; Held 1995). This last is certainly a noble ideal, but it requires a common basis of rights and values, which is far from undisputed. The 'Asian values' debate, for instance, has revolved around the argument that existing human rights declarations are not necessarily universal, and that achieving a truly global consensus would be neither possible nor desirable (Sutherland 2006). The present text is not post-national in its orientation, because it does not seek to transcend nationalism or nation-building analytically. Instead, it aims to explore precisely how these ideologies respond to the cosmopolitan challenge, leading us to the next key term of cosmopolitanism.

Cosmopolitanism

The word cosmopolitan derives from the Greek term *cosmos*, or universe, and *polis*, or city. In the small-scale democracies, or city-states, of Ancient Greece, early cosmopolitans sought to undermine the boundaries of the *polis*. The concept is also strongly associated with Immanuel Kant, who argued for an individual's right to hospitality when travelling abroad (for an overview of the conceptual history of cosmopolitanism, see Axtmann 2011; Delanty 2009; Harvey 2009; Kostakopoulou 2008). In the social sciences, the study of cosmopolitanism experienced a revival at the turn of the twenty-first century (Glick-Schiller 2010), and this text is concerned with its contemporary manifestations. Like nationalism, the concept of cosmopolitanism covers a wide variety of phenomena today, which can be broadly divided into its cultural, political and ethical dimensions. Of these, the cultural cosmopolitan is perhaps the most readily recognisable, as embodied in the men and women of means, who travel the globe for work and play. One should not be too quick to associate this kind of cosmopolitan only with professional or educated classes, however, since migrant workers taking on menial jobs also build up transnational networks through diaspora communities, remittances and a concomitant hybrid culture (Werbner 1999). Politically, cosmopolitan democracy demands supranational institutions capable of tackling and managing global issues, with or without the coexistence of state governance (Archibugi 2003; Held 1995). Finally, ethical cosmopolitanism aspires to achieve a worldwide standard of human rights based on common values, and to tackle social disparities on a global scale (Guibernau 2007, 159). Examples of cosmopolitanism's normative impact would include embracing the politics of difference within nation-states, or looking beyond state-based governance to envision global systems of rights and justice. Such views need not be directed towards a global 'imagined community' (Anderson 1991) to replace the nation, even though the cosmopolitan outlook certainly transcends nation-state boundaries. Neither must these different strands of cosmopolitanism overlap, or even pursue the same goals. Ethical cosmopolitans, for instance, tend to emphasise what people have in common, whereas cultural cosmopolitans highlight their diversity. For the purposes of the present text, it is important to look at some of the consequences of a cosmopolitan perspective for how we understand the nation.

In his book *Cosmopolitanism and the Geographies of Freedom* (2009), David Harvey surveys a number of so-called 'adjectival cosmopolitanisms' that all attempt to reconcile 'respect for local differences with compelling universal principles' (Harvey 2009, 114). These include the 'rooted cosmopolitanism' and 'cosmopolitan patriotism' put forward by Anthony Appiah (1998, 2006), which echo Ulf Hannerz's view that 'home is not necessarily a place where cosmopolitanism is in exile' (cited in Harvey 2009, 169). Though keen to avoid essentialising the concept of culture, Appiah argues that local loyalties are a necessary springboard for pursuing universal goals, if these are to be historically informed and respectful of diversity. In other words, the multiculturalism explored in Chapter 3 is an important basis for Appiah's approach. David Harvey, on the other hand, sees in this and other cosmopolitan projects the need to convert those who do not conform, to denounce violence and fundamentalism in the name of recognition and tolerance, and thereby run the risk of sliding into the very forms of chauvinism and exclusionary nationalism they seek to condemn (Harvey 2009, 119). According to Harvey, simplistic constructions of the 'Other' writ large, which are such a potent part of nationalist ideology, are partly to blame here. For instance, both former United States president George W. Bush's depiction of an 'Axis of Evil', and the British Labour government's use of a diffuse terrorist threat to link conflict in Afghanistan with security on Britain's streets, created an evil 'Other' designed to foster international solidarity and support for foreign wars. Indeed, the so-called 'coalition of the willing' and the 'war against terror' could also be read as a form of ethical cosmopolitanism long championed by the United States in its self-professed role as a beacon of liberty for the world (Billig 1995, 90; Harvey 2009, 8). At the same time, however, this cosmopolitan conceit is built around nation-states as unitary, unified entities that can allegedly be rendered more secure through interstate warfare. In such cases, then, the demands of nation-building coincide with appeals to shared, cosmopolitan values.

States' continuous need for nation-building demonstrates that notions of belonging are never cemented and secure; maintaining a sense of national solidarity in order to support nation-state legitimacy is an ongoing process. For instance, soldier and civilian morale must be boosted with assurances that the country's cause is right and good, and even the most patriotic citizen's loyalty can be eroded if the state continually disappoints or fails to deliver. To take another example, government appeals for individual sacrifices during an economic downturn are routinely justified on grounds of national solidarity, but this is not always a winning argument. In the wake of the global, so-called 'credit crunch' of 2009–10, strikes and demonstrations greeted news of large government cuts in Greece and Spain, which were badly hit by economic mismanagement and unemployment respectively. The scaled-down political cosmopolitanism embodied in the European currency union, one of the world's most advanced experiments in supranational solidarity, was also put under severe strain by the financial crisis. This directly pitted the need for member states to stand together in defending the single currency against public opinion hostile to transnational bail-outs. In the face of domestic opposition, for example, Germany's government eventually opted to contribute to supporting Greece, Ireland and Portugal's flailing economies. Although the issue was often presented in the German media as a fundamentally irreconcilable conflict, the strength and stability of the euro currency was as much in the national interest of each Eurozone member as that of the group as a whole (*Economist* 2010b, 48). Nevertheless, a zero-sum analysis organised around the opposition of nation-state sovereignty and supranational solidarity remained dominant, illustrating one way in which contemporary nationalism and cosmopolitanism collide in practice. How else do the cosmopolitan and the national combine?

As a geographer, David Harvey (2009) is concerned with the concepts of space, place and territory, and how they ground our understanding of everything from local knowledge, through living in our homeland, to a more inchoate sense of national belonging. He distinguishes between absolute space, exemplified by border posts and the idea of sovereign states as bounded power containers, and spaces that are partly defined through their relationship to periods in time, emotions, symbols and other associations (Harvey 2009, 250; see also Closs Stephens 2010). Harvey is interested in what links territory as a basis of political organisation with the emotional power invested in people's sense of place. He also thinks about how people's loyalties are most effectively mobilised across these dimensions: 'While regions, states, or nations may appear at one level as mere imagined abstractions, the sense of a territorial bond and of an affective loyalty to it has enormous political significance' (Harvey 2009, 171). This suggests that territorial bonds continue to shape both individual allegiances and state practices, without necessarily excluding the cosmopolitan dimension. There are scholars, like Martha Nussbaum (1996), who urge individuals to 'construct relational loyalties with everyone living on planet earth' (Harvey 2009, 163) by imagining a set of concentric circles around the self, family, community, nation and finally all of humanity. However, this approach seems to employ the same notions of bounded communities, territories and regions that an analysis of contemporary nation-building as flexible, porous and open to the cosmopolitan challenge seeks to transcend (Sutherland 2010, 22). Thinking about nations in territorial terms may make them easier to grasp, but it can also distract us from the many other markings of belonging – including myths of common descent, hostile constructions of the 'Other', heroic sacrifice and sporting symbolism – which all serve to bind people to their nation. Nation-building is also premised on enforcing borders, and the sort of policing and passport checking that are relatively recent innovations. Yet the main thrust of the cosmopolitan challenge lies precisely in confronting nationalism with the oft-divided loyalties of diaspora communities, with how to integrate migrants and other transnational flows, and with how to respond to regionalisation and globalisation. This questions the assumption that state sovereignty simply derives from controlling territory, when information, trade and population flows pierce state borders at every moment of the day or night. These flows do not magically make borders disappear, because borders continue to have life-changing meaning for the identity and status of asylum seekers, so-called illegal immigrants and irredentist movements among others. However, the increasing porosity of borders suggests the need for a reappraisal of territorial boundaries and how these relate to wider, multidimensional understandings of belonging related to cosmopolitanism. An analysis in terms of concentric circles or other bounded metaphors does not do justice to these complex networks of criss-crossing population flows and transnational allegiances (Sutherland 2010, 22). By contrast, an analysis of nationalism within the context of the cosmopolitan challenge incorporates some of these dynamics.

As discussed above, some critical studies of cosmopolitanism have moved away from its universalist tradition as a commitment to a global community of human beings, in order to locate it in a more 'rooted', particularist philosophical tradition (Robbins 1998, 1). Gerard Delanty (2009, 17), for one, 'reject[s] a purely dichotomous view' of cosmopolitanism and nationalism, pointing out that the 'national has never been entirely national, but has always been embroiled with immanent cosmopolitan orientations'. Mary Kaldor, in turn, while condemning the backwardness and violent exclusivity of much 'new nationalism' and lauding a cosmopolitan alternative, still deems it possible that 'nationalisms could be harnessed to a cosmopolitan politics that reflected the complexity of contemporary conditions' (Kaldor 2004, 176). In a discussion of nationalism and cosmopolitanism published in 2007, Calhoun sees 'tensions between two different ways of imagining the world' (Calhoun 2007, 8). A later intervention, however, suggests that we 'need not simply oppose cosmopolitanism and belonging [...] They can be complements to each other' (Calhoun 2008, 434). Similarly, the interplay between nationalism and the cosmopolitan challenge is not understood here as an inherently conflictual, zero-sum game; it is not a question of two ideologies confronting one another, or 'national identity versus cosmopolitan identity' (Guibernau 2007, 159). Instead, there seems to be potential for complementarity between the two.

Gerard Delanty's wide definition of cosmopolitanism as a transformative process, whereby the dynamics of cultural and societal interaction create the conditions for 'new ways of thinking and acting' (Delanty 2009, 252), provides a useful starting point for exploring the evolving relationship between the cosmopolitan and the national. This approach does not see cosmopolitanism as an 'alternative to globalisation or the nation-state' but rather as an orientation 'embedded [...] in current societal developments' (Delanty 2009, 250). Neither does it regard identities, ideologies or communities as either mutually exclusive or essential categories. People will flit or gravitate between any number of these depending on time and circumstance, and no single label can sum up any individual. This interpretation of identities and cosmopolitanism is also open to – and indeed premised on – transnationalism, since it is composed of cross-cultural encounters. Yet at the same time, the transnational 'signifies the resilience of nations and the state' (Binnie 2003, 599) because the concept of 'transnational' also presupposes the existence of national borders to be crossed. Accordingly, contemporary nationalism is informed by transnationalism both across and within nation-state borders, since multiculturalism also highlights the 'transnationality that is arising inside nation-states' (Beck and Sznaider 2010 [2006], 389). This suggests that the cosmopolitan challenge is not necessarily on course to clash with nationalist ideology.

Methodological Cosmopolitanism

Leading scholars of cosmopolitanism agree that classic, bounded, territorial sovereignty – if it ever existed – is being redefined, and that new legal frameworks are emerging at a supranational level (Beck & Sznaider 2010 [2006]; Glick-Schiller 2010; Held 2010, 54; Soysal 2010). In Beck and Sznaider's view (2010 [2006], 382), it is time to move on 'from a nation-state definition of society and politics to a cosmopolitan outlook [...] and raise some of the key conceptual, methodological, empirical and normative issues that the cosmopolitanisation of reality poses for the social sciences'. This provides one starting point for a critique of state-centred reasoning and policy-making spanning a whole range of ethical, legal and political issues. At the same time, cosmopolitanism refers to the global trend that Beck and Sznaider called 'the cosmopolitanisation of reality'. This approximates to the cosmopolitan challenge as defined here, and sums up the range of pressures confronting contemporary nation-states and nationalists alike. By considering how cosmopolitan theory and methodology can be applied to the social sciences – which have long been structured around nation-states – Beck and Sznaider propose a 'critique of methodological nationalism' (2010 [2006], 382). In so doing, they question the frequent equation of states with societies in both qualitative and quantitative academic analyses, as well as the assumption that nation-states are the 'natural and necessary form of society' (Chernilo 2006, 129). An alternative approach might, for instance, focus on transnational flows rather than bounded communities, or seek to deconstruct 'the unexamined territorial frame of the nation-state' (Harvey 2009, 267). This signals a shift away from nation-states as rather monolithic units of analysis and comparison towards an emphasis on relational, heterogeneous identities, and the transnational dynamics which shape our ever-evolving understanding of the nation-state. In other words; 'Methodological nationalism needs to be transcended because, rather than allowing us to capture the actual complications of the history of the nation-state in modernity, it turns the nation-state into the natural organizing principle of modernity' (Chernilo 2006, 137). According to this view, analysis of change trumps tradition, and emphasis on transformation is deemed to hold greater analytical power than the tendency towards reifying, or essentialising, national identities and interests. Following Delanty (2009, 70), examples of cosmopolitanism as a dynamic process of transformation range from the limited horizon of mutual recognition and a consumption-led appropriation of other cultures, through liberal multiculturalism, to new forms of national unity as a result of contact with the 'Other'. Far from requiring the transcendence of the nation-state, this last form of cosmopolitanism takes place through the nation-state.

The empirical encounter of nationalism and cosmopolitanism can best be grasped, then, by an analytical perspective that looks beyond the boundaries of methodological nationalism. For instance, a cosmopolitan perspective could be helpful in understanding the impact of international communism and capitalism on nation-building in the likes of Germany, China and Vietnam (Delanty 2009, 253; Sutherland 2010). The German nation-state, with its long-standing commitment to European integration, its globalised economy, its experience of reintegrating a German diaspora, and its mixed record in coping with migration and asylum-seekers, is one particularly interesting case for studying nation-building from a cosmopolitan perspective. Beyond the focus on nations and nationalism, the approach also allows for integrated study of wider international dynamics, not only in the field of migration and population flows, but also concerning security questions, international law and intervention, transatlantic relations, economic networks, and trading regimes, among other issues. From this point of view, the nation-state remains the nodal point of analysis where diverse aspects of the cosmopolitan challenge intersect. Globalisation, transnationalism, migration, diaspora and regionalisation all have an impact on the evolution of contemporary nationalism and nation-building through a transformative process summed up as the cosmopolitan challenge. Self-consciously cosmopolitan approaches seek to capture these flows both analytically and methodologically.

As we have seen, cosmopolitan thinking encompasses much more than a utopian vision for doing away with national allegiances or the existing nation-state system. Scholarly work is also well under way to link social enquiry with political theory (Delanty 2009; Harvey 2009; Kostakopoulou 2008). This endeavour has both normative and methodological implications for the way in which we study politics in general and nationalism in particular. By privileging the analysis of cross-border flows rather than stopping at state frontiers, a cosmopolitan approach disrupts the binary distinction between 'home' and 'abroad'. At the conceptual level, a cosmopolitan orientation leaves behind so-called 'methodological nationalism' by also looking beyond borders for the sources and routes of transformation. At the empirical level, it examines 'a process of globe-spanning fundamental social change that is making new theoretical insights possible' (Glick-Schiller 2010, 415). Nations nonetheless remain a key subject for investigation, because cosmopolitan transformations occur through the nation-state empirically and also offer new conceptual perspectives on those nation-states. Some forms of contemporary nationalism will emerge as more multicultural, others as less tolerant and open in response to the cosmopolitan challenge. What is certain is that, as an eminently flexible ideology, nationalism today is reacting and adapting to that challenge, and this text explores some of the ways in which this is taking place. The overall approach is therefore more 'analytical-empirical' than 'normative-political' (Soysal 2010, 409), though a brief word on ethical cosmopolitanism is warranted here.

Ethical Cosmopolitanism

In addition to its role as a conceptual framework and a tool of empirical study, cosmopolitanism has an important normative dimension, which, as we have seen, can be portrayed as a desirable alternative to nationalism. Calhoun (2008, 429) points out that as a 'normative program,' cosmopolitanism 'offers an ethics for globalisation', and charts its rise as an elite project of 'world citizenship' in which particularism, unless it is of Anthony Appiah's liberal, tolerant stripe, is frowned upon. Calhoun opines that '[c]osmopolitanism may be a cultural orientation, but it is never the absence of culture. It is produced and reinforced by belonging to transnational networks and to a community of fellow-cosmopolitans. There are different such communities – academic and corporate and NGO, religious and secular' (Calhoun 2008, 442). This raises the question as to whether, and if so how, allegiance to a cosmopolitan community can co-exist with belonging to a national community. For example, much of the debate and soul-searching surrounding Germany's 'normalisation' following its reunification in 1990 turned on exactly this issue. In normative terms, a sense of solidarity towards other human beings can conceivably go hand in hand with a sense of national belonging. To put it another way, it should be possible to celebrate at once the unity and diversity of peoples, a formula that has often been used within the European Union and other regional organisations (Sutherland 2005b). As Calhoun (2008, 444) reminds us, 'Nationalism was also (at least often) an attempt to reconcile liberty and ethical universalism with felt community. This doesn't mean that we should not seek more cosmopolitan values, cultural knowledge, and styles of interpersonal relations in modern national democracies'. When Calhoun (2008, 444) goes on to pose the seminal question 'Does cosmopolitanism actually underpin effective political solidarity, or only offer an attractive counterbalance to nationalism?', he asks whether it can potentially be reconciled with a form of nationalism that is inclusive, aware of porous borders and shifting populations, and espouses an ever-evolving self-understanding. Setting the parameters of this ideal-type nationalism has exercised many scholars (Canovan 1996; Millar 1995; Kostakopoulou 2006; Tamir 1993;

Viroli 1995). However, Partha Chatterjee (2005, 940) doubts whether it is possible to 'experience the simultaneity of the imagined collective life of the nation without imposing rigid and arbitrary criteria of membership'. This necessarily endangers the ethical cosmopolitan ideal by distinguishing a relatively privileged 'in-group' of citizens from an 'out-group' of non-members. Notwithstanding this sobering warning, a pragmatic combination of cosmopolitanism and nationalism would seem more attainable than jettisoning nationalism altogether in favour of an all-but-unrealisable global community. Contemplating such a community would simply mean constructing a form of nationalism writ large, insofar as it would replicate its need for solidarity, loyalty and legitimation on an impractical and unmanageably broad scale. Neither is the tantalising but radical alternative of uncoupling national markers from citizenship regimes likely to make much real headway in the foreseeable future (Baubock 1994; Kostakopoulou 2008). In the meantime, as Calhoun (2008, 19) puts it, 'We need to be global in part through how we are national'.

On the one hand, cosmopolitanism shines the spotlight on diversity within nation-state boundaries as they are currently recognised. On the other, insofar as it scrutinises cartographic, political and legal boundaries, it reveals their porosity and limited applicability to how people's lives actually map out 'on the ground'. However, to use this spatial metaphor suggests some sort of tiered analysis of territorial levels; namely the local, national, regional and perhaps global. Similar to Martha Nussbaum's approach to cosmopolitanism, this soon encounters its self-imposed limits, and therefore limitations, which critical geographers have done much to illuminate (see Sutherland 2010, 14). By contrast, the wider, more dynamic understanding of cosmopolitanism put forward here attempts to reflect the multifaceted nature of the cosmopolitan challenge by bringing globalisation and regionalisation together with transnationalism, migration and diaspora so as to examine their interplay and the creative challenge to nationalism that they represent. Using a term like the 'cosmopolitan challenge' to cover such a variety of phenomena inevitably masks a great deal of conceptual complexity and debate surrounding seminal questions, including the sources of human solidarity and the best way to organise societies. It may also be criticised for simply serving old wine in new bottles (Welch & Wittlinger 2011). Nevertheless, it serves as useful shorthand for describing the contemporary situation, to which nationalists and nation-builders must respond in order to remain resilient in the current global political climate.

Borderlines are useful concepts only inasmuch as we know they can be disrupted, redrawn, undermined and reorganised in the process of building nation-states and defining their members, interests and policies. A cosmopolitan perspective goes some way towards capturing the complexity of contemporary nation-states and nationalist movements. The empirical concern with the impact of globalisation, regionalisation, migration, diaspora and transnationalism on contemporary nationalist ideology can be usefully brought under the banner of the cosmopolitan challenge, because together these encourage a reassessment of the bordered definition and delimitation of nation-states, or 'methodological nationalism', which the twenty-first-century global context demands. If we look beyond Martha Nussbaum's focus on a single universe of human beings, we encounter a whole range of possibilities: 'adjectival' cosmopolitanisms, 'situated' cosmopolitanisms and cosmopolitanisms, which commingle a global perspective with a national or local level. Writing in 1998, Bruce Robbins already observed that '[f]or better or worse, there is a growing consensus that cosmopolitanism sometimes works together with nationalism rather than in opposition to it' (Robbins 1998, 2). Despite the changes to sovereignty and control over populations wrought by globalisation, states and sub-state movements still use appeals to national solidarity in order to mobilise loyalty and foster legitimacy. This is reason enough to explore the implications of the cosmopolitan challenge for contemporary nationalist ideology.

Structure of the Book

The very flexibility of nationalist ideology does not preclude support for regionalisation, globalisation, migration or another ideology. If nationalism is viewed as a 'thin' ideology capable of being supplemented with a variety of policies and strategies (Freeden 1998), then it is not necessarily incompatible with the cosmopolitan challenge. This is one of the text's core contentions, and provides the basis for discussing a range of contemporary nationalist cases. The first three chapters focus on nationalism theory and nationalist ideology, in order to understand why nationalism is so wide-ranging and how it is combined with other ideologies. The second three chapters of the text look at nationalism from a sub-state, state and supra-state perspective in turn, using the cross-cutting nature of the cosmopolitan challenge as a unifying theme.

The first chapter examines theories of nationalism. A long-standing academic debate between so-called ethno-symbolist and modernist scholars has sought to pinpoint the origins of nations and nationalism. As their moniker suggests, ethno-symbolists trace the roots of nations far back in time to a symbolic ethnic community, whereas modernists variously argue that nations are a product of modern industrialisation, urbanisation or mass communication. Few scholars adopt positions at these extreme poles, however, and most share some common ground. The chapter examines the usefulness of these established theories in explaining contemporary nationalism. Theoretical approaches to contemporary nationalism are also surveyed, and so-called 'neo-nationalisms' (McCrone 1998) are shown to be extremely flexible in their pursuit of legitimacy. Postcolonialism is also addressed in the final section. The chapter concludes that contemporary nationalisms differ from older variants, but that the debate between ethno-symbolists and modernists continues to be relevant today insofar as many nationalists themselves claim to represent an ancient nation, and demand recognition on that basis. National divisions are not immutable but constructed, and yet nationalist ideologues continue to mobilise followers using appeals to primordial symbols.

Chapter 2 explores some of the many variants of nationalism. Just as nationalism can be chauvinistic and exclusionary, so it can be defined more openly by offering a share in a common project. The analytical distinction between 'civic' and 'ethnic' nationalism is used as a starting point for discussing the question of precisely 'who belongs?' Another useful way of thinking about nationalism is to contrast 'hot' nationalism, which may be virulent and violent, with 'banal' nationalism (Billig 1995), understood as taken for granted markers of national loyalty and belonging. The chapter argues that it is a mistake automatically to associate 'hot', or violent nationalism with atavistic ethnic loyalties and long-standing tensions. Such animosities can also be instigated for political ends where previously there was peaceful cohabitation. The chapter discusses a few of the many forms that nationalism has taken in providing the ideological underpinnings for both peaceful and violent struggles to create new nations. It suggests that the reasons for an extreme response must be sought in the degree of economic, political, social and cultural conflict in each case. What emerges from the discussion is that nationalism is an infinitely adaptable, protean ideology which continues to play a central role in politics all over the world.

Chapter 3 explores how nationalism interacts with other ideologies, principally communism and liberal democracy. All forms of nationalism draw on a recent or more distant past in their reading of the current climate, be it the injustices of the Soviet system or pre-modern myths. The ideological cleavage of the Cold War may have largely melted away, but post-communist countries continue to grapple with its legacy. In Eastern Europe, the break-up of the Soviet Union formed the basis for demands formulated in ethnic nationalist terms, which have proved difficult to reconcile with multiculturalism. Estonia provides a case in point. Elsewhere, as in Vietnam, combining nationalism and communism is still a current concern. The chapter also considers whether democracy is compatible with nationalism. It argues that the people, or *demos*, can be equated with the civic nation in an ideal-type nation-state based on the principle of popular sovereignty, but that a concomitant sense of national belonging cannot be taken for granted. The cases of Fiji and India are used for illustration here. The practical strategies and successes of communists and democrats alike often rest on a combination of their core ideological principles with nationalist appeals. The precise form these take will depend on many factors, including economics, leadership, emotion, (perceived) injustice, oppression, conflict and the nature of the 'Other' with which campaigners are confronted.

Chapter 4 focuses on sub-state nationalism. Every variant of nationalism – from terrorist nationalists, through democratic independence movements, to established nation-states – aims to represent the nation through some control of territory and institutions. Minority nationalists seek to reinvent sub-state territories as hubs of social, economic and political activity, as well as an alternative locus of identity to the existing nation-state construct (Keating 2001). Today, these nationalists tend to show flexibility in articulating the link between the individual and the collective. To be successful in achieving greater autonomy, competence in economic matters is also important. Indeed, some use 'emotional-economic' rhetoric in an attempt to channel potentially conflicting sentiments into support for their movement. Contemporary sub-state nationalism therefore often displays a mix of civic and ethnic markers, mobilised differently according to the changing constellations of power at state and international levels. Yet the nationalist ideology of individual parties must be carefully distinguished from a more diffuse sense of national identity, which is not (party) political. With reference to cases spanning three continents, the chapter argues that contemporary sub-state nationalism is capable of adapting evidence of long-standing community links to the current political environment, but also of manipulating and inventing traditions along the way.

Chapter 5 looks at nation-building, or official state nationalism, and its links with citizenship and migration. The chapter argues that a decoupling of the concepts 'nation' and 'state' remains unlikely in contemporary politics, where citizenship legislation still derives from nation-based criteria. Further, some forms of nation-building continue to emphasise ethnic or cultural markers over civic ones, which are usually understood as shared rights, obligations and democratic values. This has important implications for migrants and their wish, or ability, to naturalise as citizens. In practice, contemporary nation-states tend to advocate some cultural homogeneity in the population through integrative measures. Once avowedly multicultural states such as the Netherlands and the United Kingdom, for instance, are now using citizenship and language tests as a response to fears of social fragmentation. The chapter concludes that nationalist principles continue to underpin government legitimacy at the state level, and permeate current debates surrounding immigration and citizenship.

Chapter 6 asks how contemporary nationalism responds to globalisation and regionalisation. Like their nineteenth-century predecessors, contemporary forms of nationalism have evolved in an environment where statehood and sovereignty play a central role. Unlike them, however, they now also have to contend with globalisation and supranational integration. Some states are accustomed to international cooperation. Indeed, nation-builders may even use globalisation's economic potential to bolster their legitimacy through rising living standards, in return for national and labour solidarity (Brown 2000, 87). In turn, regional integration may be deemed to underpin rather than undermine nation-building, as in the case of the Association of Southeast Asian Nations (ASEAN), and in some interpretations of African regionalism. The chapter begins by discussing the evolution of the Southeast Asian region, which, like the nation, is itself a construct. The tensions inherent in reconciling nationalism and supranational integration are then discussed in the context of African regionalism, before returning to Southeast Asia to examine the interplay of nationalism and globalisation there. The chapter looks at different responses to reconciling nationalism and nation-building with supranational cooperation and globalisation, concluding that they can be complementary.

Since the end of the Cold War, the ideological rift which once divided the world has been superseded by the cosmopolitan challenge to nation-states and sub-state nationalisms. Nevertheless, nationalism continues to provide states with a sense of community on the one hand, and helps fuel movements for self-determination on the other. The text concludes that contemporary nationalism is a multi-faceted and evolving ideology, which shapes both state legitimacy and demands for sub-state autonomy. Regardless of whether it is 'hot' or 'banal', primordial or modern, nationalist ideology is here to stay, underlining the need for a differentiated understanding of its many variants. It is a powerful and flexible political instrument which resonates with every individual – the vast majority – who identifies with a particular nation. The distinction between state and sub-state nationalism may become less relevant to a globalising world, in which the locus of power and authority is increasingly fluid and diffuse. The cosmopolitan challenge has prompted reappraisals of nationalist ideology and strategy, but it will not change the fact that nationalism remains a nodal point of twenty-first-century political debate, since the global political map is still established and reconfigured in predominantly nationalist terms.

1

Why the Nation?
Theories of Nationalism

Can any one theory explain nationalism? What are the differences between today's nationalisms and nineteenth and twentieth-century nationalisms?

Definitions of the nation are necessarily linked to different theoretical approaches that attempt to explain nationalism. Theories of nationalism have tended to revolve around the issue of origins, principally through the long-standing academic debate between so-called primordialist, ethno-symbolist and modernist scholars, which turns on the question of how we can date nations and explain how they came about. This controversy is only of indirect relevance here, as the present text is more concerned with how existing nation-states and nationalist movements respond to current challenges. Nonetheless, the question of origins does matter to how nationalists and nation-builders define their respective nations. The point at issue has been summed up as 'do nations have navels?' (Gellner 1996). In other words, were they born of some pre-existing entity, such as an ethnic group, or were they new creations brought about by a unique concatenation of events? Did they spring from the European industrial revolution of the late eighteenth and nineteenth centuries (Gellner 1964; 1983), the exploitation of print technologies by dissatisfied, colonised intelligentsia (Anderson 1991), or the evolution of a form of 'proto-nationalism' from the medieval period onwards (Greenfeld 1993; Llobera 1994)? The first section of the chapter examines the (limited) usefulness of established theories of nationalism for explaining contemporary nationalism.

The second section of the chapter goes on to look at some theoretical approaches to contemporary nationalism. So-called 'neo-nationalisms' (McCrone 1998) are shown to be adaptable in articulating the link between the individual and the collective in the pursuit of legitimacy. The discussion looks at how contemporary nationalisms are different to nineteenth century forms, in order better to understand their response to the cosmopolitan challenge. The chapter's final section then turns to postcolonial theory, and its impact on nationalist ideology. A large proportion of the globe was under European imperial domination by the nineteenth century, with colonial powers only gradually withdrawing between the end of World War I and as late as 1980 for the likes of Zimbabwe (and 1990 for Namibia, controlled by Germany and then South Africa). It is therefore important to investigate colonialism's lasting impact on nationalism in successor states, not only in former colonies, but also former colonising powers. The evolution of post-war attitudes towards British citizenship and identity, for instance, had much to do with migrants arriving in the UK from the Commonwealth. The chapter concludes that contemporary nationalisms do indeed differ from older variants, and not least because of their need to respond to the cosmopolitan challenge. Nevertheless, nationalist ideologues continue to mobilise followers using appeals to primordial symbols or claims to represent an ancient nation, and demand recognition on that basis. This, in turn, can affect their relative openness to newcomers, or their protectiveness of traditions. The nation's putative origins therefore continue to be relevant to contemporary nationalist ideology.

Theories of Nationalism

One ongoing debate within nationalism theory divides ethno-symbolist and modernist scholars. It confronts the claim that nations are rooted in some ancient *ethnie*, symbolic or otherwise, with the contention that nations are a product of the last two centuries of modernisation (cf. Hutchinson & Smith 1996, 40–56). Another key debate juxtaposes ethnic and civic variants of nationalism, and tends to depict them as irreconcilable opposites. In this instance, discussed further in Chapters 2 and 5, a form of nationalism based on exclusive criteria of belonging such as language, religion or blood is contrasted with a nation defined according to state citizenship. These two sets of perspectives, although having the merit of clarity, very much over-simplify possible approaches to explaining and classifying nationalisms. Consequently, the pairings are most usefully seen as labels denoting end points on a scale, rather than as strict dichotomies (Brown 1999, 300). Most scholars would not situate themselves at either pole of these discussions. For instance, in the celebrated debate entitled 'Do nations have navels?', which pitted the 'ethno-symbolist'

Anthony Smith against the 'modernist' Ernest Gellner, each made considerable concessions to the other's position (Gellner 1996, 90).

This section briefly surveys some explanatory theories of nationalism in order to evaluate their relevance to contemporary nationalism and its responses to the cosmopolitan challenge. They are discussed at much greater length in Kellas (1991), Hutchinson (1994), Özkirimli (2000), Lawrence (2005), Ichijo and Uzelac (2005) and Delanty and Kumar (2006), among others. In attempting to account for the rise of nationalism, each theory emphasises different factors as crucial. Michael Mann (1993), for instance, points to the importance of nationalism as a means of mobilising men to aliment the military machines of nineteenth-century states. Benedict Anderson (1991) highlights the influence of what he calls 'print capitalism', understood as the ever-more rapid and wide dissemination of the printed word, in fostering a sense of shared national identity among the nineteenth-century bourgeoisie. Miroslav Hroch (1985) depicts intellectual elites as the force fuelling the growth of national consciousness, dividing the process of nationalist mobilisation into phases, in which first intellectuals, then the bourgeoisie and finally the masses throw their weight behind a political project.

Ernest Gellner (1964; 1983; 1994), who ranks as one of the most influential modernist theorists, characterised nineteenth century European nationalism as a response to the dislocation brought on by the uneven development of industrialisation and urbanisation. He claimed that, by being uprooted from their homes and thrown together in unfamiliar urban surroundings, people were forced to reassess their loyalties in order to recreate a sense of belonging, and did so by identifying with national constructs. Nationalist ideology also had strong mobilising potential among those disappointed by the promise of social mobility and equality in the new urban centres. That is, a frustrated intelligentsia would strive to create its own national arena in which to exercise the power it had been denied under imperial or aristocratic rule. In turn, Gellner's much-quoted aphorism, 'every man is a clerk', referred to a concomitant spread of education in local languages, which helped to foster mass participation in these newly-configured nations (Gellner 1964, 159). The present text's focus on nationalist ideology shares Gellner's concern with elite constructions of the nation, rather than their mass dissemination and consumption. However, contemporary nationalism evolves in very different circumstances to the nineteenth-century European context that Gellner described.

Alongside that of John Armstrong (1982), Walker Connor (1994) and Josep Llobera (1994), among others, the work of Anthony D. Smith has a strong focus on ethnicity as a precursor and foundation of the nation. Smith, who describes his own approach as 'ethno-symbolist', asserts the existence of pre-modern *ethnies* and contends that modern states have been built around ethnic communities. He uses the term *ethnie* to mean 'a named human population with myths of common ancestry, shared histori-cal memories and one or more common elements of culture, including an association with a homeland, and some degree of solidarity, at least among elites' (Smith 1991, 13). According to Smith, the development of a nation from an *ethnie* is equivalent to the transition from a passive community to an active, organised and assertive one: 'We are not talking here about actual descent, much less about race, but about the *senses* of ancestry and identity that people possess' (Smith 1986, 150, emphasis in original). Walker Connor's (1994, 75) definition of the nation as 'a group of people characterised by a myth of common descent' supports Smith's view. These scholars do not dispute that nationalists make selective readings of the past, but argue that the selection must take place within limits set by pre-existing myths, symbols, customs and memories (Smith 1986, 154).

A. D. Smith (1981, 90) has sought to marry his 'ethno-symbolist' approach with a theory of 'ethnic historicism'. This posits an elite in search of a political arena, which it set out to create through the historical derivation of an age-old nation. Like Elie Kedourie and Ernest Gellner before him, Smith has emphasised the central role played by an ambi-tious and frustrated educated elite in fostering nationalist movements, linking the emergence of secular intellectuals to a rejection of religion and the growing popularity of evolutionary theories of human development. Influenced by the rationalism of the Enlightenment, but rebelling against its universalising tendencies, these secular intellectuals found themselves in conflict with the Church and other traditional authorities, which feared for their own legitimacy. Asserting a nation's ancient origins, in turn, was designed to burnish its credentials as an alternative source of legitimacy (Smith 1981, 102). According to Smith (1981, 87), nationalist elites vari-ously chose what he calls a neo-traditionalist, assimilationist or reformist route, but all uncovered 'submerged ethnic ties and sentiments', judged to be essential in shaping every nationalist movement. Simply put, ethnic historicism describes a search for identity, one founded on a remote point in time and a myth of common ancestry.

Despite the sophistication of some of the theories outlined above, they are for the most part deterministic and universalistic, as they purport to find their favoured factors at the root of *all* nationalist movements. For example, Gellner (1983, 39) asserts that 'a homogeneity imposed by objective, inescapable imperative eventually appears on the surface in the form of nationalism'. Although Gellner did divide nationalism's different manifestations into geographical and historical zones, these categories describe very general processes and are of limited applicability to specific cases. For instance, he divided Europe into four historical time zones, describing the Atlantic seacoast zone, for one, as based on strong dynastic states (Gellner 1994). Critics of Gellner also accuse him of being both ahistorical and apolitical in underestimating the reach and influence of nationalism as a political doctrine (O'Leary 1996, 110). Similarly, Liah Greenfeld (1993) accuses Gellner of ignoring the historical contingency of many nationalist phenomena. Greenfeld herself, on the other hand, charts the rise of English nationalism, among others, *before* the advent of industrialisation, which Gellner takes as his starting point. Yet at the same time as acknowledging the huge variation in nationalist movements according to their situational constraints, Greenfeld also proposes a universal explanatory model of nationalism based on an identity crisis, or anomie, of the relevant social actors (Greenfeld 1993, 14–17).

Like Gellner, Elie Kedourie (1966) is also a modernist. Contrary to Gellner, however, Kedourie concentrates on the history of nationalism as an idea. To this extent, he shares the present text's focus on ideology. Kedourie offers a detailed account of the philosophical roots and development of nationalism, discussing its ideological links with left and right, liberalism, democracy and civil rights. He also discusses the social standing of nineteenth-century European ideologues such as Johann Gottfried Herder and Giuseppe Mazzini, and throws light on the professional frustration, political inexperience and intellectual idealism motivating their writing. Kedourie's argument is that such men initially shaped nationalist politics, but that later figures like Hitler, Stalin and Lenin were responsible for distorting and debasing sophisticated intellectual debate. Kedourie also tends to see nationalism's chauvinistic, German and ethnic form as its archetype, leading him to conclude that 'nationalism is unknown' (Kedourie 1966, 143) in the likes of Great Britain and the US. This analysis differs starkly from that of the present text, which considers both 'banal' nationalism and 'hot' nationalism – as discussed in Chapter 2 – to be variants of the same core ideological principle of prioritising the nation.

Paul Brass (1991), like Kedourie, also emphasises nationalism's ideological nature. Like A. D. Smith and Gellner too, he highlights the importance of elites in shaping and propagating nationalist ideas. Brass (1991, 13) argues that elite competition, rather than ethnic identity per se, constitutes the basic dynamic of ethnic conflict. He underlines the importance of the political and economic environment in shaping the expression of ethnic identity and its politicised form, nationalism, in line with notions of 'invented tradition' (Hobsbawm & Ranger 1983) as well as constructed social realities. Similarly, John Breuilly (1993) points to the central role of state authorities in manipulating nationalism to mobilise the population. This supports his thesis that nationalism is used to create an ideological link between the cultural and the political, or society and the state (whether actual or desired.) Breuilly puts state structures and their need for legitimation at the forefront of his approach to nationalism. Like the present text, he does not claim to explain nationalism, stating that there 'is no valid explanatory theory of nationalism, only a number of ways of describing and comparing various forms nationalist politics have taken' (Breuilly 1993, 338). According to Breuilly, nationalism is simply a product of 'the need to make sense of complex social and political arrangements' (1993, 343). He also points to nationalism's adaptability as an important element of its appeal, and highlights the construction of national stereotypes, histories and enemies as crucial to the success of a nationalist party. Here we encounter the flexibility of nationalist ideology, which is particularly relevant in the context of the cosmopolitan challenge. Kenneth Minogue's definition of the nation as 'something to be found largely in the aspirations of nationalists' (1967, 31) and his emphasis on 'legend-making' is also similar to Brass and Breuilly's view of nationalism as a political construct. One of Minogue's central contentions about modern nationalism is that 'the politics come first, and the national culture is constructed later' (Minogue 1967, 154). He thereby underlines both the power of national symbols to inspire political action and the fact that nationalism is an ideology largely empty of content, less akin 'to a theory than to a rhetoric' (Minogue 1967, 153). M. K. Flynn also contends that 'a precise ideological content, outside of a loyalty to the nation, for nationalism *per se* is impossible to establish' (2000, 30). These views recall Michael Freeden's (1998) definition of nationalism as a 'thin' ideology, whose core principle of prioritising the nation needs be supplemented with elements from across the political spectrum. This is a useful insight that helps to account for the wide variation in nationalist movements. It also suggests that elements of the cosmopolitan challenge can be integrated into nationalist thought.

Paul Brass (1991) claims that symbols and myths are selected and manipulated instrumentally according to their political usefulness, concluding that '[t]he important goal for nationalist movements in this regard is exclusivity, the drive to become the sole political representative of the community' (Brass 1991, 49). Such a reading chimes well with this text's focus on how the boundaries of the nation are being challenged by the cosmopolitan moment. Responding to Brass's case study of Muslim nationalism in India, Francis Robinson takes issue with this stance, however, arguing that Islam had a far greater limiting effect on elites and the form of political mobilisation they adopted than Brass admits. In his critique of Brass, Robinson acknowledges that Brass does not dismiss the importance of primordial elements altogether. Nevertheless, Robinson emphasises that the influence of primordial factors on nationalist movements should not be underestimated, as these shape not only 'the range of legitimate actions for the elite [...] but also form their own apprehensions of what was possible and of what they ought to be trying to achieve' (1994, 217). Breuilly and Brass do recognise that pre-existing factors influence elites to a certain extent. For instance, Breuilly (1993, 344) states that elites 'begin with a fund of intellectual assumptions about what society is and how it is organised' (cf. Greenfeld 1993, 15). This suggests that a balanced approach lies somewhere in between a primordialist and a constructivist theory. The debate between Brass and Robinson provides one illustration of the middle way that many scholars seek to navigate between the modernist and primordialist, or ethno-symbolist poles, which marked the starting point of this discussion.

More recent anthologies on the origins of nations revisit the debate between primordialists, modernists and ethno-symbolists, in an explicit attempt to move the discussion forward (Ichijo & Uzelac 2005). However, despite fine-grained efforts to splice questions of origins by distinguishing the sociological (when is *a* nation?) from the historical (when is *the* nation?), substantially different approaches persist (Ichijo & Uzelac 2005, 5). One advantage of focusing on nationalism as an ideology is that these disputes fade into the background; nations are primarily of interest here as a component of ideologies. For example, if nationalists make a strong case for the primordial origins of their nation, the present text is less concerned with the objective 'truth' or the historical accuracy of that claim, than with the role it plays in furthering their cause. Adopting this perspective also escapes what A. D. Smith identifies as the tautology of defining the nation in terms of European and North American modernity, thereby excluding other variants (Smith 2005, 95). Further, it appears that the relative modernity of nationalist ideology – as opposed to nations – is not at issue among theorists of nationalism: 'Since there is a consensus that nationalism itself is a modern product, any study on nationalism should deal with the nature of modern society in which we live' (Ichijo & Uzelac 2005, 3–4). Accordingly, the present text proposes to leave behind the fraught terrain of nations' origins to focus instead on the construction of the nation in contemporary politics, and how nation-building is responding to the cosmopolitan challenge. The prolific and influential A. D. Smith also has something to say on this question.

At the turn of the twenty-first century, Smith modified his long-standing definition of the nation to place less emphasis on the requirement of a mass public culture, a common economy and shared legal rights and duties. Instead, his more recent definition of the nation is 'a named community possessing an historic territory, shared myths and memories, a common public culture and common laws and customs' (Smith 2002, 15). Nevertheless, this too has been criticised for conflating state characteristics, such as common laws, with those of the nation, while neglecting the political dimension of self-determination or statehood, which is so central to nationalist ideology. His silence on how 'the state seeks to base its legitimacy on the idea that it represents the nation' (Guibernau 2004, 131) or how his definition of pre-modern nations translates to the contemporary era has also been noted. As a result, many aspects of Smith's work are of limited help in assessing the impact of the cosmopolitan challenge on contemporary nation-building and sub-state nationalism.

Smith's definition of the nation appears to be a checklist of rather vague, objectifying criteria, despite his claims to the contrary (Smith 2004, 205). To consider the definition as only an ideal type – following Smith's own advice – merely introduces further difficulties with classification, and still does not do justice to stateless nations without 'common laws and customs'. Smith is right to point out the importance of antiquity in bolstering claims to the continuity and longevity of the nation. Analyses of contemporary nationalism, however, are most interested in how markers of cultural and historical belonging can function as components of nationalist ideology. Smith is also right to be cautious of those who dismiss today's nationalisms as predominantly closed, backward, homogenising and violent (Smith 2004, 204). Instead, he regards so-called 'nationalist globalisation', understood as an 'open, flexible adaptation to the emerging global economy, but as a consciously national collectivity' (Smith 2004, 205), to be a more accurate way of approaching nationalism in the contemporary context. This view of nationalism and globalisation as potentially complementary forces offers a useful springboard for evaluating the impact of the cosmopolitan challenge on nationalist ideology. In the final analysis, however, the bulk of Smith's work has been devoted to elucidating the ethnic origins of nations, and so his focus diverges substantially from that of this text.

The deep-rooted nature of national loyalty and its strong mobilising potential led Josep Llobera (1994) to entitle his early book on nationalism *The God of Modernity*. In distinguishing between phases of national consciousness, he demonstrates that the distance between the primordialist and modernist positions is not as great as might be expected: 'Nationalism *stricto sensu* is a relatively recent phenomenon, but a rudimentary and restricted national identity existed already in the medieval period' (Llobera 1994, 220). Nevertheless, the extent to which a given ethnic heritage is real, imagined or invented still constitutes an important point of difference among theorists. Another key issue is determining whether intellectual elites, as the driving force behind a nationalist movement, are keepers or creators of the ethnic core. Their penchant for history is certainly not to be considered pointless nostalgia, but rather as a strategic reappraisal and reinterpretation of ethnic heritage for present purposes. It remains to be seen how this compares with forms of contemporary, or neo-nationalism.

Evidently, neo-nationalisms go about mobilising people in quite a different environment to the nineteenth-century variants studied by the likes of Ernest Gellner and Benedict Anderson, who give contemporary nationalism short shrift (McCrone 1998, 125). Therefore, an alternative analytical framework is called for, one that incorporates the cosmopolitan challenge. This text does not seek to establish the antiquity or the authenticity of ethnic origins or national legitimating myths. Instead, it accepts Hobsbawm and Ranger's (1983, 7) view of traditions as invented – whatever the source and pedigree of the components used – and focuses on the contemporary products of that ideological process. Neither does this text try to explain 'the rise of nationalism' as a single phenomenon. Rather, it examines the impact of the cosmopolitan challenge on selected contemporary nationalisms, in all their variety and diversity. Nor does it seek to attribute objective characteristics to the nation or its antecedents. Instead, it analyses nations only as a product of the political ideology of nationalism.

This accords with what Peter Alter (1985, 16) calls the simplest definition of the nation, as a 'politically-mobilised people'.

Neo-Nationalism

Tom Nairn (1981) was among the first to distinguish between different eras of nationalism. He refers to 'old nationalism' as the process of nineteenth-century European state-building, which took place in the context of industrial revolution and the breakdown of agrarian society. Nairn's Marxian standpoint leads him to link nationalist movements' varying forms to the different stages of capitalist development in their respective nations. According to him, 'new nationalism' is a product of relative deprivation in an already modern, industrialised environment (Nairn 1981, 128). Nairn's account of uneven development highlights the relevance of mate-rial circumstances to political mobilisation, while acknowledging the importance of symbols in cementing national solidarity. He also empha-sises that each new manifestation of nationalism is *sui generis* – a product of unique circumstances – while retaining the core principles of national-ist ideology at its heart. This is another important insight informing the present analysis. Contemporary nationalism is faced with a very different set of circumstances to its nineteenth century counterparts. There is conti-nuity in the fact that the nation is still 'the idea which lies at the core of nationalism' (Greenfeld 1993, 4) and its enduring nature as a 'thin' ideology (Freeden 1998), but the definition of that nation has often evolved to meet the cosmopolitan challenge. Nairn points out that the context in which a nationalist movement develops helps to explain the way its ideology is structured. This section surveys several other scholarly approaches to contemporary nationalism before returning to Michael Freeden's focus on nationalism as an ideology, as laid out in the introductory chapter of this text.

In his book *Nations against the State*, Michael Keating discusses the cases of Scotland, Catalonia and Quebec, three sub-state nations that enjoy substantial autonomy from the British, Spanish and Canadian governments, respectively. Keating links sub-state political mobilisation there to the revolution in governance that has further undermined central state power in each case. However, Keating does not believe that the state is in general decline. Instead, he argues that it has been penetrated and destabilised by both supra-state and sub-state factors (Keating 2001, 28). His discussion of 'new nationalisms' in these liberal democracies depicts them as generally civic movements that incorporate a broad social base and are progressive in their discourse. That is, they accept both the concept of limited sovereignty and the existence of multiple identities. For such movements to be successful, evidence of their competence in economic matters is also of utmost importance. Furthermore, he emphasises the role of nationalism in articulating a new political arena and thereby providing a focus for collective action. Given declining loyalty to the existing 'nation-state' construct in the cases he considers, sub-state territories are re-invented as an alternative focus of national identity. The way in which conflicts between the sub-state group and its state-level 'Other' are managed is therefore central to Keating's analysis. It illustrates the effects of today's political environment on the dynamics of sub-state movements, but is also helpful in considering nationalist ideologies and strategies more generally, supporting the case for a fresh approach to contemporary nationalism.

Keating (2001, 28) recognises that nationalism is an ideology but does not explore its implications. Jenkins and Sofos (1996), on the other hand, focus on nationalism as a political, historically specific ideology while highlighting, like Keating, the importance of social negotiation in shaping the strategies and interests of collectivities. The nation emerges from their account as a conceptual tool manipulated by nationalist movements in order to legitimate their political project. David McCrone's discussion of 'neo-nationalism', which generally tallies with Keating's, also underlines its flexibility and context-dependency. For instance, McCrone (1998, 129) asserts that in contemporary nationalism 'different ideological elements are mixed and mobilised: right/left; ethnic/civic; past/future; local/global; corporatist/neo-liberal; separatist/autonomist'. This portrayal suggests that nationalism must constantly develop and be ready to adapt its articulation of the link between the individual and the collective. To this extent, contemporary nationalism appears well equipped to respond to the cosmopolitan challenge. Montserrat Guibernau (1999) examines the relationship between sub-state nationalism and the changing global political order by focusing on three issues: the conceptual triad of state, nation and nationalism; the role of intellectuals in promoting nationalism; and the means nationalist movements use to achieve their aims. This corresponds to a concern with the legitimacy, agency and strategy of nationalist ideology. Much like Michael Freeden, whose work is considered further below, Guibernau points to the necessity of supplementing nationalism, as a 'thin' ideology, with principles from other ideologies. Although she does not elaborate on this theme, she considers that the 'political ideologies to which nationalism is attached are crucial to understanding the significance and character of nationalism in each particular case' (Guibernau 1999, 7).

States' need for the legitimating function of nationalism has not been eroded by the cosmopolitan challenge. On the contrary, this challenge has only emphasised nationalism's importance in maintaining the nation-state construct. In stark contrast to Delanty and Kumar's (2006, 3) view that 'the state disengages from the nation' as a result of transnationalism, the present text contends that nation-building is adapting to transnationalism and other aspects of the cosmopolitan challenge in order to retain state legitimacy. As Delanty and Kumar (2006, 3) correctly note, nationalism is indeed 'embroiled in the public culture of the democratic state', and it is important to add that appeals to national solidarity are also central to legitimating authoritarian regimes. Given this recognition of nationalism's enduring influence, any talk of its retreat – particularly in an age when communism and fascism no longer threaten its dominant position – is perplexing. This may be attributed to competing categorisations, which distinguish nationalism as a well-defined ideology or social movement on the one hand, from its more diffuse presence as an emotion, an identity or an element of public discourse on the other (Hearn 2006, 6).

Siniša Malešević (2006, 89) divides ideology into what he calls its 'normative' – or ideological – and 'operative' levels, which partly overlap with the characterisation of nationalism as an emotion, identity or discourse. What he aims to show through selected case studies is that the core 'normative' principles of ideologies like political Islam, socialism and liberal democracy tend to be expressed through nationalist rhetoric at the 'operative' level. For instance, he finds the same discourse of national pride, heroism and wartime sacrifice in speeches by British, Iranian and Yugoslav leaders, and in the history texts taught to schoolchildren in all three cases. Although Malešević's analytical focus on ideology is refreshing, it does not equate to the interpretation adopted here. In Freeden's view (1998), discussed in the introduction to this text, Malešević's case studies represent three 'thick' ideologies, which are supplemented and in some cases supplanted by nationalist rhetoric. By contrast, the present text looks at variants of 'thin' nationalist ideology and the peripheral principles and strategies supporting their core commitment to prioritising the nation, ranging from highly inclusive policies to terrorist activities.

As one of a series of recent monographs reviewing nationalism theory debates in the light of globalisation (Day & Thompson 2004; Hearn 2006; Özkirimli 2005), Spencer and Wollman's (2002) contribution to the literature stands out for clearly aligning itself with those 'contemporary theorists [who] find nationalism utterly unacceptable, in whatever shape it appears' (Vincent 2002). Their critical stance is explicitly motivated by the wars in Yugoslavia. In their view, national identity is problematic in 'that the cohesion it secures is essentially pre-political' (Spencer & Wollman 2002, 201). This assertion fundamentally conflicts with the present approach to nationalism as an inherently political ideology. Spencer and Wollman ultimately recommend more cosmopolitan forms of solidarity as a lesser evil than nationalism, since it 'is not difficult to expose what is ideological about these' (Spencer & Wollman 2002, 197) if and when these provide a front for sinister, less than altruistic agendas. Unfortunately, however, the authors do not look at nationalism in the same light. Taking issue with scholars who see a relatively progressive, inclusive form of nationalism in the likes of Scotland, Quebec and Catalonia (such as Keating 2001), Spencer and Wollman (2002, 179) contrast statements by leading nationalists with surveys and – in one rather bizarre example – comments by a nationalist leader's wife, in order to show that nationalism must be inherently intolerant. They use opinion poll evidence to the effect that not all respondents supported an inclusive definition of nationalism, in order to assert that inclusive nationalism must be inherently unviable. This seems a rather shaky basis from which to conclude that nationalism equates with chauvinism, because it would also mean that no ideology could be deemed coherent unless a majority of people supported it. To take another example, their basically sound argument that democratic accountability should justify political devolution would have been more convincing had it not been set against the narrow assumption that all nationalism is essentially chauvinistic (Spencer & Wollman 2002, 181). In analysing nationalism, Spencer and Wollman's prejudice against it clouds their reasoning. It is part of their refusal to see the same core principles at work in both 'banal' and 'hot' nationalism, which are discussed in Chapter 2 of this book.

All of the authors surveyed agree that contemporary nationalism should be approached differently to its nineteenth-century counterparts, and that strategic flexibility in the face of changing state, sub-state and supra-state relationships is a key component of 'neo-nationalism'. They also tend to recognise nationalism as an ideology without exploring the analytical implications of this. By contrast, the stated aim of David Brown's

Contemporary Nationalism is to 'unravel nationalism by isolating and examining its ideological components' (Brown 2000, 152). Brown adopts what he calls a constructivist approach to nationalism, defining it as 'an ideology offering a distorted perception of reality, containing selective simplifications and elements of myth' (Brown 2000, 1). He then goes on to distinguish civic, ethnocultural and multicultural nationalisms, arguing that the last has recently emerged from the 'unravelling' of the first two. However, Brown also highlights the inter-penetration of these three variants. This evocation of competing constructions of the nation identifies key aspects of contemporary nationalism, which are explored throughout this text and specifically in Chapter 2.

As we saw in the Introduction, Freeden's account of 'thick' and 'thin' ideologies makes a clear distinction between core and peripheral ideological principles. According to Freeden, nationalism is a thin-centred ideology, as it has few core characteristics beyond prioritising the nation. He cites feminism and environmentalism as other examples of thin ideologies, since they have no inherent principles with which to implement their basic commitment to women's rights and environmental protection respectively. These ideologies therefore require peripheral policies, such as opposition to nuclear fuel, demands for limits to toxic emissions, or measures to promote sexual equality, in order to translate their core goals into a practical strategy. Similarly, today's nationalists must interpret their core goal of prioritising the nation in a way suited to their political environment. Self-determination, therefore, has no precise, immutable form within nationalist ideology, as every nationalist movement combines it with a different set of peripheral principles.

Despite their shared commitment to self-determination, then, nationalist movements interpret this core goal in myriad ways. This proposition helps us understand the wide variations in contemporary nationalist ideology and strategy. The core of a thin-centred ideology like nationalism must be supplemented with elements from other ideologies. Conversely, a thin-centred ideology like nationalism can be used to supplement an otherwise 'thick' ideology lacking in one fundamental area. For example, most governments implicitly accept the nation-state's existing boundaries and use them as the basis for nation-building. Whether conservative, liberal or socialist, governments thereby incorporate first and foremost a basic element of nationalism into their 'thick' ideologies (Freeden 1998). According to Freeden, core principles are the bare bones of a belief system, which require fleshing out. A combination of nationalism and cosmopolitanism is therefore thinkable within this conceptual framework.

Freeden describes nationalism as a thin-centred ideology with five core principles: first, the prioritisation of the nation as a key defining framework for human beings; second, the positive valorisation of the nation; third, the desire to give a political and institutional form to the nation; fourth, the importance of space and time in determining social identity; and fifth, a sense of belonging closely bound up with emotion (Freeden 1998, 751–2). The first of these elements sums up nationalism's core commitment to self-determination. However, as Montserrat Guibernau (1996, 63) rightly points out, nationalist ideology 'does not indicate the direction to be taken or the methods which should be adopted to achieve [this goal]'. Hence the 'chameleon-like' nature of nationalism, a flexible ideology *par excellence*, capable of being moulded to fit every situation. For instance, fascist ideology has sought to prioritise the nation by 'purifying' it of foreign elements. To take a very different example, anti-colonial nationalism has sometimes been combined with communist principles, or has simply sought to create national solidarity on the basis of opposition to the colonial oppressor. Finally, a relatively inclusive form of nationalism is also thinkable, which makes its appeals on the basis of shared and easily attainable citizenship. These examples show how some of nationalism's many variants can be incorporated into Freeden's typology of 'thick' and 'thin' ideologies. As such, this conceptual framework 'accounts for the flexibility of nationalist ideologies in application and development' (Flynn 2000, 14).

Freeden's distinction between thick and thin ideologies goes beyond recognising the wide variation in contemporary nationalisms; it also provides a framework for examining their similarities. All forms of contemporary nationalism, including nation-building, share the same core principle of national self-determination. In addition, nation-building also seeks to legitimate the state by equating state and nation (Sutherland 2010, 5). To indicate one's nationality as Italian, Nigerian, Brazilian, Australian or Japanese is to evoke a national construct. This is because every nationalist variant, whether terrorist, democratic or 'banal' (Billig 1995), pursues the political goal of embodying its interpretation of the nation through territory, institutions and, in some cases, the national diaspora (Barabantseva & Sutherland 2011). Freeden has shown that the differences between these examples are a result of variations in peripheral principle and strategy, but that the focal point of national mobilisation remains the same. A world of nation-states, then, expresses the all-pervasiveness of 'thin' nationalism. Similarly, Smith has proposed his own analysis of the 'core doctrine' of nationalism. Two of its basic propositions are the division of the world into nations, on the one hand, and the nation as the source of all political and social power on the other (Smith 1991, 74).

Many aspects of our daily lives are constructed around a concept of the nation that is taken for granted. People everywhere are exposed to this kind of 'banal nationalism' (Billig 1995), which will be examined in more detail in Chapter 2. The more entrenched the nation-building discourse of a given state, the harder it is to impose an alternative interpretation of the nation. However, to describe 'thin' nationalism as all-pervasive does not lead to the analytical redundancy of the concept. On the contrary, it permits a clearer and more dispassionate categorisation of its possible variants. There is an unjustified tendency to neglect the concept of ideology in studying contemporary nationalism, when ideology can structure the analysis by attending to both flexible and immutable principles. In other words, the strategic element in the definition of ideology allows scope for analysing nationalism's flexibility and pragmatism in responding to the cosmopolitan challenge, whereas its conceptual core provides a touchstone for identifying and categorising very different cases of nationalism. This approach comes into its own when studying postcolonial nationalism.

Postcolonial Nationalism

Inevitably, imperialism shaped anti-colonial nationalism, which often used the language and concepts of its European oppressors in order to organise resistance (Chatterjee 1993). Schooled in the ways of their 'masters', anti-colonial intellectuals demanded that principles like liberty, equality, fraternity, democracy and self-determination be extended to them. On achieving independence, the preservation of national sovereignty remained paramount to decolonised countries. Indeed, the prospect of regionalisation and globalisation still makes some states nervous about losing autonomy only recently wrested from colonialists. Most Southeast Asian states, for instance, are unwilling to cede sovereignty to their regional grouping, the Association of Southeast Asian Nations (ASEAN) (Narine 2004; Sutherland 2009). Alongside imperialism's legacy in postcolonial states, it has also had a lasting impact on nation-building in former imperial powers. Decolonisation after World War II entailed the reorganisation of much of Africa and Asia – but also Europe – into nation-states, as former empires like the UK and France contemplated their loss of global influence (Berger 2003, 422; Wilder 2005).

Benedict Anderson (1991) has proved extremely influential in theorising anti-colonial nationalism, as has his use of concepts like 'print capitalism' and 'homogeneous empty time' to help explain its development. His account of 'Creole pioneers' in the Americas charts the growth of nationalist sentiment among the wealthy, landowning classes at the turn of the nineteenth century, before the growth of comparable European movements and, at first, independently of 'print capitalism' (Anderson 1991, 47). This does not correspond to the frustrated intelligentsia Ernest Gellner credits with establishing European nationalism. Rather, these Creole elites were frustrated in another way, namely by their inability to achieve power and status within the bureaucratic hierarchies of the colonial state, which were largely reserved for those born on the Iberian peninsula. According to Anderson, solidarity grew among those sharing the 'fatality of trans-Atlantic birth' (Anderson 1991, 57). This gradually extended to as yet illiterate, non-Creole natives, and would be consolidated into the nineteenth century with the rapid spread of 'print capitalism' across the Americas.

Print capitalism is a key concept in Anderson's work. It refers to the explosion in newspaper circulation and novels made possible by printing technology, the move away from Latin texts to publishing in a range of vernaculars, and the capitalist production process itself. Taken together, these elements provided the basis for imagining a community of fellow readers, whose dialects might make it 'difficult or even impossible to understand one another in conversation [but who] became capable of comprehending one another via print and paper' (Anderson 1991, 44). For instance, David Marr (1971; 1981) charts the exponential rise in book and newspaper publishing in early twentieth century Vietnam, then a part of French Indochina. The use of a relatively accessible romanised script known as *quoc ngu* – meaning national language – and the prominence of nationalist themes, were designed to encourage the spread of the national imaginary as part of the anti-colonial struggle. According to Anderson, and with specific reference to Southeast Asia, twentieth-century movements also arose – particularly among indigenous functionaries and the native intelligentsia – from a comparable sense of frustration to that felt by earlier Creole pioneers in the Americas (Anderson 1991, 126). In the case of these low-level bureaucrats, or clerks, it was the limited educational and employment opportunities afforded by the colonial system which made them hungry for more, and for the freedom to fulfill their potential. According to Anderson (1991, 116), their nationalism came from exposure to European education, and formed the basis of an anti-colonial solidarity, which often rested on ambivalent, colonially influenced territorial foundations. For instance, the Vietnamese Communist Party, as the leading group in the Vietnamese League for Independence (*Viet Minh*), was originally called the Indochinese Communist Party and remained undecided as to the limits of the Vietnamese nation right up until the 1940s (Goscha 1995).

Although Anderson's work is generally recognised as path-breaking in looking beyond Europe for the origins of nationalism, he has been criticised for applying concepts like print capitalism too readily across the globe, resulting in the neglect of marginal groups and anti-colonial particularities, including the way in which local intelligentsia adapted European models to their own context (Kelly & Kaplan 2001). Anderson does tend to focus on the urban, reading public and pass over certain sections of the population in his broad analytical sweep. For instance, he quotes the opening of a novel by the Filipino nationalist José Rizal to illustrate its appeal to a nationalist audience (Anderson 1991, 27). However, he ignores those *not* invited to the glittering Manilan party evoked in Rizal's book, such as the marginalised minorities living in the hinterlands (Rosaldo 2003, 6). This raises the issue of agency: was anti-colonial nationalism merely an elite, ideological undertaking and if so, how did it become an instrument of mass mobilisation? How did 'the people' interpret and internalise a sense of national belonging? This is one area investigated by so-called 'subaltern scholars', who are concerned with those rarely given a voice in official histories.

The subaltern has been defined in the Indian context as 'the demographic difference between the total Indian population and all those we have defined as elite' (Guha, cited in Loomba 1998, 199). Rather than pit coloniser against native, then, this approach introduces a different distinction to help understand the postcolonial legacy. On the one hand, it groups the indigenous entrepreneurs, the bourgeoisie and the bureaucrats at all levels of seniority who adopted an 'all-India' perspective. On the other, it places those like the lowest-caste Hindu Dalits, who did not feel represented by India's postcolonial nationalist discourse. Although there is a danger of merely replacing one simplistic dichotomy with another by essentialising these groups, such an approach does alert us to the enduring influence of 'the state's practice of co-opting the ruling strata of native society and reshaping their traditional authority' (Cheah 2003, 284). This can be observed in both colonised and postcolonial countries. However, even within relatively centralised postcolonial states, these co-opting strategies have varied according to regional particularities (Boone 2003). In post-war Senegal, for instance, the nationalist leader Léopold Senghor sought to accommodate regional elites in order to gain their support and, by extension, that of the local population. Ironically, anti-colonial nationalists might label themselves progressive and democratic – as Senghor's parties did – while relying on a 'fusion of elites' (Boone 2003, 60) composed of entrenched aristocratic families and local Islamic marabouts, who always seemed to find a privileged place within the evolving hierarchies of pre-colonial, colonial and postcolonial rule.

The cultural and postcolonial theorist Gayatri Chakravorty Spivak warns that the subaltern voice cannot be captured or recorded as a coherent whole, like some sort of authentic ethnic experience (Leonard 2005, 106). This approach has close affinities with poststructuralist theories, which highlight the inconsistencies and fissures in discourse that prevent any actual closure or completeness (Laclau & Mouffe 1985). Poststructuralism has been criti-cised, perhaps unfairly, for failing to move beyond this key proposition to develop a critical response to colonialism, globalisation, transnationalism and revolutionary nationalism (Leonard 2005, 2). By contrast, such concerns are central to postcolonial theory, which extends to investigations of enduring colonial structures and legacies, and their contribution to current global inequalities that might be considered 'neo-colonial'. As such, postcolonial theory promises insights that are highly relevant to contemporary nationalism and the cosmopolitan challenge.

Spivak (2008, 6) argues that any search for the essence of the subaltern subject will be in vain, but instead sees critical potential in recognising both the coloniser and colonised as heterogeneous and mutually consti-tutive. For example, dominant modes of thought are often shaped by paradigms emanating from Western academia, so that postcolonial schol-ars themselves may be unwittingly perpetuating imperial ideas (Leonard 2005, 108). This leads us to the notion of hybridity, which suggests an interdependence rather than a dichotomy, or strict opposition, between coloniser and colonised. Often associated with the theorist Homi Bhabha (1990a; 1990b), the concept of hybridity is useful in understanding how nations are shaped through relationships, rather than representing any essential characteristics. For instance, the coloniser's sense of superiority can only exist in relation to the inferiority imputed to the colonised 'Other'. Similarly, the bond of national belonging often derives from a shared, negative rejection of the outsider, rather than a positive and independent celebration of oneness. According to Bhabha (1990a, 296), however, even this source of solidarity has been ambivalent among colonisers. The conflicting characteristics they have attributed to the 'native' – innocent yet threatening, savage yet servile, primitive yet calculating – mean that we cannot begin to paint a clear picture of either the colonised or their colonisers (Leonard 2005, 128). In sum, we should not seek to essentialise postcolonial communities or generalise about any shared characteristics.

Bhabha shows that the identities that colonisers themselves construct and propagate are necessarily unstable, thereby providing an opportunity for the oppressed and disempowered to undermine and resist those identities that paint them as inferior. The concept of hybridity thus breaks down the division between 'them' and 'us' by pointing to the relativity of national, racial and ethnic categories, leaving the way open for the possibility of transnational alternatives in the contemporary arena (Bhabha 1990b; Leonard 2005, 134). Again, this suggests that some form of cosmopolitan nationalism is thinkable. Nevertheless, Bhabha and Comaroff also point to a conservative backlash against this trend:

> Current 'origins' of nationalism and fundamentalism have everything to do with an anxiety provoked by the complex process of cultural hybridization that challenges atavistic definitions. Such hybridization is as much part of the national scene as it is a global phenomenon [but] there is also the pressure to create a kind of coercive, lethal closure.
>
> (Bhabha & Comaroff 2002, 27).

This highlights the problems inherent in denying the nation's unfixity and ambivalence, and aiming for closure by positing an ancient, homogeneous nation and unquestioningly anticipating its future progress and preservation as a unitary whole. Ironically, however, Bhabha's critics point out that he presents hybridity as a universal phenomenon, thereby adopting precisely the universalising tendencies that he seeks to question (Cheah 2003; Leonard 2005). The all-pervasiveness of nationalism also makes it a universal organising principle because it purports to associate every human being with a nation. Indeed, 'the putative antithesis between cosmopolitan universalism and nationalist particularism misleadingly obscures the fact that both philosophical nationalism and cosmopolitanism articulate universal institutional models' (Cheah 2003, 2). Nationalism's all-pervasive-ness has also been expressed through Benedict Anderson's conception of 'homogeneous, empty time'. Understood as people's ability to imagine the 'steady, anonymous, simultaneous activity' (Anderson 1991, 26) of their compatriots, and members of other nations beyond their own, this provides the basis for appeals to members of the nation as an 'imagined community'. According to Anderson, it is also at the root of organic metaphors depicting the nation's progress towards the future as a bounded, interconnected whole.

Asserting the universality of nationalism's foundations risks denying nation-builders and nationalist movements any originality or independ-ence in the way they imagine the national community. In response, Partha Chatterjee, both an admirer and a critic of Anderson's work, has sought to trace anti-colonial nationalism's subtle blend of borrowing and differ-entiation through the case of Bengal. Chatterjee (1996, 217) describes a unique and spiritual cultural nationalism that 'creates its own domain of sovereignty within colonial society well before it begins its political battle with the imperial power'. According to Chatterjee, this cultural domain embodied the originality of Indian nationalism. It was a key site of resist-ance outside of the state apparatus and independent of the more derivative political nationalism, which had pervasive colonial associations. Thus, anti-colonial nationalism did not merely extend a Western ideology into new lands, but adapted it. Importantly, this created a realm outwith the reach of the state in which to develop non-Western conceptions of literature, the family, gender roles and other aspects of society 'that would be modern and at the same time recognisably Indian' (Chatterjee 1996, 220).

A further interesting perspective on colonialism and nationalism comes from Shalini Puri (2004), who points out that Caribbean nationalists could never draw on a purist, primordial sense of nationhood. This leads her to question why hybridity and nation-building should ever be considered mutually exclusive in the first place. Instead, Puri explores so-called 'hybrid nationalisms', focusing on transnationalism as a way of 'studying aspects of human experience and societies which cannot be contained within the nation-state' (Puri 2004, 6). She rejects post-nationalism, however, which purports to transcend the nation-state altogether. According to Puri, focus-ing on transnational flows, from migrant labour to 'five-star tourists' (Puri 2004, 24), may be one way of imagining the nation anew. Although she does not consider nationalism as an ideology, preferring its Andersonian gloss as a framework for political activity and emotional attachment (Anderson 1991, 5), Puri's critique of the post-nationalist position is highly relevant to the present text. It draws our attention to the wide variety of more or less empowering hybrid identities, and more or less oppressive nationalisms. Though we should be wary of essentialising the nation, it may yet be imaginable in a more inclusive form, one more clearly attuned to transnationalism, diaspora and other aspects of the cosmopolitan challenge. One possible approach, which is formulated explicitly in terms of the nation, contrasts territorially and monolingually defined nations 'imposed by subordinating regions and ethnicities within more or less arbitrarily delimited spaces' with new forms of transterritorial and multilingual nations linked to the logics of markets and globalisation (García Canclini 2001, 29). This suggests that focusing on the marginalisation of minorities, such as is championed by subaltern scholars, need not entail jettisoning the nation-state construct in its entirety. Indeed, demonstrating an awareness of the enduring influence of the nation-state in dispensing privilege and status, and the diverse ways in which national borders are crossed, are useful starting points for conceptualising the heterogeneous, hybrid nationalisms that can arise as a result of the cosmopolitan challenge.

Both Shalini Puri and Partha Chatterjee are concerned by the universalism implied in associating nationalism with a shared experience of (Western) capitalist modernity, privileging Enlightenment values of rationality, secularism and a belief in science and the state. For instance, Anderson's (1991, 26) understanding of 'homogeneous, empty time' is premised on the decline of pre-modern perspectives, so that alternative interpretations of time and place tend to be dismissed as remnants of a bygone age. However, Chatterjee (2005) points out that people today draw on many heterogeneous ways of constructing and experiencing the nation, which cannot be dismissed as atavistic or invalid simply because they do not fit the Enlightenment mould. He also cautions against Anderson's rather utopian depiction of the nation as promoting horizontal bonds of solidarity, when nation-building often goes hand in hand with enduring inequality. For instance, the formal, legal equality of Dalits (once termed Untouchables) as Indian citizens exists alongside continued caste discrimination, decades after India's independence (Chatterjee 2005, 939).

Similarly to Chatterjee, John Kelly (1998, 844) criticises Anderson's view of nations as 'symmetrical units of imagined, communal self-love', because this suggests a horizontal leveling of individuals through notions of national solidarity and comradeship, which is belied by the hierarchies that pervaded colonial rule and often persisted thereafter. Such a view can also detract attention from the upheaval of diasporic movements, and cases in which diasporas are denied a role in nation-building. For example, Kelly cites the case of Indo-Fijians, which is discussed further in Chapter 4. Brought by British colonialists to the Pacific Islands as indentured labourers in the nineteenth century, their descendants still remain subordinate to the principle of ethnic Fijian paramountcy. Kelly also charges Anderson with anachronistically projecting back into history a picture of a world divided into nations – arguing that this organising principle can really only be traced to the creation of the UN following World War II – and should not stand in the way of seeking a 'clearer understanding of the asymmetries in global flows' (Kelly 1998, 869). According to Kelly, the neatly delineated nation-states we see represented on political maps or embodied around negotiating tables do not correspond to people's lived experience. They are part of 'an international normative order [...] based on sovereign nation-states' (Delanty 2006, 363), but as Chatterjee (2005, 928) puts it, this 'is not located anywhere in real space – it is utopian'.

Although this text is chiefly concerned with nationalism as a political ideology, and the way in which nationalists mobilise cultural symbols, it must also be alive to how these symbols shape and are shaped by people's way of life, and this is discussed further in Chapter 2. Postcolonial theory is but one strand of a multifaceted approach to cultural nationalism, which looks beyond the 'one-sided transmission of ideology from above [towards] an on-going consumption (and therefore reproduction) of culture in which various sections of the population participate' (Yoshino 1999, 2). These questions continue to be particularly relevant in postcolonial societies, which are confronted both with the legacy of the Western 'Other' and the impact of globalisation. The postcolonial legacy includes the cultural continuity, or 'path dependency', of colonial relationships, which still colour international relations, trading regimes and development flows to this day (Bebbington & Kothari 2006, 852). One example is France's cultural and military engagement in many of its former African colonies, which are also members of the language alliance known as *Francophonie*. Similarly, the Commonwealth brings together many former British colonies, and Portugal played an important part in the international intervention leading up to the independence of its former colony of East Timor from Indonesia in 2002 (Burke & McDonald 2007, 13).

In the British context, the 'unfinished contestations' (Clifford 1997, 3) of decolonisation can be observed in the way former colonial officials in Africa, India and elsewhere were redeployed in UK government development agencies. Not only did this degree of continuity affect nation-building in post-independence states but, as Uma Kothari (2006) has shown, it also helped perpetuate a rather stereotypical view of the UK (particularly England) among its expatriates. An 'imagined geography' of England 'was sustained and reproduced as it circulated within colonial networks' (Bebbington & Kothari 2006, 857), upheld through ritual and reverence. This was a deterritorialised depiction of the nation, which existed outside the 'home turf' in the imaginations of these expatriate citizens, illustrating how the postcolonial legacy has resonance for former colonising countries as well as those colonised. In the words of one expatriate; 'they weren't living their nationalism; it was all in the head, it was a myth' (cited in Kothari 2006, 245). It could well be argued that the nation is no less mythical at home than away, especially if we understand a myth as 'an abbreviated world outlook, an ideology in miniature' (Nothnagle 1993, 6). The notion of expatriates 'living their nationalism' highlights the strong assumption that the nation is realised through a close bond with and, ideally, proximity to the homeland. Yet, as will be shown, transnationalism and the cosmopolitan challenge more generally are undermining that assumption (Barabantseva & Sutherland 2011).

There is a long-standing tendency in the media and political discourse for the outsider, the immigrant, or the foreigner to be constructed as somehow threatening, thereby encouraging members of a national community to close ranks in order to preserve jobs, traditions, or some vague notion of national heritage (Stratton & Ang 1994). To use Edward Saïd's terminology, this is a product of 'imaginative geographies', which create difference through distance (Gregory 2004, 17). The postcolonial moment, on the other hand, disrupts the neat dichotomy between 'us' and 'them' by excavating the colonial past in order to uncover its continuing influence over the present (Gregory 2004, 7). The cultural theorist Stuart Hall (1997, 24) expresses this vividly with reference to his own emigration from Jamaica to England; 'There is a tremendous paradox here which I cannot help relishing myself; that in the very moment when Britain finally convinced itself it had to decolonise, it had to get rid of them, we all came back home. As they hauled down the flag, we got on the banana boat and sailed right into London.'

The situation faced by those nation-states that successively gained independence in the post-war era prefigured the cosmopolitan challenge. Their self-determination was internationalised from the outset, influenced by enduring economic ties with the former imperial power, bureaucratic legacies, cultural accretions and often a privileged path for emigration. Catapulted into a globalising world where transnational exchanges and localised adaptation were intensifying as never before, governments still had to meet the challenge of nation-building. 'Postcolonies, even where they did constitute more or less integrated nation-states, could seldom achieve the autonomy promised by nationalist ideology precisely because they confronted global capitalist markets and unequal terms of trade' (Calhoun 2007, 18). Amid a confusion of intermingling cultures, they had to construct a sense of national unity and solidarity. In so doing, nation-builders used nationalist symbolism to squeeze ethnic, cultural and religious diversity into a common crucible of national belonging. Whether privileging the 'dominant *ethnie*' (Smith 1995, 106), as in Vietnam or Thailand, or espousing an official multiculturalism, as in Malaysia or Singapore, ethnic categories often originating in colonial times were imposed to help govern a clearly delimited people and pursue nation-state legitimacy within defined territorial borders (Anderson 1991, 168). But the difficulties of nation-building have not abated in the contemporary era; quite the contrary. Indeed, 'the difficulty of creating national cultures that might preserve, indeed nourish internal differences has emerged as a major issue in our time' (Loomba 1998, 203).

The preceding discussion of anti-colonial and postcolonial nationalism has questioned the view of nationalism as a Western export to the colonies. However, as Spivak (2008, 1) has pointed out, we should also be wary of trying to capture the subaltern voice as somehow unsullied by the colonial associations of certain indigenous elites. Rather, we should take note of these colonial associations, their lasting effects on postcolonial nation-building and, by extension, their influence on sub-state ethnic and nationalist movements. This applies both to postcolonial states and former colonising countries, whose own national identities continue to be influenced by decolonisation. Most obviously, their approach to citizenship and nation-building has been strongly affected by migration and diaspora from former colonies. Finally, students and scholars of nationalism would do well to remind themselves that as citizens of any given nation-state, and perhaps also as patriots, migrants, members of a diaspora or sympathisers with sub-state movements, they are also subjected to nationalist ideology.

Conclusion

Analysing nations as 'imaginative geographies' or 'imagined communities' acknowledges the creative licence inherent in every nationalist ideology. In turn, placing contemporary nationalism and nation-building in the context of the cosmopolitan challenge points to the transnational flows that complicate neatly delineated accounts of national territory, history and heritage. Just as young children learn to categorise objects differently according to the rules of their respective mother tongue, so the 'encapsulated' (Lieberman 2003, 6) study of, say, French history or Uruguayan geography serves to consolidate these countries' borders. This is a form of educational nationalism to rival the methodological nationalism discussed in the introduction to this text (Beck & Sznaider 2010 [2006]). Alternatively, and as Martha Nussbaum (1996) has argued, a curriculum covering cross-border trade, transnational culture and multinational corporations might prompt children to understand the organisation of space rather differently. At an analytical level, at least, we need to 'step away from an ethnographic focus on separate, integral cultures [...] to focus on hybrid, cosmopolitan experiences as much as on rooted native ones' (Clifford 1997, 24). Postcolonial theory also teaches us to be wary of the dominant nation-building narrative and interrogate what it leaves unsaid, or who is being silenced.

Even though political enquiry such as that undertaken here may privilege the analysis of governments, movements, ideologies and global trends, nation-building is not merely a top-down process. Approaching nationalism as an ideology still leaves enormous scope to study its many facets, from particular, individual interpretations (Cohen 1996), through its institutional manifestations, to party political pronouncements. Analysing nationalism as an ideology also helps to show how the nation is constructed and perpetuated through political discourse, international relations and everyday interaction (Billig 1995). In so doing, it becomes clear that linear accounts of national history are skewed, and that seemingly fixed borders of belonging are constructed. The nation is not 'natural', nor does the nation-state represent the inevitable organising principle of political life. Instead, it is the product of constant ideological work to create and maintain what remains a remarkably potent mobilising force. Nationalism's resilience in the face of the cosmopolitan challenge is a result of its flexibility and adaptability, as subsequent chapters will show.

This chapter has argued that theories relating to the emergence of nineteenth-century nationalism are of limited use in exploring contemporary responses to the cosmopolitan challenge. While Benedict Anderson's concepts of print capitalism and homogeneous empty time have been enormously influential in framing studies of nationalism within the colonial context, they tend to overlook marginalisation and difference, which are some of the very issues pushed to the fore by transnationalism, migration, diaspora, regionalisation and globalisation. Yet the universalising assumptions underlying much 'classical' nationalism theory continue to influence assessments of contemporary nationalism. Alternatively, more recent examinations of contemporary nationalism tend to focus on specific case studies. These pragmatic, empirically founded approaches offer useful insights into the recent evolution of contemporary nationalisms in response to the cosmopolitan challenge, by addressing the 'difficult interplay between their local and global contexts' (Loomba 1998, 257). Similarly, the following chapters use a series of case studies to illustrate some of the range of nationalist responses to aspects of the cosmopolitan challenge.

2

Who Belongs to the Nation? From Patriotism to Terrorism

How do we distinguish between the many types of nationalism and understand its extreme manifestations? Is there a difference between patriotism and nationalism?

This chapter looks at different variants of nationalism, examining ethnic nationalism, 'banal' nationalism and 'hot' nationalism in turn. 'Hot' nationalism, which tends to be virulent and violent, can be contrasted with 'banal' nationalism, understood as taken for granted markers of national loyalty and belonging. For example, South Asia offers examples of both 'hot' nationalism in Sri Lanka, discussed below, and attempts to foster a pan-Indian nationalism, considered in the context of nationalism and democracy in Chapter 3. This chapter argues that it is a mistake automatically to associate 'hot', or violent nationalism with atavistic loyalties and long-standing inter-ethnic tensions. Indeed, ethnic animosities can be instigated for political ends where previously there was peaceful cohabitation. There are also nationalist movements that spurn electoral politics for terrorist tactics. The reasons behind such extreme campaigns for self-determination must be sought in the degree of economic, political, social and cultural conflict in each case. By approaching nationalism as an ideology that combines principle and practice, it is possible to see how the core aim of prioritising the nation is pursued using different strategies, ranging from the mundane to the murderous. Sub-state nationalist tactics, for instance, range from ruthless terrorism to mainstream democratic parties.

This chapter looks at how nationalism has provided the ideological basis for both peaceful and violent struggles to create new nations and maintain existing nation-states. It examines some of the effects and implications of ethnicity, arguing that the concept of ideology is a better framework for analysing these dynamics than that of identity. Discussions of banal and hot nationalism follow in the second and third sections respectively. Selected examples attempt to give the reader a sense of the unique context of nationalism in specific cases, namely the US and Sri Lanka, thereby offering an empirical focus which is often missing from theoretical studies of nationalism (Day & Thompson 2004; Hearn 2006; Spencer & Wollman 2002). What emerges from the discussion is that nationalism is an infinitely flexible, protean ideology that continues to play a central role in politics all over the world, and is responding to aspects of the cosmopolitan challenge.

Ethnic Nationalism

Like nations, ethnic groups claim to have 'distinctive attributes' (Brown 2000, 6), but they do not necessarily express these through a political ideology or demands for self-determination linked to a given territory. Indeed, Michael Mann (2001, 217) understands nationalism to be the politicisation of ethnicity. The respected scholar of nationalism A. D. Smith used the French noun *ethnie* to designate ethnic groups, defining them as 'named human populations with shared ancestry myths, histories and cultures, having an association with a specific territory, and a sense of solidarity' (Smith 1986, 32). As such, there are many points of comparison with nations, which Smith argues are derived from *ethnies*. Smith's theory of ethno-symbolism emphasises a shared *belief* in common origins, rather than *actual* descent. Other scholars have taken up the notion of myths of shared ancestry to define the nation as 'a group of people who feel that they are ancestrally related' (Guibernau 2007, 12). In turn, the ideal-type distinction between civic and ethnic forms of the nation helps us identify the components of nationalist ideology and thereby understand its different variants.

The distinction between ethnic and civic forms of nationalism has often been used to categorise and judge nationalist variants; '[Civic nationalism] sees the nation as a territorial association of citizens living under the same laws and sharing a mass, public culture, ethnic nationalism regards the nation as a community of genealogical descent, vernacular culture, native history and popular mobilisation' (Smith 1996, 363). In practice, it is impossible to find either of these ideal types in a 'pure' form. For example, the civic 'public culture' to which Smith refers in the above quote is likely to contain some of the elements he identifies in an *ethnie*, such as a shared history, territory and sense of solidarity. But the frequent combination of civic and ethnic components in nationalist ideologies throws up some problems of its own. For example, defining the nation as a belief in shared ancestry can be considered anachronistic and exclusionary towards those of its inhabitants – an ever-increasing number – whose ancestries cannot be traced through sedentary generations. Making links between ancient ethnic markers and national belonging is also of limited use in meeting the contemporary challenges of migration and diaspora. With the loosening of territorial ties, an individual's ethnic heritage may not correspond to their state citizenship. It may instead be a composite of where they were brought up and their parents' and grandparents' cultures, which might themselves only partially overlap. This is not in itself a cause for concern, but the challenge for contemporary nation-building is clear. How to create a sense of solidarity among people of many different backgrounds? Nation-states tend to be shaped 'by the norms and culture of the privileged (usually, majority) national community on the territory' (Moore 2006, 95), or what Smith (1995, 106) has called the 'dominant *ethnie*'. It remains to be seen how nationalist ideologies adapt their interpretation of the nation to reflect the lack of fit between the dominant ethnic group and the increasingly multicultural make-up of societies. This is an important facet of the cosmopolitan challenge.

As will be shown in Chapters 3, 4 and 5, conditions of access to state citizenship, practical policies designed to foster inclusion, and the principles of nationalist ideology in stateless nations, are all good indicators of relative national inclusiveness. For instance, nationalists may reappraise shared bonds and move away from ethnic markers of belonging towards a more voluntaristic form of national solidarity as part of their response to the cosmopolitan challenge. Nonetheless, belonging to the 'dominant *ethnie*' (Smith 1995, 106) continues to confer symbolic and material advantages in many countries today, suggesting that multiculturalism and cosmopolitanism have yet to overcome the enduring link between ethnicity, nation and state. For instance, despite Malaysia's official multiculturalism, the ethnically derived *Bumiputra* policy has long been in place. This is a form of positive discrimination in favour of the Malay ethnic group and the peoples of Sabah and Sarawak on the island of Borneo, ostensibly in order to help them reach economic parity with Malaysia's other ethnic groups. Although the term *Bumiputra* literally means 'sons of the soil', the status has not been extended to peninsular Malaysia's indigenous people, the *Orang Asli*, who are instead caught up in a long-term government policy of assimilation to the Malay majority (Endicott & Knox Dentan 2004). Malays may be the main beneficiaries from pro-*Bumiputra* policies, but there are now growing income inequalities within this ethnic group (Balasubramaniam 2007, 39), since only a privileged few tend to gain access to the educational, economic and employment advantages linked to their Malay ethnicity. In Malaysia, then, formal civic equality is paired with the principle of positive discrimination in favour of the dominant *ethnie*. This is just one illustration of the many ways in which civic and ethnic components can be combined in contemporary nation-building.

Ethnicity is an inchoate cultural allegiance, which can be instrumentalised for good or for ill. Ethnic markers often form the basis for informal cultural and institutional bias, as well as legally based positive discrimination, such as access to education and scholarships. Unsurprisingly, then, the link between ethnicity and nationality, or citizenship, can be highly charged. For instance, the ethnic affiliation included on Soviet identity cards was widely associated with discriminatory policies and therefore unpopular in the days of the USSR, but an attempt to abolish this category in the post-Soviet Russian federation also met with opposition, due to fears that minority identities would be lost in a process of Russification (Danks 2001, 38). In a different context, the struggle for recognition of Canada's First Nations and Australian aborigines are two examples of peoples claiming rights by virtue of native title to territory and resources, independently of their respective state's current multiculturalist policies. In Australia, for instance, 'the individual contracts made with the Australian state by migrants have not been extended to indigenous Australians. This remains a powerful challenge to the new civic nationalism in Australia' (Wesley 2000, 191). These examples show how definitions of ethnicity and belonging have crucial consequences, ranging from the way in which land ownership is allocated, to how the state targets discriminatory practices. A stark reminder of this is Serbia's role in the break-up of Yugoslavia and the status of Kosovo.

At various times in its history, Serbia has clashed with the Ottoman Empire, the Austro-Hungarian Empire, Croatia and, most recently, the combined forces of NATO, giving rise to a widespread and enduring sense among Serbs of being victimised and misunderstood (Gilberg 2000, 29). It is interesting to note how Serb nationalism was strengthened by this interpretation of history. In the context of the Bosnian wars of the 1990s, it has been argued that Serb defiance at being represented as beyond the pale of mainstream European societies forced 'more moderate voices, people estranged by violence, even Sarajevans fully endorsing the values of multiculturality of old Bosnia and Yugoslavia' (Armakolas 2001, 55) to take sides. Yugoslavia had provided a convenient umbrella term for its inhabitants' frequently hybrid identities. Escalating conflict as the Iron Curtain crumbled, however, combined with misleading appraisals of that conflict's ancient, atavistic roots, had a polarising effect among the population, providing fertile ground for radical nationalists to ratchet up mutual hostility among erstwhile friends and neighbours. It is also argued that international perceptions helped to shape conflicting identities and hence the wars themselves, by proposing diplomatic solutions that essentialised ethnic groups into distinct, bounded communities; 'Through its insistence on an essentialist treatment of ethnicity, in which Serbs, Croats and Muslims have immutable identities, Europe has played a part in legitimating nationalist leaders' (Sorabji, cited in Armakolas 2001, 49).

Serbia's dominant religion of Orthodox Christianity has long played an important role in identifying the country's allies – such as Russia today – and its alien 'Others', including Albanian Muslims and Catholic Croats. The crusading battle between Muslim Ottoman Turks and Serbs at Kosovo Polje in 1389 remains a defining moment in Serb history, and a core justification for their refusal to relinquish claims to the present-day territory of Kosovo where it took place. Slobodan Milošević, president of Serbia in the 1990s, played on images of ancestral battlefields and religious entitlement to lay claim to the territory of Kosovo, oppose its independence from Serbia, and carry out notorious 'ethnic cleansing' against Kosovo Albanians. Like the Tibetan nationalists discussed in Chapter 4, Serbia has thus found itself involved in 'an issue for the global public' (Armakolas 2001, 47). Contrary to the Tibetans, however, Serb nationalism has tended to be viewed internationally with suspicion at best. Just as Tibetan nationalism is personified by the Dalai Lama, a figure widely perceived as a peace-loving defender of human rights, Serb nationalism continues to be associated with the late Slobodan Milošević and his translation of an extremist ideology of national purity into a murderous policy of 'ethnic cleansing'. Milošević himself was tried at the International Criminal Court for crimes against humanity, though he died before the trial concluded. However, this legacy still affects outside perceptions of Serbia today, whose foreign policy options tend to be reduced to a stark choice between isolating, radical nationalism or 'rehabilitation' through projected membership of the European Union (*Economist* 2010c). The

Serbian example underlines the importance of exploring the ways in which national belonging is constructed and defined as more or less civic, inclusive, ethnic and chauvinistic. It also shows how nationalists are called upon to respond to aspects of the cosmopolitan challenge. Even within this transnational context, the distinction between ethnic and civic nationalism remains a useful conceptual framework for analysing different forms of nationalism, few of which will conform to either of these ideal types. Despite being hampered by unhelpful stereotyping as Eastern and Western, bad and good respectively, the distinction between ethnic and civic nationalism is also useful in uncovering the ethnic bias underpinning what some hold up to be expressions of civic nationalism, such as the citizenship tests discussed in Chapter 5. We now turn to a second analytical axis for exploring the variations in contemporary nationalist ideology, which runs the gamut from all-pervasive 'banal' nationalism to hostile 'hot' nationalism.

Banal Nationalism

One much-cited definition of the nation, coined by Benedict Anderson (1991), is the 'imagined community'. More precisely, Anderson understands the nation as 'an imagined political community – and imagined as both inherently limited and sovereign' (Anderson 1991, 6). It is important to stress that Anderson defines nations as imagined, not imaginary. That is, they may be creations, but are not thereby false fabrications: 'Communities are to be distinguished, not by their falsity/genuineness, but by the style in which they are imagined' (Anderson 1991, 6). Bringing together the political and the personal, Anderson's definition of the imagined community suggests individual identification with a larger social whole along the lines of shared kinship and religion (Anderson 1991, 5). This leads us to the notion of national identity and belonging. Identity is a psychological term related to people's self-understanding as individuals and members of a group (Reicher & Hopkins 2001). In turn, the 'crucial question relating to national identity is how the national "we" is constructed and what is meant by such construction' (Billig 1995, 70). As such, it is closely bound up with the notion of banal nationalism, considered below.

According to Walker Connor, the nation as a 'psychological bond' approximates the sense of belonging to a large, extended family (Connor 1978, 379; 1994, 202). Montserrat Guibernau (2007, 10) argues that, in addition, 'continuity over time and differentiation from others' are essential characteristics of national identity. That is, a shared set of well-established attributes will distinguish a particular community from others. Any search for a homogeneous national essence is doomed to fail, however. Attempts to essentialise identity are misguided and potentially dangerous. For example, consider the massacres in Rwanda and Bosnia, when 'identity becomes a knife' (Hintjens cited in Malešević 2006, 21). Few people are likely to evoke the same things to explain their sense of national belonging. To some, it may be a long literary and cultural tradition. Others may feel pride in a history of national resistance. Still others may value current examples of political progressiveness or sporting achievement that make them feel part of the national whole. Furthermore, Guibernau (2007, 10) notes that national identity is constructed in a two-way process of individual identification and ideological mobilisation. The social psychologists Stephen Reicher and Nick Hopkins (2001) also highlight the importance of mobilisation in creating a sense of national identity.

Some scholars have criticised identity as an excessively vague concept, which is of limited value in explaining the behaviour of individuals and groups (Brubaker & Cooper 2000, Malešević 2006). They are understandably wary of attempts to depict it as an inborn characteristic distinct from ideology and self-interest. Identity has become so catch-all a term that it has lost much of its explanatory power for theorising nations and nationalism, and has helped to obscure other factors at work in nation-building. It has also been shown to be a Western concept of relatively recent vintage, so that its universal applicability across all communities and contexts cannot be assumed (Malešević 2006, 23). Finally, identities are often understood as bounded categories, which can be attributed and inherited. As we have seen, nationalists have used the preservation of a putatively primordial identity to justify everything from positive discrimination in Malaysia to 'ethnic cleansing' in Kosovo. This stance is subject to the same analytical criticisms levelled against imagining nation-states as neatly bordered entities, which were discussed in the introductory chapter to this text. The cosmopolitan challenge is precisely about disrupting and undermining such categories, suggesting that a concept like identity is inherently unsuited to analysing the nationalist response. The search for an alternative leads us back to nationalism as an ideological project, one that sets out to create nations and a sense of national identity as the focus of group solidarity. Analysis of this sort is not oriented towards highlighting the truth or falsity of nationalist claims, as a Marxian approach to ideology might be. Instead, it aims to explore the systems of ideas and mobilising strategies, which together make up the principle and practice of ideologies (Sutherland 2005a; Malešević 2006, 79).

In seeking to grasp the nature of nations, national identity can only tell us part of the story. Ultimately, there are as many national identities as there are individuals, and analysing these would involve the psychological or anthropological study of 'personal nationalism' (Cohen 1996; Fox & Miller-Idriss 2008). By contrast, a text like the current one, rooted in the discipline of politics rather than sociology or anthropology, focuses on the motivational power of nations and nationalism to influence state legitimacy and sub-state autonomy. It concentrates on nationalists who claim to speak for a community as part of a political ideology that aims to achieve greater national self-determination or lend authority to state power as a 'limited and sovereign' territorial entity. This element of Benedict Anderson's definition of the nation, cited above, highlights the political nature of the nation as opposed to its cultural content and, as we have seen, a claim to sovereignty or some form of political autonomy is what distinguishes nations from ethnic groups. Nevertheless, it is important to consider the people deemed to constitute the nation and their receptiveness to the nationalist ideologues who set about mobilising inchoate cultural myths and markers of identity into a strong and politicised sense of national loyalty. Even though other ideologues may also attempt this as part of their political programme, by supplementing their core claims with 'peripheral' or 'operative' nationalist principles, this is the *raison d'être* of every nationalist cause (Freeden 1998; Malešević 2006). The popular impact of nationalist strategies therefore deserves some scrutiny.

A focus on nationalism as an elite-led ideology detracts attention from 'the people in whose names nations are being made [and who] are simply assumed to be attuned to the national content of their self-appointed nationalist messengers' (Fox & Miller-Idriss 2008, 537). Yet popular support is crucial to any nationalist cause. Apart from backing nationalist political parties at the ballot box, individuals may express their national(ist) loyalties through patterns of consumption, participation in certain performances and celebrations, the adoption of apparently patriotic symbols and their own self-identification, among many other means (Yoshino 1999). These oft-repeated acts, carried out in the spirit of the 'daily plebiscite' evoked by the nineteenth-century French historian Ernest Renan, help create the nation by constructing a sense of shared solidarity. Through everyday actions, the nation 'renews itself especially in the present by a tangible deed: the approval, the desire, clearly expressed, to continue the communal life' (Renan 1994 [1882], 17). Outside of elections, as well as in authoritarian and 'low-quality' democratic states (Case 2009), people produce and reproduce the nation through the often unthinking repetition of mundane daily activities. In so doing, they engage with an idea of the nation 'cloaked by the fog of common sense' (Fox & Miller-Idriss 2008, 539).

Every citizen is subject at the very least to 'banal nationalism' (Billig 1995), which is expressed in the symbolic markers of belonging to the nation-state. For example, these include a limp flag seen hanging from a public building on the daily walk to work (one being waved would be an explicit statement), the media's emphasis on 'home' news, singing the national anthem at football matches, or the repeated use of the adjective 'national' to describe affairs of state. These instances are generally seen (or rather overlooked) as an integral part of life's routines, in contrast to the explicit expressions of allegiance that also help cement national loyalty. Banal nationalism tends to be peripheral to people's concerns, despite forming a frame of reference for locating belonging and allegiance. In other words, 'the nation is not something ordinary people talk *about*; rather, it's something they talk *with*' (Fox & Miller-Idriss 2008, 540). Nevertheless, familiar activities like watching the television news serve to maintain national identifiers as taken for granted.

It is no coincidence that the question 'where are you from?' is often among the first to be put to new acquaintances. It helps situate them within a spatial understanding of the world, one that is dominated by nation-states. This, in turn, is reinforced by most standard answers to the question. For example, if the new acquaintance assumes they are from the same country as their interlocutor, they will specify a city, town or region within it. If not, they will tend to associate what is actually quite a vague enquiry about origins, provenance or residence with nationality, and offer that up as a statement of belonging. Other everyday markers signal this belonging, such as the language or dialect spoken, dress (Yeh 2002, 240), sporting allegiances, and so on. More solemn occasions than sports events also serve to maintain a national community. For instance, the significance of the annual Remembrance Sunday ceremonies observed across the UK, commemorating those who have died in wars since 1914, rests completely on the perceived existence of this national community. Without the justification of dying for one's country, the 'sacrifice' of the fallen would make no sense. And yet, individuals' responses to national monuments like the Cenotaph in London – the main focus for these ceremonies – will vary from their official interpretation. As with any ideology, top-down, orchestrated events will fail to reach some, whereas others will be selective and discerning in consuming, or 'buying into' national symbols. For example, Nadkarni (2003) chronicles a range of reactions to communist-era monuments in Budapest, which were dismantled in the early 1990s as symbols of an unacceptable ideology. For many city-dwellers, however, they had equally strong cultural associations as meeting places, familiar features of the cityscape, or even markers of their political passivity under the communist system. There was some public debate as to whether their removal to a small, commercially run park outside the centre implicitly honoured Hungary's communist past or brushed it aside to encourage forgetting. This highlights how official symbols of an ideology, nationalist or otherwise, may actually be imbued with as many meanings as there are political perspectives.

Michael Billig's book *Banal Nationalism* (1995) examined the omnipresence of nationalism in well-established nation-states like the US. As the world's only political superpower, the US is not only at the forefront of cultural and economic globalisation, but its people also have a reputation for patriotism (Lieven 2004, 6). As such, its brand of nation-building is worthy of closer attention in the context of the cosmopolitan challenge. Generations of immigrants to the US have invested in constitutionally enshrined values and the life aspirations of the 'American Dream', pointing to the existence of 'a pervasive ideology [which] provides a country with cohesion and flexibility – useful qualities to have in a rapidly modernizing world' (Hodson 2000, 108). This form of nation-building thus appears supremely well placed to cope with the cosmopolitan challenge. Nevertheless, the so-called Christian Right (Lieven 2004, 8), with religious fundamentalist movements at its vanguard, rails against the country's perceived social and cultural decline, which it variously attributes to globalisation, consumerism and increasing diversity. Proponents of this view tend to hanker after the days of 'White Anglo-Saxon Protestant' (WASP) dominance and portray other communities as a threat to 'real' American values (Lieven 2004, 7). These self-styled 'true Americans' see themselves as the inheritors and guardians of the US as 'God's chosen country', and challenge 'the state which they see as betraying the values of the USA's founders' (Scott 2001, 91). During the early years of US independence, the noble principles enshrined in the Constitution helped fuel the fledgling nation's 'messianic view of itself' (Scott 2001, 86) as a blessed and beautiful country. US presidents, both Democrat and Republican, have routinely called their country the 'greatest' (Clinton and Bush, cited in Billig 1995, 88). The Tea Party movement, which emerged early in Barack Obama's presidency to protest against what it sees as excessive government spending and regulation, explicitly argues for a return to the basic principles of the Constitution. It draws its name and inspiration from the Boston Tea Party of 1773, when American settlers resisted imperial Britain's attempts to impose taxes. The fervour with which the Tea Party movement champions the American Constitution overlooks the difficulty of applying its lofty but vague ideals to the pressing problems of today (*Economist* 2010a). However, the important point here is that a form of 'constitutional idolatry' (Klarman, cited in the *Economist* 2010a) is harnessing the Constitution to a contemporary cause. It is symptomatic of nation-building in the US, because 'what stands out about American ideology is its extraordinary ability to survive all the changes that have come over America since the seventeenth century' (McKenna 2007, xi). This statement says more about the flexibility of American nation-building in adapting to changing circumstances than its durability in any primordialist sense. The American Constitution contributes to this flexibility because it is open to so many (competing) interpretations.

A study of the role of print culture in American nation-building points out that 'Americans have historically had a mundane faith in the infallibility of their own written origins' (Loughran 2007, xviii). The word 'mundane' highlights that a hallowed document like the Constitution has become a taken for granted symbol of the American nation, a banal marker from which very diverse causes can derive their justification without fear of being branded 'un-American'. Indeed, the language of shared American values has been invoked by figures as diverse as Martin Luther King and Ronald Reagan (McKenna 2007, xii). Today, Tea Party symbolism resonates strongly because it builds on the Constitution as a central foundation of US nation-building, which schoolchildren learn to respect and even to revere. Regardless of the anachronistic use of a document whose understanding of equality originally excluded women and slaves, and regardless of how well it reflected the state of the American nation at the time, the Constitution is now anchored in collective memory (Loughran 2007, xx; Wiebe 2002, 67). It has been elevated to the national pantheon of America's 'founding myths' (Raphael 2006), together with iconic figures like Abraham Lincoln and George Washington, as well as selected works of literature. Together, these have 'created a usable past for a nation that lacked one' (Thomas 2007, 21; Wiebe 2002, 64). Of course, the US has not always lived up to this evocative discourse. One does not have to probe far into history to see that the Constitution as an icon of banal nationalism barely masks America's fragmentation, evident in everything from the Civil War to racial segregation, from migration to the mythical melting pot. Ironically, the continued tug-of-war over how to interpret the Constitution is itself a stark reminder that national unity is merely a fragile creation of nation-building (Loughran 2007, 3).

The US has had to face up to the lack of fit between its Constitution and the realities of racial segregation until the late 1960s, as well as more recent evidence that the US military tortured inmates at Abu Ghraib prison in Iraq, that so-called 'extraordinary rendition' of terrorism suspects to third countries for torture took place during George W. Bush's presidency, and that the notorious Guantanamo Bay prison continues to exist well into Barack Obama's term of office. These have been hard to square with the US's self-appointed role during the 1990s as representative of the 'international community', and its ethical justification for the first Gulf War in 1990–91. George Bush Senior, America's president at the time, often used an encompassing 'we' in his speeches to designate a vaguely defined international coalition working towards an equally vague 'new world order' (Billig 1995, 91). This coalition, led by the US, was clearly presented as occupying a moral high ground, in stark opposition to Saddam Hussein. By invading Kuwait, the Iraqi dictator epitomised the reprehensible 'Other', the outsider beyond the pale of shared moral values (Billig 1995, 91). George W. Bush would later crystallise this sentiment in no uncertain terms with the phrase 'Axis of Evil', uttered in the aftermath of the 9/11 attacks on New York and Washington, and the subsequent US invasions of Afghanistan and Iraq. In so doing, the younger Bush drew North Korea and Iran into this orbit of moral opposites, which was premised upon state regimes being somehow representative of ethical norms. Painting US patriotism in terms of moral certainties is clearly problematic, but it is part of ingraining a sense of banal nationalism in the American people. Vilifying the 'Other' is an effective form of nation-building in that it helps to vindicate the home country and make people feel good about belonging to it. At the same time, it seeks to marry the cosmopolitan appeal of supposedly universal values with a sense of US national exceptionalism as the 'leader of the free world'.

There is a link between the belief in the universality of American values and widespread expressions of nationalist pride, loyalty and patriotism.

Referring to the US, Martha Nussbaum describes something approximating banal nationalism as an 'unexamined feeling that one's own current preferences and ways are neutral and natural [...] lending to what is an accident of history a false air of moral weight and glory'. This form of nationalism has the potential to 'demonize those who are outside that boundary' of national belonging (Nussbaum, cited in Gasper 2006, 1235). In Anatol Lieven's view, it is a recipe for hubris and chauvinism (Lieven 2004, 14). Perhaps as a way of avoiding this conclusion, the less laden term of patriotism is widely used to describe nationalism in the US. For example, one US scholar writes, 'In place of "nationalism" and "chauvinism", I would substitute "patriotism". I believe that what we have seen persistently and, until recently, even among the most radical of Americans, is an underlying and abiding affection for America' (McKenna 2007, xiii). This appears to be an attempt to rebrand American nationalism as patriotism in order to make it seem a more banal, benign and fundamentally positive phenomenon, far removed from nationalism's more dangerous, atavistic or 'hot' manifestations.

As the world's only superpower, the US is subject to particularly rigorous outside scrutiny. Its past condemnation of colonialism and its role in developing and representing the UN's Universal Declaration of Human Rights in 1948 set a standard against which it found itself judged (King 2005, 16). Added to this are the strong transnational connections between diaspora communities in the US and their homelands, as well as US presidents' own readiness – from Woodrow Wilson to George W. Bush – to present the US as a defender of self-determination (King 2005, 176). As a result, 'outsiders form an image, whether favorable or critical, of the US's nationalist ideology from what they observe and learn about America's military power, economic reach, political influence and cultural representations' (King 2005, 15). Outside observers have also always been ready to analyse this ideology in explicitly nationalist terms, ranging from an interpretive essay by the influential theorist of nationalism Hans Kohn (1961), to the searing critique by the academic and journalist Anatol Lieven (2004). However, there is still a sense that those more favourably disposed towards American nationalism prefer to call it patriotism, whereas its 'critics and victims' (Sheehan in Wiebe 2002, xi) label it nationalism pure and simple. This normative debate has also taken place at the more abstract level of nationalism theory.

Maurizio Viroli (1995) set out to distinguish a patriotic love of liberty from the nationalist commitment to the homogeneity and unity of a people.

He asserts 'a charitable and generous love in the case of patriotism, an unconditional loyalty or an exclusive attachment in the case of the nationalists' (Viroli 1995, 2). In his view, both patriotism and nationalism use rhetorical flourish as much as rational argument in trying to orient patriots towards defending the republic or, in the case of nationalists, 'fomenting exclusion or aggression' (Viroli 1995, 8). Viroli accepts that 'the language of patriotism has also been used to oppress, discriminate, and conquer,' (Viroli 1995, 2), but his attempt to distinguish patriotism and nationalism ultimately hinges on a normative distinction between 'good' and 'bad' nationalism (Brown 1999). Elie Kedourie (1966) also differentiates between a Whig theory of nationality on the one hand, and nationalism on the other, asserting that the former 'worked' in the US and the UK, while the latter led to Nazism. In other words, Kedourie and Viroli are suggesting that a relatively 'benign' application of nationalist principles should have a less loaded title, like patriotism.

Dora Kostakopoulou's article titled 'Thick, Thin and Thinner Patriotisms: Is this all there is?' (2006) refers to the degree of cultural belonging inherent in each of these three variants. She argues that attempts at distinguishing patriotism from nationalism by emphasising allegiance to shared institutions instead of loyalty to a cultural community are ultimately unsuccessful, as both patriotism and nationalism are necessarily founded on national identity. Any distinction between nationalism and patriotism is a normative one, which tries to rescue the latter from the negative connotations of the former. Indeed, Viroli and Kedourie seek to introduce a value-laden distinction between patriotism and nationalism. Ultimately, however, patriotism draws on the same ideological principles and strategies as nationalism, and has the same potential to be exclusionary and, indeed, virulent. This, in turn, fatally undermines attempts to establish a '"new" discourse of "patriotism as anti-nationalism"' (Kostakopoulou 2006, 75). By contrast, this text has sought to portray patriotism, including US patriotism, as a form of 'banal nationalism'. It supports the view that 'by demonizing nationalism we avoid reckoning with it' (Wiebe 2002, 5). However, the same can be said of those who try to seal American patriotism off from nationalism, so as to avoid reckoning with its nastier implications and variations.

The US's long history of trade with and immigration from Europe, Africa and elsewhere has led it to be described as 'global before it was national [...] both as a product and as an agent of globalization' (Hodson 2000, 127). Linked to this, the US is also unique in the close association of cultural globalisation with so-called McDonaldization, Coca-colaization and other strong US brands (King 2005, 175). At the same time, different strands of national self-understanding in the US also display a deep and more inward-looking nationalism. For instance, American nation-building is rich in myths, commemorations and heroes, complete with founding fathers, a war of independence and a festival of thanksgiving. The renowned 'melting pot' model of integration has proved to be something of a misnomer, however. The country's archetypal immigrant society did not form a new amalgam, but rather retained distinct ethnicities, as evidenced by hyphenated identifiers like African-American. Neither has it been open to all. For example, the transparently titled Chinese Exclusion Act put a stop to Chinese immigration in 1882 and remained in force until 1944 (King 2005, 169). Vigilante patrols along the US–Mexican border to stop migrants entering the country illegally are evidence that borders and belonging continue to be highly sensitive topics today. Yet US leaders have often referred to their country using quasi-religious rhetoric, calling it a universal 'beacon of hope, […] a light unto the nations' (Reagan cited in Billig 1995, 100) and a bringer of freedom to allegedly more benighted countries. This discourse, repeated to the point of cliché and reinforced through ubiquitous phrases like 'God bless America', helps to ground the nation as a matter of fact in the minds of people who are 'being routinely primed for the dangers of the future' (Billig 1995, 127). It is a regular reminder of where people's loyalties should lie. As such, it is a prime example of banal nationalism, the underlying purpose of which is nation-state legitimation, and mobilisation in times of crisis. When 'your country needs you', to quote the World War I poster of British War Secretary Lord Kitchener pointing out from the page, everyone should know their country and be quick to leap to its defence. If banal nationalism represents the embers of national love and loyalty, then the moment when these are fanned into flames can be equated to the 'hot' nationalism considered in the next section.

Hot Nationalism

Nationalists who are chauvinists not only assert their national belonging and loyalty, but are also convinced that their nation is inherently better than others. Expressions of this can range from claims to be a chosen people living in 'God's country' to aggressive opposition to an 'Other' deemed inferior. In the latter case, we enter the realm of virulent or 'hot' nationalism, which some incorrectly believe to typify nationalism as a whole (Mišćević 2001, xii–xiii). Chauvinism presupposes a belief in being special, but the sense of superiority it promotes does not necessarily translate into aggression towards non-members of the community. In theory, it is possible to identify forms of nationalism that profess their people to be specially blessed, as can be found in the US, without necessarily advocating hostility towards outsiders. However, nationalism also has a tendency to take fascist, expansionist and even genocidal forms. This is when principles of chauvinistic nationalism are combined with strategies of belligerence, terrorism or extermination. Yet if we dismiss all nationalism as inherently pernicious, then the current international political system and an important component of most people's identities are necessarily compromised, because nationalism also underpins the world order of nation-states and citizenship. Consequently, we should be cautious of tarring every form of nationalism with the same brush, and try to distinguish between its many variants instead. Thus, the importance of understanding nationalism in its breadth and complexity becomes all the more evident, especially if we are to explore its responses to the cosmopolitan challenge.

Terrorism in the name of self-determination is one particularly violent and destructive form of chauvinist, 'hot' nationalism. Terrorists value their cause more highly than human life; in the case of suicide bombers they value it more highly than their own life. The combination of terrorism and nationalism can be particularly potent; nationalist ideology allies principle with a practical strategy for realising its aims, and the use of violence sharpens ethnic and political divisions. For example, violent attacks can resonate with people who do not believe they are condoning terrorism, but interpret them as 'retaliation or rebellion against repression rather than acts of random violence' (Byman 1998, 154). Even failed attacks draw attention to the cause, as subsequent state crackdowns cause resentment and alienation, serving to push more people towards terrorist tactics. The essentialisation of ethnic divides has been an important feature of civil strife on the island of Sri Lanka in the Indian Ocean, which ended in 2009 after more than 25 years of conflict. In considering the Sri Lankan conflict, it is misguided to assume a simple correspondence between an ethnic group – such as the majority Sinhalese – and 'their' island (Jazeel 2009). This underlines the more general point that nationalism never simply reflects 'natural' nations, even on an island territory.

Instead, it views peoples through an ideological prism, which divides them into national communities rather like light across a colour spectrum. The conflict in Sri Lanka pitted one such nationalist ideology against another using violent tactics, hence the inclusion of the Sri Lankan case in this section.

Following Sri Lanka's independence from Britain in 1948, the rapid politicisation of ethnicity formed the basis for accusations that the minority Tamil ethnic group was being victimised and the majority Sinhalese were dominating key aspects of Sri Lankan society including language, education and employment. In the late 1970s, the Tamil United Liberation Front's political agitation for an independent homeland in the island's north and east, together with sporadic attacks on political targets, soon gave way to organised armed violence after 1983. Any account of the ensuing conflict and its protagonists immediately runs the risk of making normative judgements by choosing to define the Liberation Tigers of Tamil Eelam (LTTE), also known as the Tamil Tigers, as either 'terrorists' or 'freedom fighters' (Stokke 2006, 1021). Like so many other political concepts, the definition of terrorism is contested, which is hardly surprising given its polarising effects. Today, terrorism is certainly associated with politicised violence and negative connotations, although this was not always so (Laqueur 2003, 235). Consequently, so-called terrorists usually try to escape the label by presenting themselves in more neutral terms, such as guerrillas, insurgents, militants, activists or commandos (Laqueur 2003, 232).

Predictably, successive Sri Lankan governments chose to label their LTTE opponents as terrorists, thereby helping to legitimate their own actions in the eyes of the international community. They depicted the conflict as one between the Sri Lankan state, understood as representing Sinhalese interests, and 'Tamil terrorists'. The LTTE, on the other hand, considered itself to be engaged in a national liberation struggle for the self-determination of a Tamil homeland (known as Tamil Eelam) in Sri Lanka's north and east. Using familiar nationalist discourse, it claimed to be speaking for Tamils as a whole and to be 'articulating the wishes and aspirations of the Tamil nation' (Pirapaharan, cited in Nadarajah & Sriskandarajah 2005, 88). The LTTE thus used the principle of national self-determination to justify its cause. In 1983, however, campaigning for this goal was made illegal following a government amendment to the Sri Lankan Constitution.

The LTTE frequently refers to the 1983 wave of violence against Tamils, sparked in reprisal for the LTTE's own landmine attack that killed thirteen Sri Lankan soldiers in the northern town of Jaffna, as the event which triggered civil war and the escalation of its violent campaign (Brun 2008, 403). Widespread attacks against Tamils led to a wave of refugees and the formation of a sizeable Tamil diaspora, parts of which then helped to promote and fund the LTTE. The organisation became notorious for the scale of its suicide attacks, having pioneered this form of violence in the early 1980s around the same time as Hezbollah in Lebanon (Laqueur 2003, 79). The precarious state of 'no war and no peace' following a ceasefire in 2002 offered exhausted inhabitants in the north and east only temporary respite from the uncertainty, confinement and violence of wartime. The region slid back into conflict over the next few years, culminating in the corralling of thousands of Tamil civilians into a narrow strip of beach in the last weeks of an all-out war in 2009. This was won by the Sri Lankan military, only to be followed by the lengthy and highly internationally controversial internment of those civilians in camps. In 2011, an expert report for the UN also condemned both the LTTE and the Sri Lankan government's role in causing casualties running well into five figures, including many civilian victims of government shelling, during the final months of the war. This supported the assessments of many non-governmental observers, but the Sri Lankan government has consistently denied any responsibility for these deaths (*Economist* 2011a, 60).

As in the case of Tibet, discussed in Chapter 3, the international dimension of the Sri Lankan conflict should not be underestimated. Contrary to that of the Tibetans, however, the Tamil cause has not enjoyed the same level of international sympathy and support, partly due to its association with terrorism. References to the LTTE as 'terrorists' were not new to political discourse in Sri Lanka, as evidenced by the oft-repeated phrase 'there is no ethnic problem in Sri Lanka, only a terrorist problem' (Wijetunge, cited in Kleinfeld 2003, 109). Following the 9/11 attacks on Washington and New York, however, Sri Lankan governments placed the ongoing civil war within the wider context of the US-led fight against terrorism, which they used to justify their aim of completely defeating the LTTE (Kleinfeld 2003, 107). In so doing, they sought to ride the international wave of opprobrium against terrorism by putting the LTTE on a par with the Al Qaeda network, to gain outside support and assistance for their military campaign. The regular equation of 'Tamil' with 'terrorist' in Sri Lankan government discourse, together with its own self-identification with Sinhalese interests rather than those of the entire citizenry, hindered efforts at conflict resolution as ethnic divisions became more entrenched (Byman 1998, 155). Linked to this, the LTTE was banned in the UK, the US, Canada, Australia and India as a terrorist organisation, suggesting that its nationalist rhetoric of armed struggle was not considered legitimate internationally. This shows how the LTTE's fortunes became intertwined with the cosmopolitan challenge through its diaspora and the global ethics propounded among the international community. Only in the 1990s did the Sri Lankan government seek to distinguish between Tamils and the LTTE, ostensibly in order to 'free' the former from the latter (Nadarajah & Sriskandarajah 2005, 92). This was accompanied by attempts to defuse ethnic politicisation through limited devolution of power under president Kumaratunga (Stokke 2006, 1026). However, the LTTE rebuffed government moves towards a federal solution in 2000, continuing to demand complete independence for Sri Lanka's Tamil-majority territories in the island's north and east (Ganguly 2004, 904).

Aspects of the cosmopolitan challenge had an important impact on the evolution of the conflict in Sri Lanka. As we have seen, the repercussions of the 9/11 attacks included an international backlash against terrorist tactics. The LTTE's use of suicide bombers, women and child soldiers, its alleged links with drug trafficking and smuggling, its role in harassing, killing and expelling Sri Lankan Muslims from the east of the country, and its attacks on high-profile political figures, resulted in its being banned in many countries where the Tamil diaspora had settled. This was a major setback for its cause, as parts of that diaspora played a key role in fundraising for the LTTE and presenting a positive image of the organisation abroad. The break-up of Yugoslavia, which made support for self-determination deeply suspect internationally, only heightened the LTTE's isolation on the world stage. The LTTE's fall from grace corresponded to the heightened status of the Sri Lankan government as a co-combatant in George W. Bush's 'War on Terror' (Ganguly 2004, 908). This helped pave the way for several rounds of LTTE peace talks with the Sri Lankan government in 2002–3. By this time, the LTTE was prepared to countenance self-determination through greater autonomy within the Sri Lankan state, but insisted on retaining the option of outright secession. This only fuelled continuing government misgivings about accepting a so-called Tamil homeland as a possible precursor to de facto independence.

In early 2004, the election of a new Sri Lankan government seemed to indicate popular support for a change of tack, which included a refusal to recognise the LTTE as sole representative of the Tamils, and a renewed emphasis on seeing the conflict in terms of terrorism and law and order rather than ethnic division (Ganguly 2004, 915). This approach underlined the country's constitutional status as a unitary, centralised state. Meanwhile, the success of pro-LTTE parties in the country's north and east appeared to strengthen the LTTE's claim to be a legitimate Tamil representative, only for this to be undermined by tensions among its own regional leaders. Nevertheless, the LTTE proceeded to engage in a form of state-building in Sri Lanka's north and east through a combination of ideological hegemony and military coercion (Stokke 2006, 1027). As a result, the extent of the LTTE's popular support is difficult to gauge. For instance, the LTTE's role in establishing a legal code, court system and police force within their claimed jurisdiction of Tamil Eelam was an extension of their security apparatus, but also seemed to enjoy legitimacy among the population. The LTTE became involved in health and education service provision, as well as being indirectly linked to a humanitarian aid organisation working to heal the wounds of the very war it was waging (Derges 2009).

Research conducted in Sri Lanka's northernmost Jaffna peninsula in 2003–4 found a society characterised 'by rumour and accusations of questioned loyalties; village was often pitted against village and the extensive infiltration and observation of the populace made anonymity rare' (Derges 2009, 29). Another study of young Tamils found ambivalent attitudes; a mixture of respect, gratitude, fear and resentment at the LTTE's dominant position and the lack of space for dissenting voices. People were cautious of criticising the LTTE for fear of endangering themselves or their families, leading to a culture of silence and suspicion (Brun 2008, 415; Derges 2009, 27). Evidently, the LTTE's claim to represent all Tamils cannot be taken at face value. Instead, it seemed the organisation was 'among the people, of the people, and at the same time distant from the people' (Brun 2008, 410), highlighting the complex relationship between nationalist ideologues and the compatriots they claim to represent.

The LTTE's nationalist discourse – including racist stereotyping of the Sinhalese 'Other', the adulation of LTTE heroes and martyrs, and emphasis on Tamil victimisation to help justify violence – was certainly influential among Tamils, both within Sri Lanka and in the diaspora. It contributed to the essentialisation of Sri Lankan politics into ethnic categories, namely separatist Tamils versus unitary Sinhalese (with Muslims and other ethnic groups caught in the crossfire). At the same time, Tamils in Sri Lanka's north and east were living under the competing control of LTTE and government institutions. For young Tamils in particular, their future aspirations made them look towards Sri Lanka's capital Colombo as a bastion of modernity, compared to the island's isolated north. Some were therefore inclined to put federalism above independence as their preferred political solution (Brun 2008, 420). Clearly, categorising the LTTE as terrorists does not go uncontested, and some have argued that the US killing of Osama Bin Laden was a state-sanctioned assassination that blurred the line between legitimate violence and terrorism, since 'no enlightened moral framework allows revenge to become a synonym for justice' (Porter 2011, n.p.). It is submitted here that the LTTE provides an example of 'hot' nationalism because it combined nationalist principles with violent action. In ideological terms, its nationalist core principles were pursued through a sustained strategy of military and guerrilla warfare lasting over a quarter of a century. Finally, support from within the Tamil diaspora was an integral part of maintaining its operations, and worldwide crackdowns on perceived terrorism during the 1990s and 2000s directly affected its activities. This is not an attempt to tarnish Tamils as a whole, for that would be the sort of essentialising analysis critiqued in Chapter 1. Rather, it highlights how potent the label 'terrorist' can be in affecting the fortunes of a nationalist movement. Straddling the turn of the twenty-first century, the LTTE's struggle clearly incorporated aspects of the cosmopolitan challenge.

Conclusion

Banal nationalism refers to the everyday activities and choices that are informed, moulded and constrained by the institutions and imaginings of the nation-state. The 'unreflective, automatic' (Fox & Miller-Idriss 2008, 544) nature of many manifestations of banal nationalism is not a symptom of its weakness, quite the opposite. Ironically, the nation is at its most potent when it becomes banal, a taken-for-granted source of loyalty and belonging. The acceptance of a given national configuration as common sense necessarily puts any competing interpretation of the nation at a disadvantage, since it will have to overcome a well-established, unquestioned frame of reference. This is reinforced by national institutions like schools, which tend to 'silently structure' (Fox & Miller-Idriss 2008, 545) people's choices by streaming and socialising them within national categories. Banal nationalism aims to instil an unthinking loyalty in people, which can be galvanised and mobilised in times of need; overcoming 'intermittent crises depend[s] on existing ideological foundations' (Billig 1995, 5). Banal nationalism takes its strength from the familiar, and also from the 'universal code of nationhood' (Billig 1995, 83), which characterises the current world order. Banal nationalism keeps the embers of nationalism glowing, ready to be stoked during elections and referenda, through authoritarian legitimation by acclamation, or in times of war. Finally, banal nationalism is designed to keep support for nation-building or a nationalist movement at the level required to ensure its legitimacy. The nation-building strategies, discourse and rhetoric adopted to promote the nation can thus be subsumed under the practical, 'action plan' aspect of ideology.

Simply imagining the home nation as one among many helps to undermine chauvinistic nationalism, which focuses on a sense of superiority that purports to justify aggressive policies like expansionism and 'ethnic cleansing'. Universalist nationalism imagines the 'Other' as different in order to justify nation-state borders and legitimacy, whereas chauvinist nationalism paints the 'Other' as inferior and therefore unworthy of protection or respect. Colonialism's self-legitimating 'civilising mission', for example, notwithstanding the euphemistic use of the term 'protectorate' in some cases, clearly fits the latter category. This helps to explain the widely differing strategies adopted across variants of nationalism. If nationalists respect and value the community of nations and their place within it, they will strive for international recognition of their own authority and autonomy, and accord it to others. The motivation of nationalist chauvinists is more complex, for it acknowledges the international order while construing it as a threat to national survival. Nazi propaganda's creation of a worldwide Jewish conspiracy is but one example. Chauvinism is certainly a variant of nationalism, but it is misguided to equate chauvinism with *all* nationalisms. The way in which the nation is defined is what opens the fault lines between nationalism's many variants, ranging from 'hot' to banal. In other words, just as nationalism can be chauvinistic and exclusionary, so it can be defined more openly by offering a share in a common project. Nationalism necessarily creates in-groups and out-groups, but these can be more or less exclusive and the barriers to entry more or less porous. Membership of some national communities will be defined very restrictively by the likes of descent, linguistic ability or religion, whereas others may adopt a voluntaristic model, according to which anyone wishing to do so may join by living on the national territory. The difficulties of negotiating these hurdles to national belonging, both for the governments imposing them and the migrants on whom they are imposed, is a key aspect of the cosmopolitan challenge discussed further in Chapter 5. Ultimately, however, nationalists aspire to win and retain the loyalty of 'their' people and to command that loyalty at key moments in the life of the nation they have done much to create or maintain.

3

What Kind of Nation: Communist, Democratic, Multicultural?

Is it possible to reconcile communist and nationalist ideologies? How does nationalism relate to multiculturalism? What is the relationship between nationalism and democracy?

This chapter looks at how nationalism interacts with communism, democracy and multiculturalism. All forms of nationalist ideology draw on a recent or more distant past, be it the injustices of the Soviet system or pre-modern myths. The chapter begins by looking at communism, which may seem more suited to critiques of the Cold War, but which has not disappeared from today's world. Like the lasting legacy of colonialism discussed in Chapter 1, post-communist countries are still marked by the experience, and a few communist states still remain in place today (Sutherland 2010, 165). Communism trumped nationalism within the USSR and its satellite states, but cases like Yugoslavia and Estonia – which is discussed below – show that Soviet-era territorial units could quickly be rearticulated in ethnic nationalist terms. Beyond the core ideological principle of prioritising national autonomy and culture, however, nationalist strategies and success will depend on many factors, including economics, leadership, emotion, (perceived) injustice, oppression, conflict and the way the 'Other' is constructed. The first section of the chapter explores how the two apparently incompatible ideologies of communism and nationalism are combined in the Socialist Republic of Vietnam, one of the last few remaining communist states.

The second section of the chapter discusses nationalism's links with multiculturalism, a concept that requires further clarification. Multiculturalism, in the wider sense, refers to collectivities seeking public recognition for their heritage and culture. In the narrower, political sense prevalent in the UK, for instance, it denotes 'the recognition of group difference within the public sphere of laws, policies, democratic discourses and the terms of a shared citizenship and national identity' (Modood 2007, 2). This definition highlights the way in which a multiculturalist response to diversity and immigration affects nation-building. Rather than promote a unitary sense of national belonging, multiculturalism recognises a range of loyalties, though this is usually premised on the acceptance of certain core societal values. That is, different ways of life are tolerated, except for specific practices deemed repugnant to prevailing laws and principles. Of course, multiculturalism also throws up questions about national solidarity and social cohesion: how to maintain national identity and legitimacy on a relatively meagre shared basis? How to deal with divided loyalties? Multiculturalism is also essentialising insofar as it groups people into categories according to putative shared characteristics, as will be seen in section three below. A retreat from the multicultural model in the likes of the Netherlands and Germany (*Guardian* 2010b) suggests that some states have not found satisfactory answers to these questions.

In his book *Rethinking Multiculturalism*, Bhikhu Parekh makes a crucial distinction between fact and ideology: 'The term "multicultural" refers to the fact of cultural diversity, the term "multiculturalism" to a normative response to that fact' (Parekh 2002, 6). According to this definition, a nation-state may be multicultural in practice but pursue a monocultural idea of shared citizenship in principle. France is one example of a country that is in fact multicultural but does not officially recognise or protect ethnic diversity as a matter of policy. Monoculturalism advocates some form of assimilation to the culture, values and norms of the 'dominant *ethnie*' (Smith 1995, 106), whereas multiculturalism, by contrast, makes the nation-state's cultural diversity 'central to its self-understanding' (Parekh 2002, 6). Parekh points out that conservative thinkers are often reluctant to accept that their country is in fact culturally diverse, for fear of ceding ground to those who argue for a multiculturalist, rather than a monoculturalist approach to nation-building. Successive German governments' reticence in recognising Germany as a land of immigration (*Einwanderungsland*) is one instance of this (Holmes Cooper 2002, 97). Highlighting the link to the democratic context discussed further below, these multiculturalist and monoculturalist approaches to nation-building have also been termed democratic nationalism and assimilationist democracy respectively (King 2005, 6). The following discussion adopts the distinction between multicultural demographics and multiculturalist policy, and shows in its second section how a multicultural country like Estonia has responded to diversity in a less than multiculturalist way. Instead, Estonia's policy has tended to be monoculturalist in giving the Estonian language 'pride of place' (Parekh 2002, 6) in official culture and making competence in it a condition of access to citizenship. This has proved a significant barrier to Estonia's sizeable Russian-speaking minority.

The chapter's final section goes on to examine the compatibility of democracy and nationalism. It looks at the world's largest democracy, India, whose matchless cultural diversity has coexisted with a democratic resilience that has puzzled many observers. The notion of national unity, which under-pinned India's first decades of independence, has come under sustained attack from promoters of Hindu monoculturalism, and the question is whether shared citizenship can continue to overcome communalist tensions in the long term. Another case in point is Fiji, where planned elections were postponed and the Constitution suspended in 2009. This represents the failure of democracy in the face of a long-standing communal divide between ethnic Fijians and Indo-Fijians. The concluding comparison between Fiji and Estonia is instructive, because these represent two examples of multicul-tural states that are wary of multiculturalist rhetoric. Both Fiji and Estonia are multicultural according to Parekh's definition, with a large Indo-Fijian minority to match Estonia's Russian-speaking one, and in both cases the indigenous ethnic group plays a predominant role in government. Democracy is one means that nation-builders can use to manage pluralism and diversity (Vincent 2002, 173). Based on principles of popular sovereignty and equal citizenship, the people can be equated with the *demos*, but a concomitant sense of national belonging cannot be taken for granted. Within a multicul-tural society, both democracy and nation-building can struggle with a multi-culturalist agenda. This is because each approach will be trying to represent the interests of different groups which do not completely overlap, whether it be those of the multicultural *demos*, a monocultural nation or specific ethnic minorities. It is precisely this feature that results in friction between monoc-ulturalists and multiculturalists. 'In this sense, nationalist language – reduced in scale and dimension – paradoxically accounts for much of the appeal and moral impetus of multiculturalism' (Vincent 2002, 159).

Communism

Although Karl Marx is often accused of paying scant attention to national-ism, it does feature in his work as an established phenomenon destined to be overcome by proletarian revolution. Indeed, he imagined the proletariat transcending national boundaries to form a cosmopolitan class solidarity: 'Marx envisions a historical scenario in which national states are no longer able to command the loyalty of their proletariat. The masses are able to recognize the nation as a tool of oppression because the hyphen between nation and state has been rendered so tight that it has completely disappeared' (Cheah 2003, 185). Marx thereby associates the nation with the state, rather than the people, or *Volk*. He portrays the bourgeoisie as hiding their class interests behind a façade of national solidarity, which actually smacks more of economic protectionism. As such, they may cooperate with the proletariat against outside economic forces, but in no way as fellow nationals (Szporluk 1988, 23). Marx's understanding of the nation is of course intimately tied up with the exploitative capitalist structures he describes. Therefore, he posits that the nation must necessarily disappear, along with the state, as a result of proletarian revolution. However, Marx's theoretical approach was tempered by events occurring in his lifetime.

Marx was favourably disposed towards nineteenth-century Polish and Irish nationalism, as they fought for independence from imperialism (Connor 1984, 11). The uprisings of 1848 across Europe also brought home to him the mobilising power of nationalism. Marx then sought to distinguish nation-building by the bourgeois state from the nationalism of the oppressed, which he considered to be an important force in the struggle against imperialism. Indeed, Marx identified Irish independence as a prerequisite of proletarian revolution in England, since he considered colonial exploitation to be linked to domestic exploitation within the imperialist system. When the bourgeois state sought to foster imperial pride and national chauvinism, it created an artificial divide between work-ers, thereby blinding them to their common cause with the international proletariat (Cheah 2003, 189). Therefore, in Marx's view, the English proletariat could only free itself by ending its collusion in colonialism. In sum, anti-colonial nationalism was to be viewed as a tool of emancipa-tion, whereas state-led nation-building was a means of oppression (Connor 1984, 7). Marx thereby supplemented his narrow economic view of state nationalism with an anti-bourgeois nationalism. This could be used as a vehicle on the road towards proletarian internationalism, but was not to be valued as a good in itself.

V. I. Lenin took up these ideas in the context of third world anti-imperialism and nationalism's obvious continued appeal into the early twentieth century. Though shocked and disappointed by nationalism's strength and virulence during World War I, Lenin opted for the more pragmatic approach to nationalism evident in Marx and Engels' later writings. He theorised that by allying communism with the nationalist aspirations of colonised peoples across the world, he could undercut the imperialist exploitation of the colonies, whose labour had temporarily eased the pressure on the European proletariat and thereby dulled their appetite for revolution. National self-determination, understood to include outright secession, thus took centre stage in the wider struggle for class emancipation from imperialism and exploitation. Lenin's purely strategic commitment to nationalism highlights his enduring belief that economic and class interests would eventually win out 'against the stupidity of the cultural-national autonomists' (Lenin cited in Connor 1984, 36). The link Lenin forged between anti-colonialism and communism would be particularly relevant in the case of Vietnam.

Still firmly in control of Vietnam's one-party state, the Vietnamese Communist Party (VCP) continues to combine nation-building with communism in order to maintain its legitimacy. Its brand of nationalism has also varied strategically, however, from its early-twentieth-century beginnings in the midst of anti-colonial resistance, through mobilising the population to endure decades of war against France and the US, to its current response to international pressures for economic liberalisation and democratisation. This account cannot begin to convey the heated debates which surrounded the gradual evolution of Vietnamese self-understanding among imperial court historians, anti-colonial nationalists and VCP ideologues from the turn of the twentieth century onwards (see Marr 1971; Ninh 2002, 242; Tai 1992; Vu 2007, 207). Resolving the apparent tension between communism and nationalism was but one of the ideological battles waged among Vietnamese intellectuals 'not only over the form of their state, but over the nature of Vietnamese society, the very identity of the Vietnamese' (Huynh 1982, 9). The VCP's own ideological focus shifted strategically during the 1930s and '40s in response to the evolving domestic and international situation, moving from an emphasis on class struggle towards 'revolutionary nationalism', anticolonial heroism and national liberation instead (Bradley 2000, 109). At the same time, communist internationalism was reflected in the peripatetic lives of leaders like Ho Chi Minh and cross-fertilisation with communists in China, the Soviet Union and elsewhere.

Following Ho Chi Minh's declaration of Vietnamese independence in 1945, his close colleague General Vo Nguyen Giap made a speech stating that '[t]he center, the south, and the north share one heart' (cited in McHale 2004, 177), thereby reasserting the unity of the Vietnamese nation after its division into three regions of French colonial Indochina. The French did not accept Vietnamese independence, however, leading to the first Indochinese war. General Giap would go on to lead the final French defeat at the battle of Dien Bien Phu in 1954, only to see Vietnam divided into two as a result of the subsequent Geneva agreement. This ideological and territorial divide along the seventeenth parallel soon hardened into two states, the Democratic Republic of Vietnam (DRV) to the north and the Republic of Vietnam (RVN) to the south. The US bankrolled the RVN as a bulwark against Ho Chi Minh's DRV and what it saw as predatory communism supported by China and the USSR. As a result, the US gradually became embroiled in one of the most devastating and traumatic conflicts of the Cold War. The Vietnam-American war, also known as the second Indochinese war due to its wider regional impact, polarised opinion among Western scholars and commentators with regard to the relationship between communism and nationalism (Vu 2007, 190). Many adopted the primordialist view of nationhood used by both the DRV and the RVN in bolstering their respective claims to legitimacy as the 'true' representative of Vietnam. In both states, national division tended to be viewed as a temporary, regrettable aberration brought about by alien forces and ideologies, thereby supporting a narrative of recurrent Vietnamese victimhood and 'natural' Vietnamese unity (Sutherland 2010, 48).

William Duiker (1981, 5) reports Ho Chi Minh's comment that 'for him, the road to communism went through nationalism', illustrating how closely the two ideologies were linked in the Vietnamese case. The interplay of nationalism and communism in Vietnam is encapsulated in a poem composed by Ho Chi Minh around 1940, likening Lenin to a stream and Marx to a mountain waiting to be 'united into one country' (Ho, cited in Bradley 2000, 110). This links the fathers of international communism to familiar mythological themes, reminiscent in particular of the Vietnamese founding legend of Au Co and Lac Long Quan, mountain fairy and water god respectively. It is typical of the rhetorical technique Ho used to bring home the relevance of a fundamentally alien and complex ideology, with its opaque concepts of 'bourgeoisie', 'class' and even 'worker' (McHale 2004, 113). The poem's reference to national unity thus expresses a central aim of both the first Indochinese war and, although prefiguring the division of Vietnam along the seventeenth parallel, also the Vietnam-American War, where both sides sought unification albeit under opposing ideological systems. Vietnam reportedly shares with Afghanistan the dubious distinction of enduring the longest period of international conflict since the end of World War II (Taylor & Botea 2008), but revolutionary ideology continued to be a potent basis for popular mobilisation and nation-building in peacetime. Today, 'Uncle Ho's' carefully constructed cult of personality as a Vietnamese father figure continues to emphasise his nationalism as much as his communist credentials. One of his most quoted phrases, emblazoned on a banner at the entrance to his Lenin and Mao-style mausoleum, reads 'there is nothing more precious than independence and freedom.'

Vietnamese unification came about in 1976 after the DRV's victory had been sealed with the fall of Saigon in April 1975. Years of hardship followed for the rechristened Socialist Republic of Vietnam. This so-called 'subsidy era', characterised by severe shortages and even famine in some areas, is only now being thematised and publicly discussed within the country (Maclean 2008). It is important to note that Vietnam was never a closed society, since it was part of the international network of 'socialist brother states' throughout the Cold War. However, the 'renovation' policy (known as *doi moi*) introduced during the 1980s marked a departure from this model in favour of a so-called 'socialist market economy', which saw an end to price controls and agricultural collectivisation. It also brought the economic liberalisation of housing and investment markets, as well as the privatisation, or so-called 'equitisation', of some state-owned enterprises. This has not been accompanied by any large-scale political democratisation, however, although there have been moves to increase public participation and parliamentary oversight of politics in recent years. The state still aims to play a 'leading role' in the economy (Painter 2005, 264), and the VCP remains in overall control of contemporary Vietnam, even though its influence is patchy depending on the administrative level, the policy area and even the part of the country in question (Gainsborough 2007; Painter 2005, 267). This illustrates how the Vietnamese state is adopting new forms of nation-building to bolster its legitimacy, without jettisoning its communist credentials for all that: 'The move towards a law governed state is a reflection of the broader strategy of the ruling Communist Party of Vietnam to create new foundations for its legitimacy' (Rodan & Jayasuriya 2007, 805).

The evidence suggests that the partnership between nationalist and communist ideology continues in a new form of creative tension. Where national legitimacy was once closely entwined with the VCP's wartime legacy, economic development and administrative reform are now playing an increasing role in its approach to nation-building. This strategy rests on the assumption that national loyalty and 'performance' legitimacy will flow from prosperity, transparency and increased efficiency. Naturally, the VCP's current nation-building is designed to underpin its continuing political hegemony. The VCP must therefore manage economic and policy innovations while maintaining its authority, and this often means co-opting the forces of private enterprise and globalisation into the state apparatus (Gainsborough 2007; Rodan & Jayasuriya 2007, 805). Here we see a pragmatic response to the cosmopolitan challenge, one that seeks to harness the impact of globalisation and international liberalisation for the purposes of nation-building: 'The selection and adoption of particular neo-liberal reforms in the face of external pressures must be understood as a domestic political process in which the state seeks to shore up its authority while accommodating emerging state–business alliances' (Painter 2005, 263). For instance, recent efforts at promoting the political participation of Vietnamese citizens are partly to comply with external pressures, such as World Trade Organisation membership and the conditionalities attached to World Bank funding (Rodan & Jayasuriya 2007, 810).

The VCP is highly attuned and sensitive to signs of popular discontent, testifying to 'the centre's domestic vulnerability as much as its strength' (Painter 2005, 267). In some high-profile cases, the government has arrested online pro-democracy campaigners, including members of the activist network Bloc 8406 and the prominent human rights lawyer Le Cong Dinh. It has also muzzled associations judged too critical of the government, like the Club of Former Resistance Fighters based in Ho Chi Minh City (Kerkvliet, Heng & Koh 2003, 17). The VCP seeks to perform a complex balancing act between upholding elements of communist ideology and governance, pursuing nation-building premised on economic liberalisation and performance legitimacy, and paying heed to the concomitant spread of corruption and income inequality that undermine that legitimacy. A further important aspect of nation-building in contemporary Vietnam is the recent resurgence in religious practice, which is tolerated and in some cases promoted by the state. Although national heroes in Vietnam have been revered throughout the VCP's time in power, many religious practices were discouraged and labelled 'superstitious' in the decades following World War II (Soucy 2003, 128; Sutherland 2010, 146). Some interpret the current religious revival as 'an assertion of nationalism meant to counterbalance influences from the West' (Soucy 2003, 129). Similarly, others have shown how the VCP now approves of the widespread practice of ancestor worship, in particular its potential to promote 'a sense of national belonging in the post-war, late socialist moment' (Jellema 2007, 61). The leisure activities associated with places of pilgrimage and religious festivals are a further aspect of this trend, with entrepreneurs often leaving the most generous offerings. 'Until very recently the powerful intervention of the state upon the desires and needs of the populace was successful in implementing a regime of pleasure associated with nationalist ideals' (Drummond & Thomas 2003, 7). Now it seems that long-standing spiritual beliefs and religious practices are also being rehabilitated and co-opted into official nation-building.

What can we conclude from the Vietnamese case about the compatibility of communism and nationalism? Early communist cadres were faced with the gargantuan task of introducing a new discourse to Vietnam. In the event, the communist-led *Viet Minh* preferred to appeal to the people (*dan toc*) and the fatherland (*to quoc*) rather than highlight class divisions. To this extent, nationalist and communist goals could be complementary, but only if ideological links were forged between core elements of each, such as communist revolution and anti-colonial struggle, patriotic heroes and proletarian workers, capitalist exploitation and national liberation. Scholars have long debated whether nationalism or communism dominates the Vietnamese nation and where the loyalties of its chief exponent truly lay (McHale 2004, 180; Vu 2007, 193). One is tempted to let Ho Chi Minh himself have the last, slightly ambiguous word on the matter, if we recall that Lenin merely paid lip service to nationalism: 'At first, it was patriotism (*chu nghia yeu nuoc*) not yet communism (*chu nghia cong san*), which led me to have confidence in Lenin, in the third international' (Ho, cited in Vasavakul 1995, 261).

In its various guises, the VCP has continued to marry nationalism and communism in its nation-building, by repeating core messages, myths and stories in its propaganda until they have become taken for granted elements of official discourse. Today, although the VCP is aware of the need for international aid and investment to achieve economic growth, it is not always prepared to accept external conditions regarding the pace and content of reform without question, and some agreements have foundered as a result. In what can be taken as a reference to decades of wartime resistance, Vietnam's then Minister of Planning and Investment is quoted as saying in 1999 that 'no one is going to bombard Vietnam into acting' (Tran Xuan Gia cited in Painter 2005, 274). This shows how the contemporary reform process is intimately bound up with nation-building in

Vietnam. This continues to draw on national myths, while also relying on popular beliefs, economic growth and limited democratic participation in order to bolster state legitimacy without endangering the VCP's pre-eminent position within the Socialist Republic of Vietnam.

Multiculturalism

The break-up of the Soviet Union resulted in the creation of a 25 million strong Russian diaspora overnight, without any population movement whatsoever. Fifteen new states were created from the former Soviet republics and the tables were turned. Having been the majority 'dominant *ethnie*' (Smith 1995, 106) in the USSR, many ethnic Russians living within its former borders suddenly found themselves a minority – albeit a size-able one – in the likes of newly independent Estonia and Latvia. This illustrates the way in which nation-building involves categorisation, and how labels like 'ethnic minority' are not a given, but rather highly potent points of departure for a whole range of policies. These have a tendency to discriminate either positively or negatively (why else create the category in the first place?) in ways that can have a huge impact on individual lives. The Russian federation today, for example, depicts itself as the historic homeland of its diaspora. As such, it considers itself within its rights to intervene in neighbouring countries in order to protect Russians, as demonstrated by the short war with Georgia in August 2008. Some of Russia's newly independent neighbours, by contrast, are suspicious of what they see as an imperialist attitude. The Russian state thus has a significant role to play in Estonia's relations with its large Russian-speaking minority. The Estonian case illustrates how a de facto multicultural polity may resist multiculturalist policies, despite pressure from the international community on Estonia to extend citizenship and the franchise to all of its residents. As in the case of Vietnam, part of the cosmopolitan challenge for this recently independent country is to reconcile its obligations as a member of regional and international organisations with the consolidation of its own nation-state.

Along with the other Baltic republics of Latvia and Lithuania, Estonia was briefly independent between the two World Wars, only to be annexed by the Soviet Union in 1944 under the terms of the secret Molotov-Ribbentrop pact. On becoming independent again from the defunct Soviet Union in 1991, however, it did not enfranchise its sizeable Russian-speaking population. Today, Estonia tends to score relatively highly on democratic indicators such as press freedom, judicial independence and free and fair elections. On a descending scale of 1 to 7, the non-governmental organisation Freedom House gave the country an overall average rating of 1.93 for the year 2009 (Pettai & Molder 2009, 199). Estonia's accession to the EU and NATO in 2004 entrenched its orientation towards Western powers and away from Russian influence, but its treatment of ethnic Russians, most of whom settled in the Baltic region during the Soviet era, has been a cause for concern among its Western partners (Steen 2010).

Predictably, independent Estonia's nation-building has focused on legitimating its new contours and valorising its heritage. For instance, it has 'rediscovered' the traditional appeal of indigenous ethnic groups like the Seto (Kaiser & Nikiforova 2006). Interestingly, in terms of the cosmopolitan challenge, this has taken place within the regionalist framework of EU membership and funding to support minority groups. Inevitably, however, it has not gone uncontested, especially as border zones are key sites of conceptual and physical nationalist conflict, and the Seto homeland straddles the current border between Estonia and Russia. This has led the Estonian government to support the resettlement of Russian-based Seto, who identify as Estonian, on the Estonian side of the border, while ruing the resulting loss of Seto influence and culture inside Russia (Kaiser & Nikiforova 2006). At the same time as the borders of EU, Estonian and Russian influence are being defined, and the return of Estonian co-ethnics is being facilitated, there is dissatisfaction among ethnic Russians living on Estonian territory about their situation. About one third of Estonia's total resident population of 1.3 million is currently identified as ethnic Russian.

In 2007, riots sparked by the contested symbolism of a soldier's statue signalled a festering issue in need of urgent attention, though there are no signs as yet that ethnic divides threaten Estonia's democratic system itself. It is worth noting that the unrest sparked by the case of the bronze soldier – discussed further below – was an exception to the rule, which had been 16 years of peaceful community coexistence in independent Estonia. The emergence of an Estonian nationalist movement from the late 1980s onwards and its rise to power in an independent Estonia could potentially have provoked much uglier confrontation at an earlier stage. As it was, the nationalists' political dominance was expressed through control of, rather than compromise with the ethnic Russian community (Pettai & Hallik 2002, 506). According to Parekh's (2002) distinction, this was evidently a case of a multicultural state without a multiculturalist policy.

On Estonian independence, ethnic Russians who had arrived during the Soviet period were deemed non-citizens and thereby excluded from the democratic process, except for local elections. This was a result of the government's decision to accord citizenship only to those who had been citizens of the independent Estonian state prior to 1940 and their descendants, thereby excluding all those who had settled during the Soviet era. However, choosing to 'forget' decades of Soviet rule as a temporary aberration in the *longue durée* of Estonian history in this way, was complicated by the fact that ethnic Estonians now officially constituted only some two-thirds of the country's population, compared to 88 per cent before 1940 (Pettai & Hallik 2002, 509). Integration programmes were designed to encourage non-citizens to join the newly configured Estonian nation-state. This was in stark contrast to the Soviet system, which had helped create cultural segregation by providing all sorts of Russian-language services, including mass media and education. At first sight, this move appeared to entrench and thereby exacerbate existing ethnic divisions within Estonia, making them more 'real' by linking them to the ability to exercise important citizenship rights. After several months of limbo following the declaration of eligibility for automatic citizenship, the criteria of 'belonging' required for naturalisation were handed down in February 1992. This arrangement did not provide an immediate solution to the fact that those deemed non-citizens under the new legislation were effectively stateless; they were no longer Soviet citizens but now neither Estonian nor Russian citizens. Rather, they were officially called 'aliens' and given temporary, Estonian-issued 'alien passports' as a stop-gap measure. Some 90,000 people opted to become Russian citizens while continuing to live in Estonia, leaving 230,000 registered stateless and therefore disenfranchised (Pettai & Hallik 2002, 513). In 1995, the link between Estonian ethnic belonging and citizenship was strengthened by introducing an Estonian-language exam to the naturalisation procedure, leading to a drop in applications.

Although Estonia's democracy appears well-established almost 20 years after independence, a 2009 survey suggested that many ethnic Russians 'feel uneasy about their place in Estonian society' (Pettai & Molder 2009, 201), raising questions as to how inclusive Estonian democracy can be under the present system. What was it that motivated the government of newly-independent Estonia to link citizenship so tightly to ethnic Estonian belonging, thereby denying a democratic voice to a substantial minority of the population and risking discontent and instability as a result? Loyalty and legitimacy are two central planks of the nation-building process, and doubts as to the loyalty of the Russian minority seemed to override the need for them to lend legitimacy to the fledgling Estonian nation-state. The official reason for denying citizenship to most ethnic Russians turned on the legality of Soviet rule in Estonia. One motivation for this can be found in differences of collective memory, an important component of nation-building that hindered a move towards official multiculturalism in the Estonian case.

A major source of tension between Estonians and Russians lies in how to interpret twentieth-century history. This was brought into stark relief by the events of late April 2007, when the Estonian authorities' attempt to move the bronze statue of a Soviet soldier from the centre of the capital city, Tallinn, to a small park on its outskirts triggered two days of rioting. The violence reportedly resulted in one death, 100 injuries and 1000 arrests (Wertsch 2008, 133), shocking the country and prompting ripples of reaction beyond its borders (Pääbo 2008, 21). In a clear reference to the event, Russia's then president Vladimir Putin later condemned 'those who desecrate monuments to war heroes' (cited in Wertsch 2008, 136), as did many Russian press reports. Furthermore, a series of subsequent cyber-attacks on Estonia's electronic information systems apparently largely originated in Russia and were widely interpreted as a reprisal. Erected to commemorate the Red Army's entry into Tallinn in 1944, the contemporary significance of the bronze soldier lies in its ambivalent symbolism. This depends on whether the Red Army's arrival is interpreted positively as Estonia's liberation from German Nazi control, or negatively as the beginning of occupation by Soviet forces. As a result of their socialisation into a particular form of collective memory (and at the risk of over-simplification), the positive narrative tends to be favoured by ethnic Russians, whereas ethnic Estonians adopt the negative view. The statue's increasing use as a place of pilgrimage for ethnic Russian school trips and pro-Soviet commemoration prompted the official decision to sideline it as a possible source of conflict. However, the Estonian authorities were caught off guard by the violent reaction to this measure.

Disagreements over interpretations of the past are by no means confined to Estonia. Continuing controversy between the People's Republic of China and Japan over how their school textbooks interpret the events of World War II is but one other example of history arousing popular passions and souring present-day diplomatic relations. Collective memory simultaneously simplifies history to fit a wider narrative – such as that of dogged and repeated resistance to invasion in Estonia, Vietnam and elsewhere – and telescopes past events together to give them continued, contemporary significance (Wertsch 2008, 147). In the Estonian case, the status of ethnic Russians on Estonian soil raised the additional issue of democratic inclusion and equality, and Estonia's decision to implement a large-scale minority integration programme in the aftermath of the riots apparently acknowledged this (Pettai & Molder 2009, 201). Also important in this context is whether those Russian-speakers living in independent Estonia, who in 1991 lost Soviet citizenship overnight, identify with their new membership of a putative Russian diaspora.

As will be discussed further in Chapter 5, membership of a diaspora entails some sort of cultural affinity and loyalty towards a recognised homeland. Given that, on finding themselves non-citizens of Estonia, only about one third of its ethnic Russian residents opted to become Russian citizens, we can infer at least an ambivalent attitude towards diasporic identity among those who did not. Regardless of their personal identification, they are nonetheless associated with a country that Estonia perceives to be its greatest external threat. Without the Estonian linguistic and cultural competence required for naturalisation (Pettai & Hallik 2002, 517), they are effectively left in a legal limbo (see Laitin 1998). Official figures for 2007 recorded that although some 40 per cent had naturalised, 25 per cent still remained stateless, with the rest either emigrating or adopting Russian or other citizenship (Pääbo 2008, 9). From being the ethnic majority in the Soviet Union, Russians were thus suddenly redefined as a minority in Estonia as part of its nation-building process, illustrating how ethnic categorisations are both relative and flexible in their import and impact.

The government of newly independent Estonia evidently felt that a monocultural national identity had to be fostered and invigorated after 40 years of subordination to the Soviet system (Pettai & Hallik 2002, 506). The same logic was applied to the citizenship question and to the symbolism of the bronze soldier, based on the assumption that Soviet forces illegally occupied Estonia. Among the strengths of this narrative are its simplicity, and its ability to unite the different Estonian nationalist factions that emerged in the last years of the Soviet Union under one banner. Neither is it an ethnically-derived argument, insofar as it demands restitution of Estonian statehood on a legal basis. On the other hand, if one takes the view that Soviet citizens of all ethnicities suffered under the system – Estonians and Russians alike were deported to Soviet gulags under Stalin, for example – it seems unjust to exclude from citizenship ethnic Russians who moved within the Soviet Union, but awoke one morning to find themselves in the new Estonian state (Pääbo 2008, 12). The dilemma also hinges on the form of nation-building Estonia chose to adopt; it could have opted for one that took Estonia's current residents as its starting point and sought to build a multiculturalist nation around them, or one that sought to erase the Soviet era and its consequences completely, in order to reconnect to Estonia's pre-war past. It chose the latter, thereby privileging an approach to nation-building centred round ethnic Estonians as the country's 'dominant *ethnie*' (Smith 1995, 106). Ironically, this was made explicit in Estonia's first minority integration policy, agreed in 1998. It declared that 'the Estonian version of a multicultural society' would be premised on individuals' readiness to adapt to a 'common core' derived from Estonian culture and accept 'Estonian cultural predominance' (cited in Pettai & Hallik 2002, 522–3). Insofar as this approach was based on a unidirectional model of individual acceptance and acquisition of Estonian language, social norms, values and so on, it appears to correspond better to Parekh's understanding of monoculturalism than multiculturalism (see also Neuliep 2003, 354). In the year 2000, however, with a new government in power, a revised and expanded integration policy moved away from Estonian ethnic predominance in favour of cultural pluralism, albeit retaining Estonian language competence as a key marker of integration and a means for prospective citizens to 'prove their loyalty' (Pääbo 2008, 9).

The minority integration programme introduced in 1998 was expanded after the bronze soldier riots in 2007, but remained within a clear framework of Estonian cultural predominance. As in Fiji, discussed below, there was little sign of a newly emerging, overarching Estonian nation-state identity because nation-building continued to revolve around the dominant *ethnie*. Politically, self-identifying ethnic Russian parties are represented at the municipal level and have succeeded in having a few naturalised Estonian candidates elected to parliament. However, tighter Estonian language requirements for standing for office introduced in late 1998 (and repealed three years later under OSCE pressure) helped to fuel their sense of marginalisation in Estonian politics (Pettai & Hallik 2002, 514). This sentiment was reflected in the ethnic Russian population during the controversy surrounding the bronze soldier, through the widespread sense that Estonian politicians were not responsive to or understanding of their perspective. Ironically, government reluctance to permit Russian language media in Estonia, so as to entrench Estonian as the only official language, is partly to blame here. As a result of this policy, Russian speakers get much of their information from media channels based in Russia. During the bronze soldier controversy, these conducted a concerted negative campaign against the Estonian government (which responded in kind) (Pääbo 2008, 22).

Democratic elections are a key means of legitimating the nation-state, and excluding a sizeable minority of the population from this process is regarded as a regrettable anomaly by several of Estonia's Western partners (Pettai & Hallik 2002, 525; Steen 2010). Indeed, a relatively high degree of Euroscepticism among the Estonian population – as distinct from its government – has been explained in part by the fear that Estonian identity might be under threat from EU membership. This popular perception is further reinforced by a documented decline of trust in Estonia's own political elites, who engineered the so-called 'return to Europe' (Vetik, Nimmerfelft & Taru 2006, 1086). In turn, this suggests that outside pressure to review the 'dominant *ethnie*' model of nation-building may have limited popular support within the country (Vetik, Nimmerfelft & Taru 2006). That is, Estonians may react against an external expectation to conform – negatively connoted as 'catching up' – with international norms promoted by the EU, the OSCE and others (Steen 2010, 198). There is a sense that the involvement of international organisations is welcome in order to guarantee external security, but less so when it comes to Estonian nation-building, especially now that membership of the EU and NATO has been achieved. It has also been argued that Estonian elites, though open to instrumental modifications of citizenship legislation in return for EU and NATO membership, remained opposed to or actually hardened against legally integrating minorities, partly as a reaction against external conditionality (Steen 2010). Estonia is therefore having difficulty reconciling regional organisations' expectations with the form of nation-building it has hitherto pursued. A combination of external pressure and domestic unrest has made it move closer to a multiculturalist approach in response to this regionalist aspect of the cosmopolitan challenge. It remains to be seen how two other multicultural democracies, namely India and Fiji, have sought to represent their diverse communities.

Democracy

By way of contrast to Estonia, a small state struggling to come to terms with ethnocultural diversity, we turn to India as one of the world's most multicultural states, and also its most populous democracy. Indeed, official nation-building derives much of India's overarching sense of identity from its democratic status, although this is challenged by those who prioritise its Hindu heritage above all else. India is home to a bewildering array of ethnic groups, languages and religions, and also a number of nationalist movements. At the sub-state level, Sikh and Muslim-inspired militant movements have long struggled for power in Punjab and Kashmir respectively. Elsewhere, Tamil nationalism in Tamil Nadu was most virulent in the 1950s and 60s, before being largely incorporated into India's federal system (Sridharan 2000, 304). These forces for self-determination contrast with secular, pan-Indian nation-building, which Prime Minister Jawaharlal Nehru championed following independence. This was designed to create an overarching and unifying sense of Indian belonging to complement other loyalties (McMillan 2008, 740). According to this so-called 'tributary theory' of nationalism, 'small nationalisms build into larger identities and eventually flow into the great cosmopolitan sea' (Yapp, cited in Sridharan 2000, 301). Yet this approach has had limited success in bridging religious divides, in particular. It was also bound up with the long-standing political dominance of the Congress party in the decades following independence, which had given way to a more fragmented system of coalition governments by the 1990s (Roy 2001, 262). Neither is this form of Indian nationalism purely civic.

Despite the fact that the Indian Constitution does not disallow naturalised, as opposed to 'natural born' Indians from holding the highest offices in the land, there was a political outcry against Sonia Gandhi, the Italian-born head of India's Congress Party, becoming prime minister in 1999. The suggestion was that she could not possibly be sufficiently patriotic, thereby raising the issues of suspect loyalties and acquired citizenship, discussed further in Chapter 5. Conversely, India accords a whole range of rights short of citizenship to its diaspora, in the form of a 'Persons of Indian Origin' card. These contrasting examples show that in India, 'citizenship and nationality, although used interchangeably in common legal parlance, are not one and the same thing' (Sridharan 2000, 315). It also illustrates how India is responding to its diaspora – one important aspect of the cosmopolitan challenge – by delinking markers of national belonging from the territorial boundaries of the state.

India's politics of communalism and quotas also conflict with the principle of individual equality inherent in democratic citizenship (Alam 2009), highlighting the tension between multiculturalism and democracy discussed above. There is evidence that communal interests, particularly religious ones, tend to dominate other group interests – such as women's rights – in India's public and political discourse (Burlet 1999). As such, an individual's tendency to embody multiple identities is undermined by their primary political classification within an ethnic or religious community. Nevertheless, some feminist organisations have tried to bring together Hindu and Muslim women, for instance, thereby working against perceptions of communal conflict while making sure that 'participants in their organisations can simultaneously assert themselves as women and as members of communities defined in terms of religion' (Burlet 1999, 45). Achieving a 'productive tension' between nation-building, communalism and individual rights is one of the major challenges India faces.

In order to function, a democracy must designate the people, or *demos*, which will rule indirectly through elected representatives or express itself directly in the likes of referenda. The concept of the nation is currently the most widespread form of delimiting the *demos*, and provides a convenient container with which to help determine members of a political community. However, Chapter 2 examined some of the pitfalls inherent in defining national belonging, and a look at the cases of India and Fiji will be quick to dispel any notion that equating the *demos* with the nation offers a neat and simple solution to issues of participation. Indeed, India's diversity exemplifies the difficulties of reconciling democracy and nationalism. Indian democracy is even termed 'deviant' by some scholars of modernisation, whose theories cannot account for how it was established and consolidated across such a large, diverse and poor territory, with relatively low levels of literacy and urbanisation (McMillan 2008, 734).

Following independence from the UK in 1947 and the partition of Pakistan from colonial India, the new Indian republic pursued policies of non-alignment, economic self-reliance and secular nation-building under the leadership of Jawaharlal Nehru and his Congress Party. From the outset, postcolonial nationalism was thus partly premised on self-strengthening and independence from the Western 'Other', sentiments that would periodically resurface in populist electioneering against 'neo-imperialism' and the meddling of 'foreign hands' (Ray 2002, 42). India's democracy has also seen setbacks, including the suspension of elections and many civil liberties during the 'Emergency' period of 1975–7. There are also questions as to how far Nehru's ideal of liberal democracy has ever resonated beyond the country's westernised elite, or reached out to include all sections of society (Bhatt 2004, 143). Nevertheless, democracy continues to play a crucial role in official nation-building, as was evident during the celebrations of 50 years of independence in 1997. These centred, significantly, on the parliament buildings, where politicians gathered to hear recordings of speeches given by Nehru and Mohandas Gandhi half a century previously (Roy 2001, 258). In order to transcend ethnic and linguistic diversity, official nation-building has presented the democratic state as central to a vision of 'Indianness in terms of citizenship rather than ethnic belonging' (Roy 2001, 263).

In India as elsewhere, individuals' relative status, education, institutional contacts and personal networks mean that the principle of equal citizen participation is extremely difficult to realise in practice. Furthermore, the Estonian case has already shown that nation-building practices can hinder inclusion. '[W]hen the national identity is defined in an exclusivist way and it tries to make the idea of citizenship subservient to it, then minority groups feel less equal, less at home' (Mohapatra 2002, 169). India's democratic system faces its own challenges, both domestic and international. There has been a splintering of party representation into regional and religious blocs, for one. Added to this comes supranational pressure from international NGOs, often allied with domestic civil rights groups, to address environmental, gender and child labour issues. These often cite rights enshrined in India's Constitution as the basis for their demands (Ray 2002, 49). Ironically, the recognition that a degree of economic well-being and social acceptance is crucial to full citizenship has led to corrective policy measures that derogate from the equality principle. For instance, forms of 'positive discrimination' have been designed to raise the status of disadvantaged groups such as the *Dalits*. The use of this name for low caste Hindus, formerly known as 'Untouchables', is one way of encouraging their social rehabilitation, together with a system of quotas to ensure their parliamentary representation.

A strong challenge to India's state secularism and possibly its democracy has come from Hindu nationalists, who emphasise Hinduism's religious, historical and cultural heritage as the core identity of the Indian nation. Central to these beliefs is the concept of *Hindutva*, which can be defined as 'the essence of the Hindu, comprised [of] a common nation, a common civilization and a common "race"' (Bhatt & Mukta 2000, 413). Not only does *Hindutva* politicise a highly diverse faith, which is understood to include Sikhs, Buddhists and Jains, but it also seeks to forge and represent a single Hindu identity. Essentially, *Hindutva* condenses fatherland and holy land into a single, sacred Indian nation (Bhatt 2004, 134).

To right-wing proponents of this view, such as members of the political and cultural organisations collectively known as *Sangh Parivar*, efforts to integrate Muslim and Christian minorities into Indian society smack more of appeasement (Bhatt 2004, 135; Mohapatra 2002, 177; Mukta 2000, 446). For instance, they rail against impoverished Muslim (but not Hindu) immigrants from Bangladesh, so-called 'infiltrators', whom they accuse of seeking to undermine India's identity in an alleged Muslim conspiracy (Ramachandran 1999, 244). By painting these migrants as an existential threat, Hindu nationalists seek to 'reconstitute the parameters of the Hindu nation-space' (Ramachandran 1999, 240) as coextensive with the Indian nation-state. By seeking to mobilise Hindus against Muslim and Christian 'Others', the *Sangh Parivar* also tries to minimise internal differences between Hindu castes and sects (Sarkar 2005, 306). Thus, *Hindutva* notions of identity are essentially bounded and closed, predicating a loyalty to the Hindu nation above all others. Discourses of Hindu victimisation, marginalisation and insecurity come together in the similarly essentialised construction of Muslims and Christians as threatening and dangerous 'Others', thereby helping to legitimise violence against them (Mukta 2000).

Building on the political structures of earlier Hindu nationalists, the *Bharatiya Janata Party* (BJP) came to prominence and power in the 1980s and 1990s, advocating an Indian national community constructed around the majority Hindu population. As the BJP argues on its website, the Hindu values and culture infusing Indian identity can be shared by all: '[The BJP] has nothing against Muslim Indians – as distinguished from Muslim invaders [...] But it has no doubt that we were and are a Hindu nation; that change of faith cannot mean change of nationality' (BJP, no date). The use of the phrase 'Muslim invaders' refers to the BJP's favoured discourse of Hindu victimhood and gradual marginalisation within India (Mukta 2000, 446). Similarly, the *Hindutva* movement's interpretation of history evokes a millennium of resistance against Muslim, then colonial invasion (Bhatt & Mukta 2000, 417). Hence 'an irresolvable politics of revenge against a real or imagined medieval period is central to Hindu nationalism' (Bhatt 2004, 135).

The *Hindutva* movement is well-represented among sections of the Indian diaspora, and bolsters its legitimacy through their support (Mukta 2000, 462; Shiladitya Bose 2008, 126). Ironically, *Sangh Parivar* activism on behalf of Hindu ethnic minorities within host nations like the UK and the US may have influenced *Hindutva* discourse within India, which argues that, despite representing over 80 per cent of the population, Hindus' rights are under attack from positive action to protect and promote minority rights there (Bhatt & Mukta 2000, 438; Mukta 2000, 448). If the *Sangh Parivar's* goal is indeed to change 'the quality of the relation between nationalism, the state and democratic citizenship' (Bhatt 2004, 142), then their ultimate goal is to challenge India's current democratic system (Sarkar 2005, 305). The BJP led a national coalition government in India for six years from 1998, but its influence was checked when it lost the 2004 election to a Congress-led coalition. This illustrates the power of Indian democracy to choose and check its rulers. However, serious and periodic pogroms, epitomised by the violence following the demolition of the Babri mosque at Ayodhya in 1992 and the murder of a Christian missionary and his sons in 1999, remind us of the potentially explosive nature of exclusionary nationalism.

Notwithstanding the potential threat from some strands of *Hindutva* nationalism, democracy seems to be regarded as an overwhelmingly positive identifier in India and across the world. Ironically, it is something to which even the most authoritarian regimes lay claim: 'It is almost universally felt that when we call a country democratic we are praising it: consequently the defenders of every kind of regime claim that it is a democracy' (Orwell, cited in Lawson 1996, 31). For example, Burma/Myanmar's notoriously repressive military junta has long been following a so-called 'roadmap to democracy' despite ignoring the results of the country's 1990 general election and holding the leader of the victorious National League for Democracy, Aung San Suu Kyi, under house arrest for over 14 of the following 20 years. She was only released in November 2010, following an election that many Western countries, though not China or Russia, condemned as a sham. In Burma and elsewhere, then, leaders have adopted and adapted the language of democracy to suit their political agenda, rejecting what they see as Western attempts to impose their own understanding of the concept. Institutional trappings – parliament, parties, elections, constitutions and the like – may be held up as evidence of a procedurally democratic system, even though the 'performative' democratic freedoms to vote, organise, debate and associate may be lacking. In the Pacific state of Fiji, for instance, the 1990 Constitution promulgated in the aftermath of a military coup in 1987, ostensibly married the protection of indigenous rights with democratic principles. In effect, however, it limited the rights of Fijian Indians vis-à-vis the indigenous population, and its hereditary chiefs in particular. The leader of the 1987 coup, Colonel Sitiveni Rabuka, claimed that democracy was a 'relative' term and that European and Fijian views of what constitutes a democracy might differ (Lawson 1996, 44). While ushering in a discriminatory system, then, he was careful to do so using democracy as a positive frame of reference.

Fiji's experience of democracy and nation-building contrasts with the Indian case, since it has been under the military rule of Commodore Frank Bainimarama since 2006. As a result of his refusal to hold elections planned for 2009, the country was suspended from its main regional organisation, the Pacific Islands Forum. Fiji's experiments with democracy and the events leading up to this latest coup are an excellent example of Bhikhu Parekh's distinction between multicultural fact and multiculturalist policy, as set out in the introduction. They illustrate the difficulties of reconciling communal representation with attempts to develop a democratic nation-state based on equal citizenship. Indeed, Fiji's failure to foster an overarching sense of shared belonging across its indigenous and Indo-Fijian population has been diagnosed as the reason for democratic collapse (Ghosh 2004, 124). The following discussion sets out to show how nation-building and democratic participation have clashed in the Fijian context, concluding with a comparison of Fiji's confusing attempts to reconcile the 'paramountcy' of indigenous Fijian interests with democracy on the one hand, and Estonia's approach to multiculturalism on the other.

The source of ethnic divisions in Fiji must be sought in its experience of colonialism, which employed racial hierarchies and putative chiefly privilege to govern the islands (Prasad 2008, 954; Kelly & Kaplan 2001, 147; Larson & Aminzade 2008, 171). Fijian Indians, first brought to the islands as indentured labourers five years after the British colonised Fiji in 1874, have added a further, oppositional dimension to the country's politics, which is unique among South Pacific states (Lawson 1996, 38). Party politics has only served to entrench the ethnic divide, with the likes of the Fijian Nationalist Party claiming 'Fiji for the Fijians' in the late 1970s (Prasad 2008, 955). Indigenous Fijian leaders have long constructed the Fijian Indian population as an essentialised and potentially threatening 'Other'. For instance, they allege that Fijian Indians are more prosperous than ethnic Fijians, in order to help bring indigenous Fijians together as a putatively homogeneous community (Robertson & Sutherland 2001, xvii; Prasad 2008, 955). Ethnic Fijian leaders have also stressed the perils of being outnumbered and losing their lands, although this was legally impossible under the 1970 Constitution marking Fijian independence, let alone the 1990 constitution (Lawson 1996, 58). Some go so far as to draw parallels between the colonising British and Indo-Fijians (Ghosh 2004, 127).

The vast majority of Fiji is owned by indigenous Fijians, with Indo-Fijians mostly leasing the land. Land rights have huge symbolic as well as material importance, because the 'way of the land' is considered synonymous with indigenous Fijian culture and tradition (Ghosh 2004, 123). Linked to this, the nineteenth-century Deed of Cession signed by the British colonising power and a group of Fijian chiefs guaranteed Fijian land ownership. Flowing from this original accord, the principle of paramountcy of Fijian interests has been enshrined in every Fijian constitution, even that of 1997, which also referred to 'our multicultural society' in its preamble. This shows that recognising a state as multicultural does not necessarily entail a multiculturalist policy of interethnic equality, since the dominant Fijian *ethnie* retains paramountcy in this case. The difficulty of reconciling equal citizenship and indigenous Fijian rights has clearly bedevilled the development of democracy there. Since the so-called 'clean up' coup against government corruption in 2006, its leader, Commodore Bainimarama, has consolidated his power, overseen the abrogation of the Constitution and put off elections promised for 2009 until 2014. His own justification for this, namely to review the electoral system and do away with its communal divisions, returns to the dilemma that has entrenched ethnic categories, fuelled inter-ethnic rivalry, and underpinned the series of coups since Fijian independence. Fiji's democratic system has buckled under the weight of its own internal inconsistencies, and given way to authoritarian rule.

Presenting Fijian society as divided by a supposedly unbridgeable cleavage between ethnic Fijians and Indo-Fijians has also been used to claim that Western-style democracy, of which Fiji's 1970 Constitution is considered representative, has proved unsuited to the country's requirements. Its 1990 replacement made this explicit in the preamble, which asserts a 'widespread belief that the 1970 Constitution was inadequate to give protection to the interests of the indigenous Fijians' (cited in Lawson 1996, 41). Colonel Rabuka, leader of the 1987 coup, has called democracy a 'foreign flower' (cited in Robertson & Sutherland 2001, 20), which had to be adapted to the local context. This is one example of how the 'narrative of indigenous rights has always posed a powerful challenge to democratic discourse' (Kelly & Kaplan 2001, 151). Interpretations of both tradition and democracy in the Fijian context are highly debatable, however. Although precolonial traditions are apparently being revived as a reaction against unwelcome Western influence, it transpires that institutions like the Fijian Council of Chiefs were established during colonial times, and only represent an approximate rendering of a pre-existing indigenous system in Fiji's eastern islands, if that (Lawson 1996, 46). Foregrounding 'time-hallowed' tradition in this way is often a pretext for preserving elite status and privilege. Despite being presented as part of the 'Pacific Way', or a non-Western take on democracy, emphasis on supposedly pre-existing tradition helps entrench social hierarchies and inequalities. This 'invention of tradition' thus runs counter to advancing democratic participation, accountability and transparency. In particular, Fijian elites long resisted defining the country as multicultural, fearing it would undermine both the rationale behind the community-based voting system designed to guarantee indigenous Fijian control of government, and the underlying presumption that social divisions 'are capable only of management and not of resolution' (Lawson 1996, 43). Here we see precisely the conservative response to the fact of cultural diversity that Parekh (2002, 6) identifies.

Colonel Rabuka's coup shortly after the reformist Fiji Labor Party defeated the long-serving Alliance Party in the 1987 election was ostensibly to protect indigenous Fijian interests (Lawson 2004, 527). In effect, Fiji's 1990 Constitution then facilitated the emergence of a one-party state, since the opposition had no realistic chance of gaining power. Although democratic institutions were in place, they served an exclusionary ethnic Fijian nationalism and the interests of its chiefly elite, rather than those of the country's population as a whole (Lawson 2004, 529). For example, the implementation of affirmative action policies for indigenous Fijians was supposed to reduce the urgency of the alleged Fijian-Indian threat, but appear to have been of more benefit to indigenous elites than the disadvantaged Fijians they were designed to help. Ironically, sidelining the Fijian-Indian issue left room for factional differences and political divisions to emerge within Fiji's indigenous community. This served to undermine the very chiefly power that the 1990 constitution sought to preserve, leaving room for other leaders to muscle in. A constitutional framework constructed around essentialised communities could only limit opportunities for inter-ethnic cooperation and some kind of rapprochement based on a more inclusive form of nation-building. Nevertheless, the influence of Indo-Fijian politicians and coalition partners helped bring about constitutional review, resulting in the revised 1997 Constitution. This featured the principle of community equality in its preamble, but retained the principle of Fijian paramountcy in its second chapter. The political fortunes of Indo-Fijians seemed to improve when one of their number, Mahendra Chaudhry, became prime minister in 1999. However, he was deposed the following year in another coup perpetrated on much the same grounds of protecting indigenous Fijian interests as its predecessor in 1987 (Lawson 2004, 532). Fiji's most recent coup in 2006 only underlined the country's systemic instability. Although indigenous nationalism was less to the fore in that case, the ongoing presence of ethnic cleavages links the fragility of democracy to the weakness of any inclusive, overarching form of Fijian nation-building (Lal 2007).

The difficulties of fostering both national identity and democratic legitimacy are particularly pressing for postcolonial states (Larson & Aminzade 2008, 170). Fiji is a clear case of the democratic principle of equal citizenship conflicting with claims for the protection of indigenous rights, a dilemma summed up by one scholar as 'nationalism versus constitutionalism' (Lawson 2004, 519). This has hindered the development of an overarching 'national "imagined community" commensurate to the postcolonial nation-state' (Kelly & Kaplan 2001, 146). Among the Indo-Fijian community, there is evidence that the 1987 coup undermined their sense of belonging to Fiji and their ability to live side by side with indigenous Fijians (Ghosh 2004, 124). Ironically, some of those Indo-Fijians who left the country because of that coup felt able to reconnect with the Fijian elements of their identity fondly and nostalgically after the 2000 coup, as they no longer saw any prospect of ever returning to live there (Ghosh 2004, 120). Much like colonisation in 1874, Fijian independence came as a result of British bargaining with Fijian chiefs, rather than through the egalitarian anti-imperialism which found an echo principally among Indo-Fijians (Kelly & Kaplan 2001, 198). Fiji's independent nation-building only began in 1970, too late for the first wave of post-war anti-colonialism and third world solidarity, but in time to latch onto the discourse of community rights (Ghosh 2004, 127). This was applied, however, to protecting the majority indigenous Fijians' inalienable right to their homeland from a diffuse Indo-Fijian 'threat', rather like the *Hindutva* movement in India seeks to hold putative Muslim 'infiltration' at bay.

Conclusion

By dividing the allocation of parliamentary seats principally along ethnic lines, the succession of electoral systems that underpinned Fijian democracy officially considered Indo-Fijians to be separate but equal citizens.

However, the doctrine of Fijian paramountcy effectively made indigenous Fijians first among equals. In Fiji, the ethnic divide distinguished between citizens, whereas in independent Estonia, it distinguished between citizens and non-citizens, since its definition of citizenship automatically created a large number of resident non-citizens. The contradictions within Fijian nation-building helped cause its democratic system to be suspended after nearly 30 years of independence. In Estonia, meanwhile, though a large disenfranchised resident population would seem a recipe for social instability, the bronze soldier controversy was the first major eruption of ethnic tensions. During the early 1990s, specific policies pertaining to the Russian ethnic minority played a limited role in Estonian politics, whose main parties did not share the widespread perception held among ethnic Russians, and supported by some empirical evidence, that they suffered disproportionately from social, economic and political inequality within Estonian society (Pettai & Hallik 2002, 519). In practice, the legal fiction underlying Estonia's transition to independence has been advantageous to the ethnic Estonian population, without the need for a Fijian-like doctrine of paramountcy, most obviously in their access to citizenship. The Estonian Constitution emphasises the 'preservation of the Estonian nation, language and culture through the ages' in its preamble. Almost two decades on from Estonian independence, however, the contested symbolism of the bronze soldier may be a sign that its brand of nation-building is faltering.

It is useful to consider possible options for Estonia in the light of issues raised in this chapter. Lessons from Fiji, as well as consociationally-ruled but chronically fractured Belgium, seem to suggest that a 'separate but equal' citizenship model that distinguishes between ethnicities is not necessarily a desirable alternative for Estonia. As we have seen, the wholesale enfranchisement of its resident alien population under such a system would likely bring its own difficulties and tensions. At the same time, one-way assimilation policies offer little encouragement or scope for ethnic Russians to feel they belong to Estonian society without investing heavily in Estonian language acquisition (Laitin 1998). A third alternative would be to institute a less ethnically-based naturalisation process by lowering linguistic and cultural barriers to citizenship and doing away with alien status. This would have to be accompanied by a form of nation-building that put less emphasis on Estonian cultural predominance. Such a step would require self-confidence on the part of ethnic Estonians that their culture could be preserved and even enriched by the give and take of two-way integration. There is the argument that Estonia's remarkably quick and decisive transformation into a market economy and a liberal democracy can be partly attributed to ethnic Estonian dominance, without which the different communities would have engaged in internecine conflict and struggled to reorient themselves towards growth and development. But there is nothing to stop Estonia becoming more inclusive, so the argument goes, now that its democracy and independence are relatively well-established. Clearly, however, the challenges of nation-building are not confined to democracies alone.

Stalin's tract entitled 'Marxism and the National Question' provided the basis for defining nations across the communist bloc (Stalin 1994 [1913]), but Vietnam developed its own unique combination of nationalism and communism in the context of anti-colonial struggle. Today, the VCP still seeks to reconcile nation-building with its one-party regime, while pursuing performance legitimacy through economic development. In India, the ongoing challenge is to manage multicultural diversity and positive discrimination within an overarching democratic framework of equal citizenship. The BJP's approach, by contrast, is to insist on the centrality of Hinduism to Indian belonging, leading it to advocate apparently oxymoronic identities like 'Muslim Hindus' and 'Christian Hindus' (Ghosh 2004, 126). Each of these cases illustrates the diversity of nation-building models across the world, and the difficulties inherent in reconciling democracy, multiculturalism and communism with nationalist ideology. The cosmopolitan challenge further complicates the picture by adding the effects of globalisation, diaspora and regionalisation to the mix. Yet nationalism continues to be used as the basic organising principle for both democratic and non-democratic states worldwide, providing further evidence of the ideology's enduring power, flexibility and diversity in the twenty-first century.

4

Whither the Stateless Nation? Integrating Sub-State Nationalism

How do sub-state nationalists define independence in an interdependent world? What roles do ethnicity and territory play in their ideologies?

This chapter focuses on sub-state nationalism and its response to the cosmopolitan challenge. Every nationalist variant – from terrorist nationalists, through democratic independence movements, to established nation-states – claims the right to represent its chosen nation. To that extent, the legitimating practices of government nation-building are no different to those of sub-state nationalist ideologues. Contemporary sub-state nationalists set out to articulate a new political arena, however. They reinvent sub-state territories as centres of social, economic and political activity, as well as an alternative locus of identity to the existing nation-state construct (Keating 2001). Sub-state nationalism in liberal democracies tends to be a mix of civic and ethnic markers, mobilised differently according to the changing constellations of power at state and international levels (Keating 2001, 12). Contrary to the focus on governments in the study of nation-building, political parties are among the dominant actors at the sub-state level, though their control of a devolved administration is also a powerful nation-building tool. As demonstrated in the cases of Scotland and Bavaria below, sub-state nationalists often attempt to manipulate a rather diffuse sense of national identity. And as we shall see in the discussion of sub-state mobilisation in Africa, ethnicity also provides an important focus for collective action. The chapter argues that contemporary sub-state nationalism is flexible enough to adapt evidence of long-standing community links to the current political environment, but also of manipulating and inventing traditions along the way. As an eminently adaptable ideology, it co-opts elements as diverse as ethnicity and supranational regionalism in some of its manifold variants across the world.

The chapter is organised into four sections designed to reflect key features of contemporary sub-state nationalism. The first looks at the meaning of autonomy and political self-determination in the context of the cosmopolitan challenge. It aims to show how sub-state nationalist movements are all bound up in different, tangled webs of state and supr-astate relations. The symbolism of sovereignty remains important to a sense of national identity and legitimacy, but the practical extent of authority and autonomy will vary greatly within these governance networks. The second section goes on to explore the apparently leading role of ethnicity in African sub-state mobilisation. This is particularly interesting because it might be assumed to result from long-standing tribal and ethnic loyalties. However, the discussion seeks to show that ethnicity is just as much of a construct as nationalism, one that is often derived from colonial categorisations rather than atavistic allegiances. This suggests that ethnic mobilisation is not enough to explain sub-state nationalism. Indeed, ethnicity in Africa is also used strategically as a response to state clientelism, just as sub-state nationalists elsewhere react to the unique form of state and suprastate governance in which 'their' nation is embedded.

The chapter's third section complements the discussion of ethnicity as a strategic tool with a look at some of the principal agents of ideology, namely political parties. It considers the case of the Scottish National Party (SNP), which has responded to the cosmopolitan challenge by embracing European regionalism, in order to counter claims of isolationism and anachronism in a globalised world. The SNP is discussed in parallel with the Bavarian *Christlich-Soziale Union* (CSU), which is not avowedly nationalist but uses the Bavarian *Heimat* as a central marker of its unique identity within the German federal system. Not only does the CSU want to come across as the best party to represent Bavarian interests in Germany and the European Union (EU), but it also wants to style itself as the only truly Bavarian party capable of representing those interests (Sutherland 2001, 28). As such, it uses key elements of nationalist ideology in its appeals. The section concludes with a look at the relationship between each party's core nationalist principles and its policies on migration, an important aspect of the cosmopolitan challenge. This leads us to another major feature of that challenge in the final section, namely diaspora. Using the sub-state nation of Tibet for illustration, it sets out to show how Tibetan nation-building is carried out among its diaspora.

The Dalai Lama and his government in exile have attempted to foster an enduring sense of national loyalty among fellow exiles, as they campaign for greater Tibetan autonomy within China. At the same time, they have successfully raised awareness of their cause across the globe, giving it a high profile among the international community. Overall, the chapter aims to give a flavour of the diversity of contemporary sub-state nationalism, highlighting how it adapts the shared, core principle of prioritising the nation to different aspects of the cosmopolitan challenge.

Autonomy

All states strive to be nations, but not all nationalists aim to achieve state-hood. Even self-defined multiculturalist states need the legitimating fiction of an overarching nation, but the reverse is not true. That is, some national-ist movements may seek statehood for the nations they claim to represent, but not all of them do so in an age when the cosmopolitan challenge questions the very meaning of sovereignty and independence (cf. Cheah 2003, 391). Nationalist movements that do not equate the political expression of nationhood with an independent state move beyond the nineteenth-century assumption that created the very term 'nation-state'. The image of all sub-state nationalists as separatist and isolationist, obsessed with having their own state and achieving absolute sover-eignty, complete with its connotations of autarchy, is an anachronistic one. It sits uneasily with the process of 'ever closer' European integration, for instance, which requires member states to surrender sovereignty across many policy areas in the name of European peace, security and economic co-operation. One of the novelties of contemporary sub-state nationalism in the likes of the EU lies in attempts to unite two apparently divergent political projects of self-determination on the one hand and regional integration on the other. Yet the difficulty in interpreting the meaning of self-determination, autonomy, independence and sovereignty remains. In the context of the cosmopolitan challenge, it is clear that none of these are absolute values to be gained or maintained.

Interpreting the core ideological principle of national self-determination to mean different degrees of autonomy can be seen as a pragmatic response to regional integration as one aspect of the cosmopolitan chal-lenge. For example, nationalist parties in Scotland, Wales and Catalonia use the process of European integration to support their political projects

(Lynch 1996; Guibernau 1999). Just as the European Community was the 'buttress [...] of the nation-state's post-war construction' (Milward 1994, 3), so some of today's sub-state nationalists use the EU to frame demands for greater autonomy from precisely those nation-states. Clearly, sub-state nationalism differs from state-led nation-building in that it has higher hurdles to cross in order to achieve its goal. Sub-state nationalists must successfully challenge the status quo, namely the prevailing common sense understanding of the nation-state. They must move people to question their acceptance of the nation-state in its already existing form, in order to promote greater sub-state autonomy through federalism, devolution or the like. Further, if the aim is to redefine the contours of the nation-state, sub-state nationalists must attack the inertia of a well-established international system. Kosovo is one example of a recently seceded state, and has struggled to be fully recognised as independent from Serbia. Some members of the international community including Russia (Serbia's ally) and Spain, which is reluctant to set a precedent for its own sub-state nationalists in Catalonia and the Basque country, do not recognise Kosovo's sovereignty.

Sub-state nationalists seek to steer a satisfactory course between the extremes of autarchy and assimilation. Should they insist on achieving their own state, one both externally recognised and domestically legitimated as a sovereign entity, or should they adopt a more flexible interpretation of sovereignty, in line with advances in regional integration, international trading regimes and increasingly mobile populations? Federalism is one means of guaranteeing a degree of sub-state autonomy through a constitutionally entrenched division of powers. Possible disadvantages include continuing disagreement over how to interpret those constitutional provisions. For instance, Germany's federal states, or *Länder*, hold long-standing grievances against the central government for apparently hollowing out their sphere of competence over time (Gunlicks 2007). Another possible disadvantage is that the formal equality between federal states leaves less room for recognising regional, or national particularities. Spain has sought to tackle this with a form of asymmetric or 'quasi' federalism benefiting its 'historic' *nacionalidades* in particular – namely Catalonia, Galicia and the Basque country. The Spanish system provides for negotiated settlements recognising well-established linguistic and cultural identities and constitutionally entrenched autonomy, which also leaves scope for accommodating emerging regional demands from the likes of Andalucia and Valencia. Similarly, the UK's devolution settlement in the 1990s allocated different powers to its sub-state nations, as evidenced by the creation of a Welsh Assembly and a Scottish Parliament. The question for nationalists, devolutionists and federalists alike is how to mould an appropriate power configuration around today's sub-state nations. Wales, for instance, has warmed to its newly autonomous status, holding a successful referendum in 2011 on whether to extend its Assembly's legislative powers.

Across the Atlantic, Quebec's nationalists have long sought a suitable mechanism for recognising its distinctiveness within the Canadian federation. Various interpretations of sovereignty have been mooted for the French-speaking province, ranging from 'sovereignty-association', to recognition in the Canadian Constitution of Quebec's 'distinct society'. Yet the meaning of any hard-won sovereignty could be lost within the dense network of international treaties and agreements of which Quebec already forms a part (Keating 2001, 125). Winning some form of sovereignty would inevitably be watered down if Quebec sought to preserve advantages of membership in the Canadian federation, such as a common currency and a common market. Highly trade-dependent on the rest of Canada and the US, Quebec would also need to consider its status within even broader structures like the North American Free Trade Agreement (NAFTA). Regional organisations like NAFTA and the EU thus represent important dimensions of the cosmopolitan challenge for sub-state nationalists trying to negotiate their position among state, regional and international governance networks. As we shall see below, the overarching state continues to be a major influence in shaping their demands. By way of comparison, it is instructive to consider examples of sub-state ethnic mobilisation and possible similarities with sub-state nationalism, given the frequent use of ethnic identifiers in nationalist ideologies.

Ethnicity

Sub-state mobilisation in Africa is a response to a combination of factors, including the legacy of colonialism, prevailing nation-building strategies at the state level, and a wide variety of regional hierarchies and dynamics across the continent. There, as elsewhere, nation-building tends to include appeals to the pre-colonial past, ethnic identifiers and territorial belonging (Forrest 2004, 4). Sub-state mobilisation also shares nationalism's characteristic flexibility. It is wide-ranging, too, covering everything from clientelist ventures promoting individual power and wealth to broad coalitions of several ethnic groups. Against this backdrop, the revival and reconfiguration of ethnic markers has less to do with resurgent tribalism and ancient antagonisms than a place-specific reaction to state structures. However, neither can we simply ascribe ethnic mobilisation in Africa to a breakdown in the state's clientelist relationships. This alone would require careful qualification, for 'even patron-client relations in Africa vary in their legitimacy, staying power, dependence on state resources, and implications for collective action' (Boone 2003, 320). In Senegal, for example, when Léopold Senghor became its first president on independence in 1960, nation-building was not simply about mobilising the masses. There, as elsewhere, practical measures to foster popular legitimacy were frequently filtered through, or subordinate to, the demands of regional representatives. These sometimes included individuals identified as leaders of ethnic groups, although sub-state activists could just as easily be mobilised along religious, urban or rural lines. In the Wolof lands of northern Senegal, for instance, rural elites enjoyed state patronage, which was designed to secure their loyalty and thereby some sort of proxy state control over the region (Boone 2003, 62). Any other strategy would have run the risk of allowing rural opposition to grow. Thus the structure of the postcolonial state in many parts of Africa sought to contain organised sub-state dissent through patronage. When opposition did emerge, it was more a calculated response to state deficiencies mobilised along ethnic lines than a spontaneous welling up of atavistic ethnic allegiances. Some of the factors affecting this mobilisation are considered below.

Prior to Africa's gradual decolonisation following World War II, a small indigenous elite had become enmeshed in colonial structures through education and, albeit limited, career advancement. This did little to prepare it for independence, however; 'When [postcolonial] leaders took over the reins of office, they were confronted with the paradoxical situation of having to operate with newly conceived pluralist institutions of alien derivation (including parties and parliaments), whereas the bulk of their own political understanding had been molded in a centralized and authoritarian colonial context' (Chazan et al. 1999, 45). Anti-colonial nationalism had been a response to the inability and unwillingness of colonisers to establish a stable political community supported by broad-based popular legitimacy. Yet in many African states, post-independence governments also failed in this important respect. Pursuing the nation-building process across states that were originally colonial creations encompassing great diversity was always going to be a difficult task, but for some leaders seeking popular legitimacy for the postcolonial state was less important than maintaining or improving their already privileged position. As a result, bonds of national loyalty were never properly forged, leading to a proliferation of sub-state claims on state resources. When these claims were articulated along ethnic lines, this could be as a means to an end rather than a true representation of an ethnic group's demands.

As we saw in Chapter 1, the 'post' in postcolonial not only refers to the period following on from colonialism, but also points to colonialism's lasting impact, influence and pervasiveness (Werbner 1996, 4). Nowhere is this more evident than in African states, which often inherited the trappings of parliamentary government, administrative bureaucracies and even ethnic categories from their former masters. These markers of domestic sovereignty were inevitably associated with colonial exploitation and therefore tended to be regarded more as vehicles for clientelist politics than as democratic, representative institutions. The early nation-building of African nationalists did aim to eradicate 'tribalism' and replace it with an overarching sense of shared, national belonging. However, this often took place in a climate of increasing authoritarianism and the personalisation of rule under a 'father figure' such as Felix Houphouët-Boigny in Ivory Coast (Chazan et al. 1999, 170), Hastings Kamuzu Banda in Malawi or Mobutu Sese Seko in Zaïre (De Boeck 1996, 81). For instance, attempts by Malawi's long-serving 'President for Life' Kamuzu Banda to forge a unifying nation-building myth centring on his own person were viewed as just that – a myth – by certain sections of the population (Chazan et al. 1999, 44). In Zaïre, Mobutu's autocratic regime did attempt to incorporate ethnic intermediaries and local chiefs in order to pre-empt any potential threat of sub-state mobilisation, such as 'some sort of Luunda "nationalism" and ethnic revival' (De Boeck 1996, 85) in the early 1990s. In turn, Luunda chiefs interpreted honours bestowed 'from above' as a recognition of their own sovereignty, thereby maintaining a strong sense of self-importance not only within Mobutu's regime, but also in dealings with diamond traders, rebel forces and the like. In this way, state leaders helped maintain their position through patronage and frequently tried to co-opt provincial power-brokers into their clientelist system. However, despite attempts to woo local kings and foster legitimacy through symbolic acts of tribute, ceremonial titles and lavish gifts, as well as mass education (Cruise O'Brien 1996, 58), Mobutu's kleptocratic rule led to a progressive collapse in state structures that continues to characterise its successor state, the Democratic Republic of Congo.

Sub-state representatives have adopted flexible identities appropriate to negotiating the perils of African politics. Ironically, however, the accepted ethnic identifiers in use are sometimes a product of colonial classification rather than well-established, pre-colonial tribes or traditions (Anderson 1991, 164). Examples include the Yoruba in Nigeria, the Ngoni in Zambia and the Karamojong in Uganda (Chazan et al. 1999, 109; Forrest 2004, 33). In Kenya, British colonialism served to consolidate a sense of Kikuyu consciousness through missionary education, a codified language and administrative categorisation, contributing to the emergence of a Kikuyu elite well versed in the stratagems of state (Breuilly 1993, 186). This privileged position undoubtedly played a key role in the relative success of their demands following independence, illustrating that although 'ethnically delimited categories may become vehicles for the articulation of political discontent' (Englund 1996, 107), these are not a priori identities that can be taken for granted. Leaders claiming to represent ethnic groups might well make primordialist claims based on putative pre-colonial traditions, but even these are invariably interpreted to fit the contemporary context.

Following independence, ethnic divisions could become more entrenched as a means of organising political competition for resources. Neither did individuals always restrict themselves to a single ethnic identity, but might switch between languages and allegiances depending on the possible benefits. Where one ethnic category had been favoured over another within the colonial system, such as the Lulua in Belgian Congo, the Kikuyu in Kenya or the Tutsis in Rwanda, this also formed the basis for postcolonial conflict. Claims to 'embody' the entire nation tend to ring hollow when there is a strong association between a national leader and a particular ethnic group, or 'dominant *ethnie*' (Smith 1995, 106). Thus ethnicity was often used strategically in attempts to secure autonomy and other advantages from the central state, something which can also be said of sub-state mobilisation more generally (Crawford, cited in Breuilly 1993, 205). Faced with sub-state ethnic movements, government responses have included what Richard Werbner (1996, 13) calls 'quasi-nationalism', where one group claiming to speak for the nation-state as a whole uses state violence ruthlessly to crush resistance. Postcolonial Zimbabwe and the Rwandan genocide are cases in point.

What parallels can we draw between ethnic mobilisation in Africa and sub-state nationalism? Far from being an atavistic loyalty or a primordial allegiance, ethnicity is often used strategically in response to the specific context of postcolonial clientelist states. This highlights the instrumentalisation of ethnicity; the African examples show how ethnic labels can be used as a legitimating device for securing patronage and privileges. Although these will tend to draw on genuinely held cultural affinities among the population, they will also be manipulated for political advantage. There is no such thing as a treasure chest of tradition that can be dug up and opened to reveal glittering nuggets of pristine, uncontested national heritage (Hobsbawm & Ranger 1983). In Africa, ethnicity has provided a useful political vehicle 'because the infinite complexity and incomprehensible fluidity of provincial and national politics could be diminished by the application of ethnic labels to contending groups' (Young, cited in Breuilly 1993, 204). This is not to suggest that all sub-state mobilisation is based on complete fabrication and purely motivated by personal gain. Although Africa's rapid decolonisation often revealed particularly weak institutions and a bald exploitation of state resources, there had to be some degree of mobilising cultural appeal for communal leaders to maintain their position as ethnic or national intermediaries (Cheah 2003, 129). Having considered the way in which ethnicity can be used to support sub-state demands, we now turn to political parties as key agents of sub-state nationalist ideology.

Parties

A key characteristic of contemporary nationalist parties is their flexibility and adaptability in responding to social and political change. Understanding the context in which they evolve is therefore vital. Although Scotland and Bavaria are not states, they nevertheless provide the boundaries of a national discourse. This is perpetuated not only by the SNP and the CSU, Bavaria's dominant party, but also by all parties who address the Scottish and Bavarian electorates as distinct entities (Llobera 1994, 199). Only nationalist parties have turned the nation into the nodal point of their entire ideology, however. Hence the SNP and the CSU's construction of the nation are designed to politicise Scottish and Bavarian identity in order to achieve an important degree of emancipation from larger polities. In turn, Scottish devolution within the UK and Bavaria's place in the German federal state are bound up with the SNP and the CSU's respective interpretations of self-determination. The choice of cases shows the very different political contexts in which sub-state nationalism can thrive. In order better to understand these dynamics, the following discussion considers each party in the light of electoral competition and the sub-state nation they have helped shape. It also considers the implications of the parties' policies on migration, as a key aspect of the cosmopolitan challenge.

On its political union with England and Wales in 1707, Scotland retained the so-called 'holy trinity' of a distinct religion, education system and legal system, as well as substantial administrative autonomy. Indeed, Lindsay Paterson (1994, 4) has provocatively questioned the extent to which Scotland ever lost its independence through the Act of Union: '[Scotland] has been at least as autonomous as other small European nations, for which the reality of politics has always been the negotiation of partial independence amid the rivalry of great powers'. This highlights the difficulty – especially amidst the cosmopolitan challenge – of defining the various degrees of self-determination, independence, sovereignty or political autonomy that nationalists crave. Nevertheless, during the decades following World War II, Scottish discontent grew at the concentration of legislative and economic powers in London. Scottish support for the fledgling SNP hovered at around 1 per cent or below until the 1960s, when the party's fortunes began to improve. In 1967, popular dissatisfaction with the status quo, successfully channelled by the SNP into demands for constitutional change, led to the party winning a by-election in the constituency of Hamilton. The shockwaves of the SNP victory made the dominant parties wish they could bury the issue of self-government once again, but they could not ignore the television and media coverage given to the victorious candidate, which helped to bridge what the SNP's erstwhile leader Robert McIntyre called the party's 'credibility gap' (Ewing 1969, 3). The UK Labour party and the Conservatives felt compelled to devise their own alternative policies on the constitutional question, in order to undermine the sudden attractiveness of the SNP. The Conservative leader Edward Heath even promised Scottish home rule in 1968, but did not honour his pledge when he became prime minister. By then, the SNP's electoral success had waned, and its opponents no longer considered the party such a threat.

The SNP's local election wins had been a baptism of fire, forcing it to supplement its core nationalist principles with a whole range of peripheral policies. The party was aware that it had to present Scottish identity as a unifying political alternative in order to overcome existing class and religious loyalties. In late 1974, eleven SNP candidates were elected to Westminster following a general election campaign in which the party had concentrated on making Scottish identity politically relevant (Brown et al. 1996, 45). The SNP was to play an important role at the UK level over the next five years, since the minority Labour government was dependent on small parties to pass legislation. During the 1970s, swings in the SNP's devolution policy suggesting indecision and a lack of clarity had a negative impact on the electorate (Levy 1986). The party was divided between 'gradualists', who saw the devolution of power from Westminster to Edinburgh as a sensible first step on the road to independence, and 'fundamentalists' who favoured the 'big bang' approach encapsulated in the SNP's 1977 slogan of 'Independence – nothing less'. A decisive swing towards the gradualists took place with the election of Alex Salmond as party chairman in 1990. By then, the party's official policy on independence had also changed to 'Independence in Europe', a response designed to counter charges of being an old-fashioned, isolationist party (Levy 1995; Newman 1996, 40–41; Sillars 1986). This shows how the party reacted to the cosmopolitan challenge by incorporating European regionalism into its goal of self-determination; it now claims to be attuned to the 'reality of independence in this interdependent world' (SNP 2011). However, the pro-European policy was a strategic supplement to its core principle of pursuing Scottish independence, which remains unchanged. Tellingly, the SNP does not consider Scotland a region of the EU, but demands a 'seat at the top table' of the organisation's Council of Ministers, alongside all other member states.

In 1997, the newly elected UK Labour government fulfiled a campaign promise to hold a Scottish referendum on devolution, leading to a resounding 'yes' vote and the establishment of the Scottish parliament in 1999 (Lynch 2001; Paterson et al. 2001). By that time, support for Scottish devolution spanned three of the country's four main parties, including the SNP. Devolution heralded a period of expansion and professionalisation within the SNP, culminating in their Scottish election win of 2007, in which they gained one more Scottish parliament seat than Labour and formed a minority government. This status differs markedly from the SNP's relative insignificance at Westminster. Nevertheless, there is no obvious parallel between its explicit claim to be 'Scotland's Party' and its electoral fortunes, since, according to opinion polls, SNP voters do not necessarily support the independence policy (Keating 2001, 227). In 2010, the party suffered a setback when it had to abandon an election pledge to hold a referendum on its core aim of independence, as it was unable to get a draft bill through the Scottish parliament. Instead, the SNP leader and Scottish first minister Alex Salmond vowed to make independence the 'transcending issue' of the 2011 Scottish election campaign (Salmond, cited in *Guardian* 2010a), although in practice economic issues largely eclipsed it. In the event, the SNP benefited from a lacklustre Scottish Labour campaign, a collapse in Liberal Democrat support, and widespread satisfaction with its first four years in office to win a swathe of new seats across Scotland. This resulted in an absolute SNP majority in the Scottish Parliament, something most electoral pundits deemed well nigh impossible under the single transferable voting system in place (*Economist* 2011b). The leaders of all three other main parties in Scotland resigned following the election.

Little more than a decade after devolution, the SNP's resounding win has put the constitutional question at the forefront of Scottish politics once again. It is likely to hold a referendum on independence by 2015, notwithstanding that opinion polls show only around 30 per cent of Scots support this, far fewer than voted SNP (*Economist* 2011b). Salmond sought to emphasise the SNP's broad appeal immediately following the election, however. Drawing attention to both national identity and the party's wider policy platform, he called the SNP the 'national party of Scotland', going on to say that it had 'reached out to every community across this country' (*BBC News* 2011b). In the short term, Salmond aims to link the core SNP issue of independence to greater financial and budgetary autonomy through enhanced Scottish parliamentary powers, in order to decouple Scotland from the effects of swingeing budget cuts by the UK's coalition government. This shows that even if pragmatism and flexibility are characteristic of the SNP's strategic thinking, keeping its ideological core intact remains crucial to its very *raison d'être*. In the past, only the unambiguous and oft-repeated long-term commitment to full independence could unite the party's gradualist and fundamentalist factions. These divisions have not been laid to rest with devolution, as the party now strives to balance its leading role in the Scottish political arena with continuing calls for full independence.

The SNP is relatively unusual among contemporary nationalist parties in Europe, because it seeks independent statehood for the Scottish nation, albeit as a member of the European Union. It tries to position itself as the best representative of Scottish interests, while portraying the UK nation-state as contrary to those interests. Crucially, in working to 'redirect loyalty of the citizens from an existing regime' (Shain 2005, 23), the party claims to embody the Scottish nation more than any other party. In sum, sub-state nationalism, just like nation-building, strives for the kind of recognition and acceptance which inheres in the sovereignty and legitimacy that have long been defining attributes of nation-states. Nationalist ideology seeks to politicise a sense of emotional allegiance precisely because successfully mobilised loyalty is a strong marker of legitimacy. In turn, sub-state nationalists aim to reconfigure the territorial and political limits of people's loyalty to match their own understanding of the nation. As agents of nationalist ideology, political parties are also key players in distilling down aspects of the cosmopolitan challenge into the language of autonomy, identity and self-determination. In Germany, something akin to nation-building goes on in the federal state of Bavaria, where the long-governing CSU has been singularly successful in cementing its legitimacy as the party of Bavarian *Heimat* (Sutherland 2001).

Today's *Land* of Bavaria roughly corresponds territorially to the kingdom it once was within the wider German Reich. Its historic regions of Swabia, Franconia and *Altbayern* also remain important markers of identity for individual Bavarians. However, these have been largely subordinated to an overriding Bavarian identity, due in no small part to the homogenising ideology of the CSU (James 1996; Mintzel 1999). As such, the party's attempts to mobilise Bavarian identity for political ends can be defined as an application of nationalist ideological principles. This is because the CSU has connected itself more credibly than its political competitors to long-standing notions of Bavarian identity through its articulation of nodal points like the *Heimat*, or homeland, which approximates to the core concept of the nation (Sutherland 2001, 17). For instance, preserving the Bavarian *Heimat* helps provide the ideological justification for other party policies such as environmental protection and city planning. The CSU's position on European integration is also argued to be in the best interests of the *Heimat* (Sutherland 2001, 18). To use Michael Freeden's (1998) terminology, these peripheral principles supplement the party's ideological core of prioritising the Bavarian *Heimat*, or nation. Crucially, the fact that the CSU is an exclusively Bavarian party standing only in Bavaria helps support its claim to best understand the Bavarian mentality, even to the point of embodying the *Heimat*. It shares this strategic advantage with the SNP in Scotland. As such, it is possible to consider the CSU as an example of a sub-state nationalist party.

The nineteenth-century nation-building efforts of Bavarian monarchs and their bureaucracies set an integrative process in motion that has been taken up and pursued by the CSU (Mintzel 1995, 195). Apart from the 12 years spent under Nazi dictatorship, the modern Bavarian state has always been a member of some form of federation, but successive governments have continuously defended its autonomy against Prussia, the Austro-Hungarian Empire and the European Union (Treml 1994). Both as a kingdom and as a federal state of Germany, Bavaria has consistently attempted to maximise its independence and promote a sense of Bavarian identity (Sutherland 2001, 30). The CSU was one of the first political parties to be authorised under the American occupation in January 1946 and immediately set about promoting a sense of internal Bavarian unity and solidarity (Schlemmer 1999). Today, the 'Free State of Bavaria' has its own constitution, government and parliament, as well as a tiered system of local government, but remains firmly embedded within the German federal system. As its name suggests, the CSU's founding members had envisaged a party that would bridge the religious divide between the predominantly Catholic south and the Lutheran Protestant north of Bavaria, in order to overcome the political fragmentation which had dogged the Weimar Republic. To this day, the CSU stands only in Bavaria and continues to present the preservation and propagation of its Bavarian identity as a central component of its ideology. At the federal level, the CSU cultivates its image as a 'sister party' (*Schwesterpartei*) and coalition partner to the Christian Democrat CDU. Not afraid to criticise the policies of its federal partner or emphasise Bavarian autonomy, the CSU's predilection for a clear, uncompromising stance on everything from immigration to EU policy has helped it to position itself to the right of the CDU on the German political spectrum. The CSU's post-unification attempts to form a parallel party in the Eastern German federal states, or *Länder*, have been laid to rest, thereby recognising that any expansion would lead to a dilution of its Bavarian identity.

At the sub-state level, the CSU has been one of the most successful political parties in Europe. It has enjoyed the consistent support of over half of the electorate in Bavaria, attracting more than 50 per cent of the vote in every Bavarian election between 1970 and 2008. But for a three-year break in the 1950s, the CSU has governed Bavaria since 1946 and without coalition partners between 1966 and 2008. In 1966, it gained an absolute majority of seats in the Bavarian parliament, which it subsequently retained and eventually bettered with a two-thirds majority in the 2003 election. Despite a significant drop in support in 2008, it still led the coalition government formed with the liberal *Freie Demokratische*

Partei (FDP). The party's electoral success has been partly attributed to its all-pervading presence across Bavarian municipalities (Mintzel 1999). Over and above the tangible benefits of representation and influence at every level of Bavarian society, the CSU also attempts to achieve conceptual hegemony there by striving to have its *Heimat*-centred ideology equated with 'common sense'. This task is facilitated by CSU governments' past success at making Bavaria an attractive place to live, work and invest. Bavaria's post-war development from a backward agricultural economy to one of the richest *Länder* in Germany is inextricably linked to CSU policies and is extremely important to the party's image. Indeed, Bavaria was the only *Land* to have become a contributor to the system of financial redistribution among the German *Länder,* after having been a past recipient (Treml 1994, 493).

The CSU's enviable election record came to an end in the Bavarian state elections of September 2008, which saw the CSU lose over 17 per cent of its vote. In the context of sub-state nationalist ideology and strategy, it is instructive to take a closer look at the reasons for this reversal in electoral fortunes. An opinion poll conducted days before the election found that 55 per cent of respondents thought the CSU no longer represented the Bavarian attitude to life (*Lebensgefühl*) 'as it once had' and that 65 per cent did not consider the CSU to be a 'modern party' (LMU 2008, no page, author's translation). A change in leadership, membership in the incumbent federal government, and voter dissatisfaction with unpopular policies, combined with a rather directionless campaign, were partly to blame for the CSU's collapse in support (*Süddeutsche Zeitung* 2008). The 2008 election results showed that the party could no longer simply rely on being equated with Bavarian identity, and had failed to adapt to the electorate's expectations. Comments such as 'respectable Bavarians vote CSU' by Bavaria's then first minister Günther Beckstein proved to be counterproductive in the run-up to the election, particularly among members of other parties, who felt unfairly besmirched (Welt-Online 2009). It seems that the CSU's complacency vis-à-vis its privileged position in Bavarian politics was also widely perceived as arrogance. This was as much to blame for its relative defeat (even though it remains in government) as the positive gains made by other parties (LMU 2008).

As 'the party to beat' in Bavaria, the CSU's overweening presence also influences opponents' responses to questions of identity. Yet it seems that the SPD's social democratic vision of Bavaria as multicultural and cosmopolitan, or the FDP's evocation of diversity and pluralism, have yet to displace the clichéd images of Bavaria that have been 'internalised' by many voters (Hepburn 2008, 195), not least through decades of CSU dominance. As the CSU's main rival for the title of 'people's party' (*Volkspartei*) in Bavaria, the SPD could not take advantage of the CSU's losses in the 2008 election, itself dropping to its lowest ever share of the vote. The disparate *Freie Wähler* group, whose principal campaign focus was to be anti-CSU, garnered a large share of votes from former CSU supporters. In spite of a lacklustre campaign, the left-wing *die Linke* actually seemed to have benefited from the CSU's vehement denunciation of its policies, which helped boost its media presence. The Green party saw a modest increase in its share of the vote, and was perhaps most successful in challenging the CSU's strong hold on Bavarian identifiers. It fielded a personable leader who, as a farmer himself, could appeal to rural voters and reinterpret traditional symbols in a positive and plausible way (Hepburn 2008, 199). What this analysis shows, however, is that other parties' fortunes partly depended on how they positioned themselves vis-à-vis the CSU, rather than on the inherent merits of their campaign. To this extent, the CSU continues to dominate the Bavarian political arena, which it has been so influential in shaping. It remains to be seen whether the 2008 election result signals the start of a shift towards a more inclusive understanding of Bavaria as a stateless nation. Linked to this, and since both the CSU and SNP are governing parties at the sub-state level, it is instructive to compare their responses to the cosmopolitan challenge of migration.

The CSU's anti-multicultural rhetoric is out of kilter with that of other parties claiming to represent stateless nations, such as the Scottish Nationalist Party, the Parti Québécois and Catalonia's Convergencia i Unió (Hepburn 2009). The CSU and the SNP's differing definitions of national belonging are exemplified in their attitude towards immigration, a key aspect of the cosmopolitan challenge. Anxious to avoid being branded anti-English or inward looking, the SNP has long emphasised its open, civic understanding of the nation (Hepburn 2009, 517). As its affiliated organisations 'Asian Scots for Independence' and 'New Scots for Independence' appear to testify, anyone who resides in Scotland and participates in its society can identify themselves as Scottish if they so wish. Similarly, the SNP adopts an open policy towards immigration and envisages Scotland as a multicultural nation. Its brand of voluntaristic nationalism presents statehood as a way of legitimating a new national arena along civic lines rather than protecting an endangered one based on ethnocultural markers. By contrast, the CSU's rejection of multiculturalism and its emphasis on ethnic markers of belonging is reflected in its sustained opposition to a German federal law extending citizenship to children born in Germany of foreign parents, a watered-down version of which was finally passed in the year 2000. This strategy was partly to counter the perceived threat of losing its most conservative voters to extreme right wing parties, and partly an expression of the CSU's long-term opposition to Germany as an *Einwanderungsland*, or 'land of immigration' (Green 2004; Holmes Cooper 2002, 93). Bavaria's then prime minister Edmund Stoiber, leading a party with a large majority in the Bavarian parliament, was also vocal in his opposition to dual citizenship and championed a Germany-wide petition against it. Of five million signatures in total, the CSU gathered 1.8 million in Bavaria (Holmes Cooper 2002, 97). The CSU's immigration and integration policies, developed jointly at the federal level with its sister party, the CDU, encourage immigrants to 'become German' (*Deutscher werden*) in a one-way process of adopting German language, culture and values (Gould 2000, 537). The CSU has also advocated reducing the numbers of immigrants and asylum seekers accepted into Germany (Kruse, Orren & Angenendt 2003), and has asked for an opt-out from the EU's common immigration provisions in order to enforce more stringent requirements on those entering Bavaria (Hepburn 2009, 522).

Much like the CSU, the SNP has also demanded that control of immigration be devolved to Scotland from Westminster, but for precisely the opposite reason. The SNP would like Scotland to enjoy the same power over immigration policy as Quebec, because both nations have experienced declines in population and birth rates which speak for an increase, and not a decrease in immigration (SNP 2008). In turn, the argument that UK immigration policy 'doesn't fit' Scotland's needs is used to canvas support for independence (SNP 2010). Quebec has also tried to 'incorporate global migration within its national project' (Blad & Couton 2009, 652) in an intriguing response to this aspect of the cosmopolitan challenge. A key factor in this has been Quebec's independent control of its immigration policy since 1991, allowing it to select migrants from French-speaking countries. This has resulted in over half of new arrivals to Montréal speaking some French, compared to 2 per cent of migrants to Toronto and Vancouver. Indeed, Quebec's linking of its language and migration policies has led its model to be distinguished from multiculturalism because 'the relatively new diversity of Quebec society is structured around a single national cultural norm, the French language' (Blad & Couton 2009, 652).

Contrary to Quebec, the need or desire to promote a national language does not figure in Scotland's immigration debate. Both Scottish party policy and public opinion tend to be more positive towards immigration than in the rest of the UK, and the Scottish media has not conveyed the same hostility towards increased immigration as some segments of the UK-wide press (Hepburn 2009, 521). Against this backdrop, the SNP in government – like the Labour-Liberal coalition that preceded it – has lobbied to attract more migrants, with the explicit aim of making Scotland a (more) multicultural nation (Hepburn 2009, 521). Parallel to this, the SNP has explicitly defined Scotland as a multicultural society since the 1990s. In stark contrast to the Estonian case discussed in Chapter 3, its policy would be to extend Scottish citizenship to all those resident in Scotland on achieving independence (Stewart Leith 2008, 88). The major differences in CSU and SNP policies on this issue illustrate the flexibility of nationalism in responding to migration as part of the cosmopolitan challenge. The two parties have supplemented their core commitment to prioritising the nation with contrasting principles. The SNP's open understanding of Scottishness, combined with the needs of the Scottish economy, the country's demographics and the party's left-of-centre agenda, allow for a positive attitude to migration, whereas the CSU's emphasis on limiting and integrating immigrants stems from its conservative orientation and ethnically tinged interpretation of the Bavarian *Heimat*. Having considered the relationship between sub-state nationalism and immigration, we turn to the opposite phenomenon of emigration and the resultant diaspora in this chapter's final section, with a look at the form of sub-state nationalism spearheaded by Tibet's government in exile.

Diaspora

The nation has been described as 'the ultimate object of competition for loyalty' (Shain 2005, 4). Whereas the state is able to *command* this loyalty using legal and military means (Shain 2005, 19), sub-state nationalists must find other ways to mobilise loyal support in their quest to undermine the existing legitimating link between nation and state. Put another way, loyalty is seen as one of the duties of citizenship, in return for state rights, security and protection, but opponents of an incumbent regime, particularly those in exile and among the diaspora, have limited resources with which to reward their loyal followers. Citizenship continues to be regarded as a badge of loyalty, as exemplified in ceremonies involving oath-taking, or the practice of stripping political exiles of their citizenship, but precise definitions of 'national loyalty' will fluctuate according to the state's incumbent government. Official attitudes towards the national diaspora are a key measure of these changes (Barabantseva & Sutherland 2011). At the same time, territory continues to be a strong focus of loyalty; states may be suspicious of diaspora communities and those who live abroad, particularly if they acquire foreign citizenship. Alternatively, states may seek to integrate their national diaspora by offering overseas voting rights or preferential investment terms, as in the cases of India or Italy, among others (Barabantseva & Sutherland 2011). The impact of diaspora communities on citizenship as a facet of nation-building will be examined further in Chapter 5, but the following section considers sub-state nationalism among the Tibetan diaspora, whose homeland is part of the People's Republic of China (PRC).

Despite China's long-standing, self-ascribed status as the 'middle kingdom' at the centre of a hierarchical cosmology, the Chinese Communist Party today emphasises and defends the sovereignty of the PRC in standard Westphalian terms (Barabantseva 2009, 133). While keen to preserve Chinese culture and society from the potentially nefarious effects of globalisation, it also attempts to market aspects of Chinese history – including colonial remnants – as a means of attracting global business, tourism and capital (Marinelli 2009). This strategy targets not only foreign entrepreneurs, visitors and investors, but also members of the extensive Chinese diaspora. It forms part of a wider range of policies designed to involve overseas ethnic Chinese in the PRC's modernisation and development, by fostering a sense of national belonging and loyalty that transcends borders. Though some of the Chinese diaspora will dislike the political propaganda that links national loyalty to support for the communist regime, this is one example of a deterritorialised form of nation-building responding and adapting to the cosmopolitan challenge. Despite the fact that the PRC officially acknowledges the country's ethnic diversity at home, however, its international appeals are unlikely to resonate with those ethnic minorities abroad who neither regard themselves as Chinese nor consider the communist regime legitimate. For example, the 2008 Olympic games in Beijing were designed to showcase the PRC's diversity and achievements (and drew many donations from overseas Chinese), but also hit the headlines as the focus for protests surrounding the PRC's policies towards Tibet. Alongside Taiwan, the status of Tibet is the most internationally controversial aspect of China's official nation-building. In considering the Tibetan case, this section focuses on the link between diaspora and sub-state nationalism.

Since fleeing Tibet in 1959, the Dalai Lama, recognised as the spiritual and political leader of Tibetans across the world, has sought to maintain a sense of Tibetan national consciousness among the diaspora, while working to reform aspects of Tibetan custom and political organisation. For instance, the Dalai Lama has introduced constitutional and democratic principles to his government in exile, but retains his position as supreme arbiter and decision-maker. Officially derived from Buddhist beliefs, Tibetan democracy is clearly influenced by Western models, but also demonstrates some of the characteristics – such as limited free speech and press – often associated with Asian democracies (Case 2009; Frechette 2007, 109). One consequence of this is the difficulty in gauging support among the diaspora for Tibet's complete independence from China. This demand is based on the contested claim that Tibet was effectively independent between the World Wars, and differs from the Dalai Lama's official support for greater Tibetan autonomy within the PRC. It is more difficult still to gain a sense of what Tibetans in Tibet desire for their homeland, given the existing PRC regime and the restrictions it places on opinion polling, journalism and academic research. What is clear is that the PRC is engaged in a political confrontation with the Dalai Lama's government in exile to win the legitimation and loyalty of Tibetans, as evidenced in the controversy surrounding the rightful successor to the present Dalai Lama.

Having undertaken worldwide lecture tours since the 1980s and won the Nobel Peace Price in 1989, the Dalai Lama is widely associated with non-violence, ethics and human rights, and is regularly received by heads of government (Magnusson 2002, 206). He is perceived as a wise and dignified man of high moral stature. To some extent, he embodies a long-standing myth of Tibet as a place of peace, harmony and simple serenity, a magical Shangri-La. In order to 'recruit supporters in the struggle with China over Tibet's future the Dalai Lama is forced to play his part in the myth' (Magnusson 2002, 210). The admiration he attracts benefits the Tibetan government in exile, helping to portray its demands for autonomy as a noble and righteous struggle against Chinese control. Although human rights abuses have been documented within Tibet (Ardley 2002, 164), this is a delicate area of claim and counter-claim. Some go so far as to describe the PRC's alleged oppression of Tibet as colonialism and genocide (Ardley 2002; 167; Houston & Wright 2003, 219), while this terminology is hotly contested as inaccurate and exaggerated by other experts on Tibet (Sautman 2006), not to mention the PRC government itself. The Dalai Lama seems to acknowledge that such accusations are a barrier to dialogue with the PRC and thus counter-productive to advancing the Tibetan cause. He himself has stated that 'Tibetan culture and Buddhism are part of Chinese culture' and 'we are willing to be part of the People's Republic of China' (cited in Sautman 2006, 246).

Tibetan sub-state nationalism is a fascinating example of a diaspora-led movement that also embraces other aspects of the cosmopolitan challenge, such as transnationalism and globalisation. Notwithstanding continuous references to the diaspora's homeland, 'Tibetan nationalism and nation building operates by necessity as a transnational force' (Houston & Wright 2003, 218). Exiled Tibetan leaders do not hesitate to harness the power of transnational alliances and global media to further their cause, as was evident from the coordinated pro-Tibet protests that greeted the progress of the Olympic flame from country to country in 2008. The Tibetan experience simultaneously underlines and undermines the importance of territory to contemporary sub-state nationalism. On the one hand, dreams of returning to an autonomous Tibet unite an increasingly disparate community scattered across the world. With the Tibetan diaspora subject to very different experiences of assimilation in its host countries, however, the government in exile's nation-building strategies must work ever harder to remain relevant across the generations. On the other hand, the transnational nature of its work testifies to the existence of an 'imagined community' (Anderson 1991) transcending borders and intimately bound up with the international and political 'Free Tibet' campaign. Inevitably, the depth and expression of national loyalty will vary from individual to individual, but the need for political mobilisation is acutely clear to the government in exile, which wants to stop its pool of potential Tibetan returnees from seeping away through naturalisation (and renunciation of refugee status) or complete cultural integration into their host society. This raises the issue of authenticity, or how to gauge 'true' national belonging.

Ironically, Tibetans in exile sometimes mistake recent emigrants from Tibet for ethnic Chinese. Resorting to racial stereotyping is not uncommon, as is politicised opposition to (Han) Chinese as the negatively-connoted 'Other' (Yeh 2002, 235). This is partly due to an exaggerated expectation of physical, phenotypical differences between ethnic Tibetans and Chinese, and partly due to the PRC-controlled socialisation and schooling of recent emigrants. In addition, those who left Tibet in the 1960s and '70s sometimes look down on later exiles. They can be stereotyped as uncouth and badly behaved (Houston & Wright 2003, 226; Yeh 2002, 243), and also suffer from a politicised association with Communist Party policies and popular attitudes in the PRC, which is heightened if they speak Chinese. This serves to show that Tibetan national identity is constantly developing and being renegotiated, but risks remaining static and essentialised within diaspora communities that are cautious of new and unfamiliar ways of being Tibetan. Predictably, younger members of the Tibetan diaspora in particular chafe under what they see as outdated and rigid interpretations of what is 'appropriate' Tibetan behaviour and 'real' Tibetan belonging.

To some members of the Tibetan diaspora, their refugee status is a key symbol of their national and political identity (Houston & Wright 2003, 227; Yeh 2002, 28). Others obtain foreign (such as Nepalese) citizenship primarily in order to facilitate business activities, while claiming to remain Tibetan 'inside' (Houston & Wright 2003, 227). The Tibetan government in exile has no means of commanding the loyalty of its diaspora in the absence of state authority or such a thing as Tibetan citizenship (Shain 2005). As such, it must work particularly hard to mobilise a scattered community that is developing in different directions. For instance, it has attempted to emphasise national unity over religious and regional affiliations, two historically important identifiers within Tibet (Ardley 2002, 163). Contrary to the SNP, however, which can stipulate residence and intention as sufficient markers of Scottishness, or the federal states of Bavaria and Quebec, which can use immigration controls and integration policies to influence understandings of national belonging, the Tibetan diaspora has no single territorial base in which to gather, organise, educate and influence its people. Instead, the Dalai Lama's government in exile attempts to administer and mobilise communities resident in India, Nepal, the US and elsewhere from their headquarters in Dharamsala, northern India. This nationalist strategy, in turn, is 'reabsorbed into the exile community's self-perception' (Anand 2002, 14).

The town of Dharamsala is important as the temporary, symbolic capital of the Tibetan diaspora and a centre of cultural preservation. As 'little Lhasa', it is also a place of Buddhist pilgrimage. The place itself thus helps to legitimate the government in exile as representative of Tibetans, and thereby protect, or help create, a religiously and culturally 'pure' form of Tibetan national identity. In turn, this identity is presented in stark opposition to the Chinese 'Other', not only ethnically and politically, but also ethically and even environmentally. For instance, the Tibetan government in exile's embrace of an environmentalist agenda, and its self-promotion through English-language materials, are means of tapping into a global network of support and goodwill. At the same time, this provides an opportunity to cast the PRC in a bad light for allegedly destroying Tibetan ecology and landscape (Magnusson 2002, 203), thereby combining 'timeless' and semi-mythical aspects of Tibetan spirituality and culture with 'progressive' features such as democracy and environmentalism. In so doing, the government in exile is also trying to mobilise international support for the 'Free Tibet' campaign, but this is simultaneously contributing to the constant evolution and further fragmentation of what it means to be Tibetan. The lack of access to the Tibetan homeland means that this form of diasporic sub-state nationalism is at a particular disadvantage in articulating modern markers of belonging that remain attractive and relevant focal points for national legitimacy and loyalty. The 'diaspora ideology of Dharamsala' (Klieger 2002, 8) is thus a multifaceted response to the cosmopolitan challenge; it exemplifies the difficulties of adapting sub-state nationalism to diverse diaspora communities while harnessing some of the potential of globalisation and transnationalism to its cause.

The government in exile's adoption of democratic principles signals a readiness to embrace change, which helps to make the Tibetan cause an attractive one for international sponsors. It also serves to draw in younger generations of Tibetans, born in exile, who are better able to relate to democratic ideals than ossified structures and traditions (Ardley 2002, 3). As ordinary exiled Tibetans become better educated and able to articulate their preferences and demands, democratic structures should come into their own (Frechette 2007, 124). The Dalai Lama himself put it thus: 'Although the Chinese have dubbed our national struggle as one aimed at reviving the old society, the steps taken by us thus far prove their accusation wrong' (cited in Frechette 2007, 113). To this extent, democratisation and reform within the Tibetan exile community are means in this 'national struggle' as much as ends in themselves. They can thus be seen as peripheral principles supporting the core principle of national self-determination. Inevitably, given the incredibly delicate nature of relations with the PRC, the Dalai Lama leaves the meaning of autonomy vague, making good use of nationalist ideology's flexibility in interpreting the core aim of prioritising the nation.

Conclusion

To quote John Breuilly (1993, 215), nationalism was 'in many ways a very controlled and advantageous way of bringing colonial rule to an end,' suggesting that, in principle, it can be a vehicle for a smooth political transition. In practice, however, the African experience shows how the illegitimacy of existing state institutions, their mismanagement, and ultimately nationalist leaders themselves, can lead to a breakdown of the loyalty-legitimacy nexus on which nationalist ideology relies. Sub-state mobilisation adds to the confusion by seeking to reform the prevailing nation-state or gain better access to its resources. In the case of sub-state nationalists, the alternative understanding of national self-determination they advance represents a revolutionary project in that it sets out to rearticulate the parameters of national discourse. All political parties use ideology in an attempt to legitimate and consolidate their bids for power, but they rarely aspire to a complete rearticulation of the political arena along new national lines. Nationalists' claims to represent a nation are problematic, however, in that many of their compatriots, though secure in their sense of national identity, do not want a particular party to politicise it for their own ends. By manipulating markers of national belonging, then, sub-state nationalists can therefore serve to divide as well as unite.

A key effect of the cosmopolitan challenge has been to force a reassessment of sovereignty and the reshaping of nationalist appeals in response. When forces of globalisation reconfigure a state's power and authority, regionalisation, migration, and the like, the nation-state needs to be redefined. The term 'stateless nationalists' has been used to describe those who see state sovereignty as having limited meaning, and therefore do not aspire to it (Keating 2001, 64). Even the SNP, one of the few parties to seek sovereignty for a 'stateless nation', espouses 'Independence in Europe', thereby wrapping its demands in regionalist rhetoric. At the same time, nationalist parties in Scotland, Catalonia and Quebec all display a form of 'free-trade nationalism' (Keating 2001, 63), which views global interconnectedness as a positive source of profit for the nation, rather than a threat to ethnocultural heritage or purity. This is also reflected in the SNP's attitude towards immigration. In the case of Quebec, however, sub-state immigration controls incorporate a form of cultural nationalism by shaping migration to fit with policies that prioritise the French language. In the final analysis, many of today's sub-state nationalists demand greater policy autonomy and flexibility not because they are inward-looking, but so as to engage on the world stage independently of an overweening state intermediary. The impact of the cosmopolitan challenge only strengthens their nationalist argument for solid sub-state institutions and interest representation in order for them to develop an appropriate response. Witness the SNP's continued marshalling of economic arguments to support the case for independence in the midst of a global financial crisis and state-level retrenchment. Sub-state nationalists from Tibet to Quebec are alive to the constraints of contemporary politics and economics, and the need to turn aspects of the cosmopolitan challenge to their advantage. Nowhere is the adaptability of nationalist ideology more apparent, then, than in the field of sub-state nationalism.

5

Where is the Nation-State? Managing Citizenship and Migration

How are nationalism and citizenship interlinked? How does migration affect nationality and citizenship?

Contrary to those who predicted the decline of nation-states (Ohmae 1996) following the collapse of communism and the alleged 'end of history' (Fukuyama 1992), this chapter takes the apparent resilience of nation-states as its starting point. It focuses on official state nationalism, or nation-building, and its relationship to citizenship. The very hyphen linking nation and state indicates how closely the two concepts are linked, with the former providing legitimacy for the latter. The chapter argues that a decoupling of the two remains unlikely in contemporary politics, where citizenship legislation still builds on nation-based criteria. It begins with a discussion of citizenship, which helps illuminate the legitimating link between nation and state. There is tension in this link, and some warn that it may snap under the pressure of migration. In order to explore this claim, the chapter's first section looks at how migrants become citizens. Do they have to possess certain skills, such as mastery of a particular language? What are the implications for those already living within that state? It will be shown that neither nation-building nor citizenship need rest on monolithic notions of national identity. Instead, they are already being redefined through multiculturalism and instrumentalist notions of 'flexible citizenship' (Ong 1999). This is one consequence of transnationalism, though its impact is neither universal nor uncontested, as will be examined in the second section of the chapter. Indeed, some national communities continue to emphasise ethnic or cultural markers of belonging over civic ones, which are usually understood as the rights, obligations and democratic values shared by state citizens. In practice, contemporary nation-states clearly tend to advocate some cultural homogeneity in their population through integrative measures. The last part of the chapter will explore the limits of this approach by discussing the notion of 'flexible citizenship' (Ong 1999) in the Southeast Asian context. The chapter concludes that nationalist ideology continues both to underpin government efforts at state legitimation, and permeate current debates surrounding citizenship. However, the protean nature of nationalism means that it can promote both inclusive and exclusionary understandings of belonging in response to the cosmopolitan challenge.

Citizenship

Many nation-states are so well established that their existence is taken for granted, but this does not make them unproblematic or somehow exempt from study in nationalist terms. On the contrary, states make particularly illuminating case studies, as they embody successful nationalist mobilisation. Nationalist symbols, institutions and rhetoric have been internalised there to such an extent that they are widely regarded as common sense, which is the ultimate goal of any nation-building project: 'It is perhaps not too surprising that *nationalism* should come to mean identification with the state rather than loyalty to the nation [when] the "nation-building" school has in fact been dedicated to building viable states' (Connor 1984, 40–41; emphasis in original). A nation always designates a people – a community – but this can be defined and represented in many different ways. For instance, as we saw in Chapter 3, representation may be organised according to democratic principles. Here, the nation is (imperfectly) equated with the people as a *demos*, or 'civic body' (Chryssochoou 2007, 359) that periodically votes for politicians to govern the state on its behalf. This model of the nation-state often goes hand in hand with the legal fiction of popular sovereignty. Alternatively, a dictator may claim to embody the popular will and present himself as 'father of the nation'. In general, '[r]elying at least tacitly on the idea of "nation" to give an account of why particular people belong together as the "people" of a particular state has historically done the double work of explaining the primary loyalty of each to all within the state, and the legitimacy of ignoring or discriminating against those outside' (Calhoun 2007, 34).

The nation-state, although the dominant form of political organisation in today's world, is by no means the only polity imaginable. Many others have existed throughout history, from the city-state – or *polis* – in Ancient

Greece, through feudal regimes, to vast empires. The conceptual link between nation and state is thus a relatively recent – and ongoing – project. In Europe, hereditary rule, military conquest and notions of divine right gradually gave way to new bases of political legitimacy; one was the people, another was the nation (Calhoun 2007, 2). Some trace the birth of the modern state to the Peace of Westphalia in 1648, marking the end of the Thirty Years War, which had engulfed much of Europe from Sweden to Spain. Westphalian sovereignty only refers to the principle of recognising state borders, however. The practice of legitimating the state through the nation only became widespread in nineteenth-century Europe. Even then, the likes of France aspired to be at once a nation-state and an imperial power (Wilder 2005), and the Ottoman and Austro-Hungarian empires continued to control great swathes of European territory until the end of World War I. In January 1918, months before the armistice, then US president Woodrow Wilson's famous 'fourteen points' address to Congress called for countries like Poland, Romania, Serbia and Montenegro, as well as the peoples of the Ottoman and Hapsburg empires, to be granted independence along 'clearly recognisable' or 'historically established lines of allegiance and nationality' (Wilson 1984 [1918], 537, 538). In contrast to the Peace of Westphalia, Wilson was calling for a post-war settlement constructed around nations, rather than states. This entrenched nationalism as a global organising principle, but remains notoriously difficult to put into practice. Far from the 'friendly counsel' that Wilson (1984 [1918], 538) hoped would determine borders, we need only look at the twenty-first-century European conflicts between Serbia and Kosovo, or Georgia and South Ossetia to understand that nationality is and remains contested, sometimes violently so.

Borders are key to nationalist thinking, because they help to distinguish those who belong to the 'imagined community' (Anderson 1991) from the 'Other'. The way in which this distinction is drawn accounts for much of nationalism's variety. For instance, the border may be territorial; national belonging is thereby imputed to all those born on a particular territory and translated into automatic citizenship according to the legal principle of *ius soli*. On the other hand, it may be ascriptive or subjective. For example, those choosing to naturalise as West German citizens were from 1977 subject to guidelines gauging their 'voluntary and lasting orientation towards Germany [...] to be determined by the applicant's entire attitude towards German culture' (cited in Green 2004, 40). Since individual federal states – and in practice the official dealing with each case – were free to interpret these guidelines, applicants had no certainty of passing the test to that official's satisfaction. Legislation enacted in 2000, by contrast, automatically ascribes German citizenship to all children born in Germany of foreign parents if one of them has been legally resident in the country for at least eight years. However, the same law also provides that the child must choose between German citizenship and any other citizenship they enjoy before their twenty-third birthday, thereby limiting legal belonging to only one nation-state. Discouraging long-term dual citizenship in this way presumably prompts citizens to examine where their loyalties lie. It is nonetheless difficult to draw borders through people's complex sense of identity. Allegiances are hardly ever as 'clearly recognisable' as Woodrow Wilson suggested. Instead, borders are often a source of tension over competing claims to national loyalty. Accordingly, some theorists have suggested that relational or network analyses are more useful ways of conceptualising communities than bounded units (Emirbayer 1997; Ferguson & Gupta 2002). As we saw in the introductory chapter, analyses that privilege transnational flows over 'methodological nationalism' (Beck & Sznaider 2010 [2006]) also question national boundedness.

Citizenship emerges from the above discussion as an important marker of belonging to the state. Indeed, it can be defined as the legal expression of national belonging, which flows from the nation-state nexus. Citizenship thereby 'entails the entitlement to belong to a community' (Wiener 1998, 22), as well as legal rights and obligations. This rather diffuse sense of identity is key in connecting national loyalty to state legitimacy, and underpins the nation-state construct as a whole. As we saw in Chapter 2, approaching nationalism as an ideology leads us to consider national identity as open to manipulation. In the case of nation-building, which seeks to forge and maintain a link between nation and state, the criteria for national belonging will therefore be ideologically laden. Indeed, the term 'nationality' is often used as a synonym of state citizenship, indicating how closely this marker of membership is bound up with the presumption of a common national identity. In fact, nationality more properly refers to members of a nation and not a state (Oommen 1997, 38). For instance, the term is sometimes officially employed to designate ethnic groups associated with a particular sub-state region or nation, such as Spain's *nacionalidades*.

The very nature of citizenship is necessarily discriminatory and exclusionary; it serves to distinguish the rights and duties of insiders from outsiders, and those who are deemed to merit protection from those who are not. Although citizenship usually regulates the relationship between the individual and a state

(Wiener 1998, 22), the 1992 Treaty on European Union (also known as the Treaty of Maastricht) created a European citizenship. Some rights, duties and privileges hitherto associated with state citizenship, such as voting in local elections, are extended to resident citizens of other EU member states as a result. As the cosmopolitan challenge unfurls, this raises the question of whether markers of national belonging could ultimately be excised from citizenship. Instead, could citizenship be considered 'an identity-generating practice with community-building capacity' (Wiener 1998, 28) in its own right? In theory, some forms of multiculturalism and even the notion of constitutional patriotism (Habermas, cited in Jary 1999, 217) can be cast in this light. In practice, however, nation and citizen tend to remain firmly linked through the likes of citizenship tests and citizenship education, which serve to perpetuate national values and markers of belonging.

Yasemin Soysal (1994) argued that a form of post-national membership is undermining the established link between national belonging and citizenship in Europe. She used the term denizens to designate those, such as Germany's so-called 'guest workers', who enjoy state-derived social, economic and welfare rights as long-term foreign residents, and can rely on universal principles of human rights as a regulatory framework beyond the state. However, as Klopp (2002, 17) points out, the fact that rights *enforcement* is still organised at the state level is of more immediate concern to migrants, and the crucial difference between denizens and citizens remains the enjoyment of political rights, with their potential to influence state policies. To this extent, post-national state membership as evoked by Soysal is a relatively toothless status, and naturalisation still provides an attractive alternative. After all, state legislation is likely to have a more immediate effect on individuals than more abstract human rights charters: 'Denizens or postnational members are reliant upon the goodwill of those members who possess full political rights (i.e., citizens). The lack of political rights makes denizens vulnerable to welfare state cutbacks and retrenchment' (Klopp 2002, 17). Contrary to Soysal's view, then, a reappraisal of naturalisation policy might well be preferable to the greater precariousness of post-national membership and the rather uncertain applicability of human rights norms. Even the supposed universality of human rights is open to challenge, as testified by the 'Asian Values' debate, which questions whether UN human rights declarations actually represent values and priorities shared by all societies (Sutherland 2006).

According to the typology famously laid down by the twentieth-century British academic T. H. Marshall (2006 [1950], 30), many European states saw a gradual extension of citizenship rights from the civil to the political and social. By civil rights, Marshall meant freedom of speech and expression, as well as the right to own property and have access to justice on the basis of equality. In turn, he considered the right to vote and stand for election to be a key aspect of political citizenship, while social rights encompassed economic welfare and security. In the European context, Marshall argued that after the establishment of the rule of law and civil rights came a progressive widening of suffrage in the nineteenth century, to be followed by the development of the welfare state after World War II. This experience was not replicated across the globe, however. Instead, many newly independent, postcolonial states found themselves catapulted into the early stages of globalisation and its attendant pressures, without having a securely established sense of national identity or a loyal citizenry. With reference to Malaysia, Indonesia and the Philippines, for instance, Renato Rosaldo (2003, 4) notes that 'these relatively new nations have undergone the daunting process of transforming colonial subjects into citizens of nation-states. They have struggled to define citizenship and elicit nationalist sentiment from their at times resistant, overlooked or indifferent hinterland populations'. This makes the important point that not only migrants, but also indigenous populations can be poorly integrated into citizenship regimes, and all the rights and obligations these entail. A fourth form of citizenship that can be added to Marshall's typology is cultural citizenship. This refers to more diffuse notions of dignity, respect and recognition of all members in the polity. In some cases, those citizens who do not fully belong in a national sense (Rosaldo 2003, 14), such as migrants and ethnic minorities, feel they are denied this cultural citizenship and are treated like 'second class' citizens as a result. One way this could be addressed is by decoupling citizenship and nationality, thereby distinguishing 'belonging to a polity' from 'belonging together' (Schwarzmantel 2003, 91). According to this view, citizens might have nothing more in common than the coincidence of living in the same territory under the same institutions and practices, and enjoying the basic, constitutionally entrenched rights guaranteed by the state. This prompts the question as to why governments should insist that citizenship be subject to additional membership criteria based on nationality.

Bernhard Giesen (2001, 41) suggests that citizenship regimes are derived from three ideal types of collective identity, which he terms primordialism, universalism and traditionalism. Giesen argues that primordialism aims to preserve the purity of the in-group by excluding outsiders, whereas universalism, on the contrary, seeks to extend community values to as many people as possible in a kind of 'civilising mission'. Traditionalism, which echoes the definition of cultural citizenship offered above, rests on familiarity with customs, traditions and practices as a way of distinguishing insiders from outsiders (Giesen 2001, 45). Although these are abstract categories, it is easy to see how they might translate into more or less restrictive citizenship regimes in practice. For instance, the question of primordial roots and the attendant issue of loyalty is raised by the continued rejection of dual citizenship in some countries: 'until most recently many countries felt threatened by citizens with allegiances to multiple countries, and withdrawal of citizenship was commonly adopted around the globe as a weapon against political exiles and even nonpolitical expatriates as a way of undermining the foundation of their national identity' (Shain 2005, xvii). Bilateral agreements disallowing dual nationality in principle have long been used to regulate migrant citizenship across much of Southeast Asia, for instance, including long-term Vietnamese residents in Thailand (Hassall 1999, 63) and China's bilateral agreements with Indonesia, Malaysia and Thailand dating back to 1955 (Li & Wu 1999, 161). Similar to the German case referred to above, a 1992 amendment to Thailand's 1965 Nationality Act also provided for children holding dual nationality to choose between them when they turned 20. In these cases, dual nationality is deemed problematic for a number of reasons. For example, how should the states concerned deal with Malaysian-Thai citizens committing terrorist acts or dealing drugs in one country and seeking refuge across their common border (Hassall 1999, 66)? The underlying presumption that citizens cannot be simultaneously loyal to two states suggests a 'thick' understanding of citizenship as an ethnocultural, 'rooted' and exclusive attachment to a single nation-state. It suggests that divided loyalties somehow undermine the unity and, by extension, the homogeneity of the nation-state, and questions whether citizens' loyalties can be relied upon to defend and if necessary, die for their 'homeland'.

Today's nation-builders are faced with the difficulties of trying to foster loyalty towards the nation-state and thereby influence the 'mental states of potential citizens' (Stoler 1997, 216). For example, criteria like language fluency and the acceptance of community values will play an important role in 'traditionalist' approaches to naturalisation – following Giesen's typology – which may seek to gauge a candidate's cultural integration through language and citizenship tests. According to this scenario, long-standing familiarity and engagement with the host society will put those immigrants at an advantage who are most fluent in the language and conversant with cultural markers of national belonging. In 2008, for instance, Germany's federal minister for integration stated that; 'social integration is not a technical process [...] the migrant's personal attitude is decisive' (Böhmer in Deutsche Bundesregierung 2008, 9, author's translation). However, it is questionable whether taking an oath, a citizenship test, or even the potentially onerous step of renouncing dual nationality, can have any measurable effect on individuals' mentality and loyalty to the nation-state. For some, naturalisation is likely to remain an instrumental, legal procedure rather than signify the adoption of a new national identity. This could be seen as one manifestation of 'flexible citizenship', to use Aihwa Ong's phrase, whereby individuals 'respond fluidly and opportunistically to changing political-economic conditions' (Ong 1999, 6). Thus, flexible citizenship seems to point towards individual pragmatism.

If we understand the concept of national loyalty as a degree of commitment to the existing nation-state (Evans 1998, 59), then this is increasingly unlikely to be either exclusive or unconditional in the context of the cosmopolitan challenge. After all, even 'the most loyalist behaviour retains an enormous dose of reasoned calculation' according to Albert Hirschman's typology of exit, voice and loyalty (Hirschman 1970, 78). It may seem inappropriate to apply ideas derived from rational choice to a sense of national belonging, but this is certainly justified in the case of time-consuming and often expensive naturalisation procedures, where prospective applicants are likely to weigh up whether it is worth their while. In sum, states continue to imbue citizenship with deeper meaning, in order to promote wider national legitimacy, loyalty and community stability, but aspiring citizens themselves do not necessarily share this rationale. There are also problems inherent in using citizenship to achieve these aims. Germany's integration minister herself identified the underlying difficulty with naturalisation: it attempts to apply criteria of belonging to a subjective attitude, a mindset that cannot be reliably modified through language lessons, citizenship tests or oaths of loyalty.

Given the limits to linking nation and citizen noted above, this brings us back to whether it is possible to decouple citizenship from nationalist notions of belonging altogether. Dora Kostakopoulou has studied this question by looking at what she calls rooted, republican and constitutional forms of patriotism in turn, but concludes that each 'fails to dislodge citizenship from the confines of the national' (Kostakopoulou 2006, 83). She argues that civic patriotism is something of a blind alley that cannot ultimately be distinguished from nation-building. In turn, this continues to influence citizenship legislation by giving it a nationalist component, so that citizenship itself is not purely civic, but is part of states' attempts to shape the national identity of aspiring citizens. In other words, the legal definition of citizenship in terms of rights and duties assumes that all citizens are equal before the law and that naturalisation is the main means of acquiring citizenship other than by birth, but this description does not do justice to the nationalist content of many naturalisation procedures (Etzioni 2007, 355). The extent to which citizenship criteria can be considered a politicised measure of national belonging will vary depending on whether they look to a candidate's ancestry (as in the case of ethnic German *Aussiedler* coming from the former Soviet bloc), upbringing, language skills and so forth. Linked to this, it is important to note that views differ on whether naturalisation should be a means of encouraging national integration or whether it should be seen as a reward for successfully completed integration. This in itself is an indicator of how 'thick' a form of citizenship is required in each case, with the requirements for 'citizenship as reward' likely to be more demanding than those for 'citizenship as encouragement'. Therefore, citizenship requirements themselves speak volumes about how nation-building ideology defines national identity.

The field of intercultural communication helps illustrate how citizenship legislation 'speaks for the nation'. For example, one way of categorising contact between migrants and their host society distinguishes the four ideal-types of separation, marginalisation, assimilation and integration (Neuliep 2003, 345). Separation denotes a strong continuing identification with the individual's native culture and a resistance to the host culture. So-called 'ghettoisation' is a good example of this. Marginalisation, in turn, entails alienation from both the native culture and the host culture, often as a result of not being accepted by the host culture. This can lead to profound disorientation. A more constructive variant of this phenomenon is the creation of a third, alternative microculture independent of native origins and host culture, such as investing in a new religious identity or integrating into the gay community (Neuliep 2003, 346). The third and fourth categories are assimilation and integration. According to this typology, which clearly essentialises the 'home' and 'host' cultures in a way that resonates with some actual state integration policies, assimilation involves abandoning one's native culture in favour of the host culture. Like separation, it is a monoculturalist solution (whereas marginalisation implies a loss of all cultural ties). Integration is the only bicultural alternative. Here the individual maintains his or her native culture while engaging with the host culture in order to achieve a synthesis. The host culture does not remain unaffected, as in the case of assimilation. Instead, it is influenced and modified by new arrivals. The US-style 'melting pot' is not a suitable metaphor for this understanding of integration, because it implies that the original cultures are ingredients in a newly created national identity that takes the place of its constituent parts. Rather, this integration is more like a piece of Venetian paper, where each culture is one colourful swirl among many that meet and intermingle, but never merge into a single blot. As such, it might be more usefully compared to some definitions of multiculturalism (Modood 2007; Parekh 2002). Assimilation and integration are prevalent terms in the discourse surrounding immigration and citizenship, and are open to a variety of interpretations. In general, however, it can be said that assimilation tends to have negative connotations, whereas integration is more widely construed to represent a desirable outcome.

Integration is a concept laden with expectations, which generally go beyond the bundle of legal rights and duties linked to citizenship. One of its aims is to encourage migrants to get involved in the community and political life of where they live. This is commonly known as civic engagement, although many of the activities it tends to encompass are not directly linked to citizenship. Pattie, Seyd and Whitely (2003, 447) list 18 forms of action used as indicators of civic engagement, ranging from donating money to an organisation and boycotting a product, through to attending a political meeting and participating in an illegal protest. None of these activities is conditional upon state citizenship; even the right to vote in local elections may flow directly from European citizenship. Citizens are not the only ones capable of wearing a campaign badge or signing a petition, suggesting that this form of integration need not actually be predicated on any kind of national belonging or naturalisation. Nevertheless, citizenship tests tend to conflate naturalisation with active citizenship, in that some of the content revolves around expressions of community solidarity and, by extension, a commitment to the nation-state as the 'imagined community' writ large. Again, this fleshes out the bare bones of citizenship as a legal construct with markers of national loyalty and belonging, of which language acquisition is a further example.

In the political discourse surrounding immigration and naturalisation, the assumption seems to be that a 'worthy' applicant will not only have mastered the language of the host country as an achievement in itself, but also thereby demonstrated integration into the host society and acceptance of its values. For instance, UK Home Office guidelines aimed at prospective citizens state that their level of English 'must be sufficient for [them] to fulfill [their] duties as a citizen, and to mix easily with the people with whom [they] live and work' (cited in Piller 2001, 268). This combines an indicator of civic activism in the first clause, with a measure of cultural citizenship in the second. To this extent, it is an example of a 'traditionalist' approach to citizenship according to Giesen's typology (2001), which emphasises cultural belonging and familiarity. Marinetto (2003, 103) points out that increasing government emphasis on active citizen participation in the UK is a relatively recent phenomenon, and that the traditional '*modus operandi* of modern liberal democracies has been a representative mode of government in which the wider citizenry has a passive role'. He links the current trend to an ideological concern with promoting a sense of community among left-leaning politicians on the one hand, and with the need to balance rights and duties on the other, more right-wing end of the political spectrum (Marinetto 2003, 117). UK Prime Minister David Cameron's promotion of voluntary work and community groups through the 'Big Society' initiative since 2010 is a good example of this trend.

German citizenship law was once considered a paradigmatic application of *ius sanguinis*, or the 'primordialist' principle of descent according to Giesen's threefold categorisation (2001). This changed somewhat with the legislative reform of 2000, only for 'traditionalist' elements to be incorporated into the naturalisation process. The limit on dual citizenship in that law, and the citizenship tests subsequently introduced, have entrenched a form of citizenship that precludes multiculturalism, understood here as 'the recognition of group difference within the public sphere of laws, policies, democratic discourses and the terms of a shared citizenship and national identity' (Modood 2007, 2). In a political parallel to this, German Chancellor Angela Merkel declared multiculturalism to have 'utterly failed' in 2010 (*Guardian* 2010b, no page). Instead, Germany's citizenship regime helps to promote the ideal of a 'dominant *ethnie*' (Smith 1995, 106) or national *Leitkultur*, defined as a guiding German culture that immigrants should both accept and adopt (Green 2004, 119). The requirement that candidates for naturalisation attend classes in German language and culture underlines this (Etzioni 2007, 356). As the previously cited UK Home Office guidelines suggest, language competence appears to be a convenient, apparently objective tool for testing potential civic activism as well as more 'traditionalist' notions of belonging to a national community of values and culture. Even in some officially multiculturalist countries, like Australia (but not Sweden), language tests are explicitly intended to gauge the applicant's ability to fulfil citizenship duties. Both Australia and the US design their language tests around documents and questions relating to the rights and duties of citizenship, although the expected linguistic competence differs (Piller 2001, 266). In the cases of French and German naturalisation, implementing the Interior Ministry's stated aim of testing the candidate's ability to hold a conversation, read and summarise an 'everyday' conversation remains very much an inexact science (Wright 2008, 4), suggesting that language-based tests are open to rather arbitrary interpretations and, ultimately, abuse.

In a discussion of the German naturalisation process, Ingrid Piller (2001, 271) documented cases where an applicant was allowed to copy out their CV as a test of language ability, or a candidate was simply asked if they had understood a text, without this being tested in any way. Practices also vary widely across German federal states, as naturalisation procedures are a decentralised competence. Neither did naturalisation officials appear to have special training in evaluating language proficiency (evident from the copying exercise). As a result, language testing was neither systematic nor uniform. The German Interior Ministry's criteria also seemed to emphasise the applicant's ability to understand (passively), thus privileging a 'traditionalist' view of naturalisation in which the applicant was expected to assimilate both literally (the text) and figuratively (Germanness), rather than play an active role in an intercultural conversation. On these terms, immigrants and candidates for naturalisation alike find the onus to integrate completely on them. As such, the ostensible goal of integration is definitely a misnomer in this case, if we understand it as the two-way process between state and prospective citizen defined above. 'Native speakers', with all the connotations of birth and descent this phrase entails, are therefore at a distinct advantage in expressing the cultural and ethnic elements of belonging to the nation-state: 'The meaning of the mother tongue is not just language. Language is the vehicle by which one knows one's roots, one's culture' (PuruShotam 1998, 89). This leads us to look at transnationalism and the way in which it disrupts assumptions of a 'native' national identity on which language tests and citizenship regimes are based.

Transnationalism

Together with diaspora, migration is a form of transnationalism, which in turn forms a significant element of the cosmopolitan challenge. Although migration is by no means a new phenomenon (Castles & Miller 2003, 50), its implications for national solidarity and state citizenship have become more prevalent in recent decades. As we have seen, there has been much debate as to how newcomers should be expected to participate in the host society. International religious and ethnic affiliations, as well as transregional trading relationships, existed well before nation-states came to dominate world affairs (Kennedy & Roudometov 2003, 3). Though individuals have always had multiple identities, these have nevertheless become more visible in today's 'technoscape' (Appadurai 1990, 297) of sophisticated telecommunications, transport and trade (Kennedy & Roudometov 2003, 10). The concept of transnationalism 'broadly refers to multiple ties and interactions linking people or institutions across the borders of nation-states' (Sørensen & Olwig 2002, ii). Although transnationalism's focus and scope remain disputed, it can be distinguished from the international activities of states and the multinational transactions of very large corporations and even religions (Vertovec 2009, 29). Instead, the study of transnationalism is principally concerned with exchanges between networks of non-governmental organisations, smaller-scale enterprises and peoples, the last of which is most relevant to nationalism and the present discussion. Transnationalism can be distinguished from globalisation – considered in Chapter 6 – in that it focuses on the way in which specific culturally and politically embedded identities evolve in their interaction with others (Ong 1999, 4). Scholars tend to agree that migration is an important aspect of transnationalism, but variously define it to cover everything from long-established diasporas to online communities. However, the relationship of exchange that is embodied in the migrant or member of a diaspora is the key element here. Transnationalism represents a challenge to the nation-state because it undermines the three-way link between identity, ethnicity and territory on which national legitimacy is based. Indeed, if residence is no longer a good measure of where people's loyalties lie, then nation-building becomes all the more difficult. Similarly, temporary, shifting allegiances are difficult to square with nation-states, which demand the ultimate sacrifice from their soldiers in wartime. Hence some nation-states' increased engagement with their diaspora as a response to the perceived fragmentation and delegitimation resulting from the cosmopolitan challenge.

Diaspora, meaning literally 'to scatter over', refers to people who live outside their homeland but retain a strong attachment to it (Cohen 1997, ix). The collective memory they perpetuate may refer to a past, idealised or even imagined home. It is this link to the homeland, together with a relatively established and cohesive community abroad, that distinguishes members of a diaspora from individual migrants. Further features of diasporas have been proposed, such as the will to return and 'traumatic dispersal', but few concrete cases will display all of these characteristics (Cohen 1997, 180). Members of a diaspora, in turn, may include refugees, traders, professionals and labourers, as well as movements resulting from colonialism. For instance, all of these types can be found within the Vietnamese diaspora which has settled across the world, but especially in the US, France, Australia and, to a lesser extent, Germany and the UK. It is important to distinguish between a migrant, who may not be at all oriented towards their country of origin, and members of a diaspora, who by definition retain some sort of emotional, economic, cultural or political attachment to their perceived homeland. Furthermore, those who self-identify as members of a diaspora may not be first-generation migrants, but their descendents. Diasporas can be considered the transnational community *par excellence* because advances in technology, particularly the advent of cheap telephone calls and the internet, have made it possible to maintain close and sustained relationships with their country of origin. This is qualitatively different to the more sporadic contact previous generations had with their homeland. Like never before, transnational communities are shaping and being shaped by the information society.

In practice, members of a diaspora may support the home country wholeheartedly or fight against the incumbent regime, as in the case of political exiles (Shain 2005). It is therefore important to stress that transnational communities are by no means monolithic and united. Neither do their members make clear and irreversible choices in their allegiance to a host or home state. There are just as many possible ways of being part of a diaspora as there are members, and the diaspora's relationship to nationalist ideologies is as complex. As suggested in the previous section, labels like assimilation, integration and even ghettoisation often say more about the host country's approach to nation-building than individuals' lived experience as migrants or members of a diaspora. States use naturalisation to define boundaries to belonging, and thereby the degree of openness or exclusivity of their own national construct. Standards of language competence and other naturalisation requirements reflect a certain national ideal to which candidates are expected to conform, but are often a poor measure of the everyday cultural competence gained by living a transnational life. This has been described as a kind of practical cosmopolitanism, or an acquired skill at negotiating different cultural systems and switching more or less expertly between them (Vertovec 2009, 71). Conversely, the challenge for contemporary nation-builders and sub-state nationalists also lies in how to include their own overseas diaspora through measures such as (quasi-) citizenship or incentives to encourage investment, remittances and even tourism, like Scotland's 2009 'homecoming year' spearheaded by the Scottish National Party in government.

Transnationalism raises 'issues concerning civic order and the cohesiveness of 'host' societies' (Vertovec 2009, 88). Nation-states have to consider not only how this aspect of the cosmopolitan challenge affects their territorial frontiers, but also how these very frontiers are being increasingly shot through not only by migrants, but also by technological and financial flows, media communications, criminal networks and environmental pressures (Appadurai 1990). Nation-states respond in different ways to these different phenomena, for example by remaining open to economic and financial flows while trying to limit and regulate population movements. These encompass both established migrant and diaspora communities, as well as more recently emerging labour mobility spurred in part by the globalising economy. Although nation-building may be undermined by the competing, international 'ethnoscapes' (Appadurai 1990, 297) embodied in these, states can also help to shape transnational movements in the guise of their 'homeland'. For example, members of a diaspora often foster links with this homeland as well as among themselves to form a deterritorialised 'nation of socially interdependent, but spatially dispersed communities' (Cohen, cited in Reid 1997).

The mobility inherent in transnationalism applies both to migratory flows themselves and to the interconnected communities they engender (Sørensen & Olwig 2002, 2). Such communities may be virtual, hybrid, fleeting or even cyclical, as migrants (periodically) return home, bringing new knowledge, experiences and financial remittances. These transnational connections should not be seen as bridges between bounded, essentialised nations, but rather 'from the point of view of mobile livelihoods that both define and cut across a range of social, economic and cultural boundaries (Sørensen & Olwig 2002, 4). Neither need migration necessarily be international. There may be cases of internal displacement within a state, which have an impact on its nation-building capacity. For instance, flows across divided nations like Korea and, previously, Germany and Vietnam have significantly affected the nationalist ideologies propounded by rival governments there (Sutherland 2010). Migrants and diasporas do not flit between predetermined social and cultural wholes, then, but rather create new transnational spaces around them. According to this understanding, newcomers to a country should not be considered as foreigners 'diluting' an established national culture or its traditions, but rather as yet another set of contributors to a constantly evolving nation-building project that has always incorporated diversity and change. This reciprocal relationship is summed up in the conception of integration as a two-way process, and not a one-way street.

In a world of nation-states, transnational communities are problematic because they do not fit into the equation of identity with territory, which underpins that world order. The idea that belonging entails a sense of 'rootedness' in a particular place is deeply engrained in our thinking about nations and nationalism (Stoler 1997, 224). In turn, the notion of 'citizenship as boundary' (Hassall 1999, 49) translates the nation-state-territory nexus into legal language. Citizenship is one means of managing the ebb and flow of populations, but it means more than gaining a passport and escaping the legal void of statelessness. It comes with the political accretions of European history, variously representing voluntary participation in the civic ideal of the French revolution, marking the covenant between ruler and ruled that underpinned the social contract, and forming the basis of the democratic system of popular sovereignty. This slow and syncretic evolution of nation, democracy and citizenship is missing in the postcolonial Southeast Asian context, among others. Yet citizenship has an important political dimension there, too, as an arena in which to demand and define people's rights and duties vis-à-vis the state. It also designates who is eligible to claim those rights. Indeed, 'why would we need to think of ourselves as citizens if there were no Others who are not?' (Weekley, 1999, 6).

The primordialist, universalist and traditionalist types of citizenship discussed above (Giesen 2001) reflect different nation-building strategies, ranging from assimilation into the culture of the 'dominant *ethnie*' (Smith 1995, 106), to integration according to the multiculturalist model, whereby the nation-state's cultural diversity is 'central to its self-understanding' (Parekh 2002, 6). Southeast Asian countries exemplify this range, from Thailand's dominant *ethnie* approach, which is shared by Vietnam, to the multicultural models of Malaysia and Singapore. What nonetheless unites these cases is a postcolonial mindset (Siam/Thailand having experienced extensive British influence though not outright colonisation) that is reluctant to countenance the dilution of national identity or sovereignty through regional integration or deep transnational cooperation. Ironically, their rigid approach to borders and territory, which finds its expression in the inter-governmentalist Association of Southeast Nations (ASEAN), is one legacy of the colonial era. At the same time, however, these nation-states are alive to the cosmopolitan challenge and respond to it in their nation-building.

Flexible Citizenship

Thongchai Winichakul coined the concept of the 'geo-body' to show how the kingdom of Siam was constructed from the mid-nineteenth century onwards to conform to the Westphalian principle 'that a nation exists in the global community of nations' (Thongchai 1994, 1). The essentialising aspects of this view, whereby nation-states interlock along hard edges rather like a jigsaw puzzle, are clear. Territorial boundaries entrench the distinction between 'us' and 'them' – those included and those excluded – that is at the core of both citizenship and nation-building. In colonial Southeast Asia, not only the nation as an abstract 'geo-body', but also human bodies were expected to fall into neat categories, usually imposed from above. Benedict Anderson (1991, 164) discusses the use of the census in British Malaya as a means to this end. In turn, Ann Stoler (1997) explores how those who transgressed ethnic or racial identifiers, namely mixed-race or Eurasian children, were classified in French Indochina and the Netherlands Indies. Their status is important because it highlights the strong link between definitions of national belonging and citizenship as the legal expression of that belonging.

The Westphalian nation-state is impatient with heterogeneity and 'frayed frontiers'. After all, even multiculturalist frameworks are inscribed within the power container of the sovereign nation-state (Billig 1995, 148). So it was too with colonial empires, where the *métis* literally embodied the liminal zone between insider and outsider, national and foreigner, and thus diluted the principle of *jus sanguinis*. Colonial authorities often looked to the child's upbringing and education in order to determine whether he or she *deserved* the rights and privileges of, say, French citizenship. A key question here was whether it was possible to grow up imbued with European culture, traditions and – importantly – morality, in the allegedly energy-sapping environment of the tropics, which colonialists widely believed to encourage moral and physical degeneracy. For instance, citizenship derived from a French father was not always enough to ensure legal protection if the child was not brought up in the French language and according to the French way of life. This was explicitly contrasted to what was deemed the corrupting influence of Asian mothers (Stoler 1997, 203). In Dutch law, a specific legal category covering Eurasians was rejected on the grounds that it might foster a potentially dangerous, subversive and destabilising group of *déracinés*, without firm roots in either the colonising or colonised country (Stoler 1997, 205). In sum, Eurasian children had to prove more than legal filiation, and demonstrate a European orientation and value-system, in order to be judged worthy of Dutch or French citizenship. This speaks volumes about the symbolism of citizenship for colonial understandings of national identity, the 'purity' of which was not to be 'diluted' by its automatic extension to culturally 'other' children (Stoler 1997, 216).

Today, nation-states still use citizenship as measures of national identity in order to regulate membership of their polities. Although the concerns of nineteenth-century imperialists with racial purity, superiority and morality should have dissipated by now, many of the markers of belonging underlying these imperialist debates can still be found in contemporary citizenship discourse. Significantly, an influential Dutch colonial legislator understood the nation to mean shared 'morals, culture, and perceptions, feelings that unite us without one being able to say what they are' (Nederburgh, cited in Stoler 1997, 215). Arguably, current citizenship regimes, which encourage common cultural and linguistic skills, attempt to foster this same, subjective state of mind. For instance, the tests governing access to citizenship in the likes of Germany, the Netherlands and the UK amount to a form of civic education, designed to instill national values into aspiring citizens. The preservation of stability, to which Eurasian children posed a danger in the colonialists' view, continues to be a key justification for immigrant integration and naturalisation. Today, stability refers explicitly to social cohesion and implicitly to national identity, the suggestion being that it could be knocked off course or 'denatured' by too many foreign elements. The case of the Chinese diaspora in Southeast Asia provides an illustration of this point.

Although Chinese communities have settled all over Southeast Asia since the sixteenth century (Reid 1997, 41) they remain at the mercy of latent racism there (Kahn 1998, 6). For instance, the Chinese minority was long constructed as an alien 'Other' to a Thai nation, which in the early twentieth century came to be defined according to the ethnic Thai majority (Kasian 1997, 76). Here, we encounter the issue of multiple citizenship once again, but this time as a tool for individuals to manage the cosmopolitan challenge, rather than as a headache for states worried about their loyalty. Aihwa Ong (1999) shows how the presumption against dual citizenship upheld in Germany, Southeast Asia and elsewhere is being undermined by those who collect passports as a form of 'insurance' against the vagaries of politics. She points to ethnic Chinese business elites from Hong Kong, Indonesia, Thailand and elsewhere, who may do business all over the world, but guard against a possible backlash or discriminatory policies by settling families in 'safe havens' so as to earn residency rights (Ong 1999, 20, 135). Ong suggests that the 'multiple passport holder is an apt contemporary figure; he or she embodies the split between state-imposed identity and personal identity caused by political upheavals, migration, and changing global markets' (Ong 1999, 2). This separation of ethnic and national identity, in turn, provides a new conundrum for the People's Republic of China, which wants to tap into the expertise and investments of its diaspora, but also questions the political loyalty and patriotic motivation of its overseas community!

According to Ong's notion of 'flexible citizenship', some individuals view passports instrumentally as evidence of status and security rather than as symbols of national loyalty and belonging (Ong 1999, 6). Ong also extends this flexibility to states, pointing out that the US practice of giving green cards to large investors is one way of attracting global capital in return for a path to citizenship (Ong 1999, 130). In countries like Cambodia, citizenship has been traded as a commodity, which potential investors can purchase to facilitate their business dealings. Here, the equation of citizens with nationals *qua* members of a national community completely breaks down and the possibility of a hierarchy within citizenship emerges, whereby naturalised citizens are excluded from election or public office for fear that they will try to exert influence in their own and not the national interest (Hassall 1999, 60–1). Nation and state are thus decoupled, but in a potentially detrimental way. The meaning of Cambodian citizenship has also been a source of tension between returning exiles – many of whom have dual nationality – and those who stayed behind during the Khmer Rouge's murderous regime and the subsequent political turmoil. In this debate, citizenship is used as a cipher for the delicate relationship between material interests and overriding allegiances, with many returnees arguing that 'the number of passports cannot measure loyalty' (Poethig 2006, 84). Again, it is clear that the significance of citizenship runs far deeper than simple legal status.

Despite citizenship's strong theoretical associations with equality, it is clear that states do not always guarantee this in practice. In order to map the different application of rights and obligations across Southeast Asia, Ong uses the concept of 'graduated sovereignty', which she sees as affording different levels of protection and privilege to citizens according to the role they play in the global economy. For instance, some designated manufacturing zones (which often straddle borders) have seen a retreat in state provision of worker welfare protection, in order to facilitate the exploitation of cheap labour (Ong 1999, 222). At the other extreme, states court an international entrepreneurial and educated elite through special incentives, facilities and privileges (Ong 1999, 219). As the Cambodian case shows, these can even extend to citizenship following the same basic principle, which affords only selected, skilled workers access to labour markets in a points-based migration system. Ong's analysis has the benefit of transcending borders and exploding the myth of the state as monolith. It shows that state governments can be selective in respecting citizens' supposedly equal rights and obligations. At the same time, individuals may choose 'flexible citizenship' in order to escape or mitigate the possible effects of state regulation. Not only do citizens' rights vary across states, then, but they also vary within those states according to a hierarchy that is as often ethnic, cultural or even financial. Malaysia's *Bumiputra* policy favouring the economic advancement of ethnic Malays is a case in point.

Migration, diaspora and transnationalism lead to a multiplication in 'irregular' identity and citizenship configurations, which burst the boundaries of nation-states. This is a key effect of the cosmopolitan challenge. In turn, the 'migrant has always been the "Other" of the nation … [b]ut if the Other is part of society (for example, as a worker, parent or taxpayer), how can national distinctiveness be maintained?' (Castles 1999, 28). This is the dilemma facing contemporary nation-states. Multiple citizenship, denizenship, residence permits and changes of domicile are among the legal tools that have been developed to cover cases where residence, nationality and citizenship are not congruent. Most, like domicile, still set out from the default principle that citizenship and long-term residence should correspond to national loyalty. Citizenship tests also follow this logic, thereby displaying the contradiction inherent in linking the potentially universal reach of citizenship to national belonging: 'The principle of citizenship for all members of society demands the inclusion of new ethnic minorities into the political community; the principle of national belonging demands their exclusion' (Castles 1999, 32).

Citizenship's role as guarantor of civic and human rights contains another potential contradiction with nation-building goals if, say, freedom of speech is deemed to endanger national unity. There can be a strong imbalance between the duties a state expects from its citizens and the rights it offers in return. The distinction between active and passive citizenship has great poignancy here; citizens cannot be active participants in political life without access to education and a minimum of economic and social security. Thus, if the state demands a 'thicker' form of civic engagement, the onus on the state to enable this also increases. This part of the equation is often overlooked, however. Southeast Asian states, in particular, tend to value citizenship less as a guarantor of rights and more as a nation-building tool (Rodan & Jayasuriya 2007, 810). For postcolonial countries, the nation-building process had hardly been set in train when the first signs of globalisation began to make themselves felt. Always an unattainable ideal, the nation-building myth of national unity was therefore being undermined before it became firmly established. Even Malaysia's former prime minister Mahathir reportedly did not expect a unifying Malaysian (as opposed to ethnic Malay) nationalism to be firmly entrenched before 2020 (Reid 1997, 38). As such, nation-building in some Southeast Asian states, such as Malaysia, Singapore and Thailand, can appear particularly malleable (Kasian 1997, 88) in response to the cosmopolitan challenge, while remaining remarkably ethnocentric or 'traditionalist' in other aspects of their discourse (Sutherland 2009). Furthermore, according to one commentator, Malaysian 'citizenship is being carefully and slowly separated from nationalism because this is required by the new economic order' (Weekley 1999, 12). Investment-friendly policies and 'high-tech' cities like the evocatively named Cyberjaya promote Malaysia's image as a 'globalized nation' (King 2008, 238), highlighting the interplay between nationalism and globalisation, which is the subject of the next chapter.

Conclusion

Nationalism theory teaches that the nation is often defined in opposition to the 'Other'. Most often associated with the 'imagined community' (Anderson 1991) of the nation, this chapter has shown that markers of belonging are now increasingly linked with debates surrounding citizenship and integration. The fluctuating borderline between the 'in' group and the 'out' group, as embodied in citizenship legislation and naturalisation in particular, is thus a key marker of how the concept of the nation is decontested. Citizenship regimes are thus an important corollary of migration in that they represent the primary means of official, legal integration into a nation-state. Naturalisation procedures constitute the borders of belonging and are a privileged point of access to contemporary nation-building. This chapter has argued that citizenship today is still imbued with nationalist ideology. However, Yasemin Soysal (1994) has pointed out that citizenship can go beyond the nation-state as a legitimating basis, to be replaced with universal human rights principles. A form of citizenship freed from national ties of ethnicity, culture or descent is also thinkable, in which residence is the ticket to political participation (Kostakopoulou 2008). According to this reading, citizenship would simply be an administrative tool to organise the polity, requiring no proof of national loyalty or identity (Davidson 1999, 235). It would not be for sale as a commodity or a reward for financial investment. These models underestimate the central importance of citizenship in regulating national membership, however, and its links to both national self-understanding and state legitimation. As we have seen, the links between nation and citizen are complex and evolving, and should be the subject of further research (Sutherland 2011). Decoupled from the nation, citizenship offers only a truncated form of political integration, and undermines the goal of nation-building to ensure state legitimation. One partial departure from the citizenship and nation-state nexus is EU citizenship, which provides for individuals to enjoy some, but not all citizenship rights when residing in another member state. However, these additional rights still flow indirectly from member state citizenship, suggesting that the principle of belonging to a nation-state is paramount even in this case. Imagining states without nations would be a revolutionary development in global politics, but the very tenacity of nationalist ideology strongly suggests that this is an unlikely response to the cosmopolitan challenge for the foreseeable future.

The current state system of policed borders has long sent a message of control to the individual citizen: 'You are mine, the state authority seemed to warn, but I benevolently allow you to travel' (Archibugi 2003, 3). Accordingly, in the age of transnationalism, labour and population mobility have not risen in line with capital mobility (Brennan 2003, 46). On the contrary, quotas and caps on immigration are important means states use to regulate this aspect of the cosmopolitan challenge. At the same time, political principles of equal citizenship and representation are confronted with the profound inequalities that characterise contemporary trade, employment, industrial relations, mobility, prosperity and access to healthcare and education across the globe; 'Any prospect of bringing humanity towards genuine unity on a global scale would have to confront the social and economic relations of actually existing capitalism' (Gowan 2003, 64). Add the need for popular legitimation to that mix, and it seems that there is unlikely to be an alternative to nation-building and the nation-state system any time soon.

6

What Now for the Nation? Responding to Globalisation and Regionalisation

Does globalisation represent a challenge to nationalism? Can nationalism and regionalism be reconciled?

Previous chapters have shown how the ideological division that characterised the Cold War has been superseded by new challenges to the enduring ideology of nationalism. This chapter asks how contemporary nationalism responds to globalisation and regionalisation as two further aspects of the cosmopolitan challenge. Like their nineteenth-century counterparts, both nation-states and sub-state nationalism continue to evolve in a political environment where statehood and sovereignty play a central role. Unlike them, they have to contend with the discourse of globalisation and supra-national integration. Global networks have been in place for centuries. Goods, capital, labour, religions and cultural influences have long radiated across the world but, as evidenced by the current intensity and speed of communication, the density, complexity and diversity of these flows are now unprecedented (Bebbington & Kothari 2006, 850). As two key aspects of the cosmopolitan challenge, globalisation and regionalism require a response from nation-builders and nationalists in today's political climate, since nation-states are being transformed by processes far beyond their borders as currently constructed. Beyond the core principle of prioritising the nation (Freeden 1998), nationalism is clearly a highly context-dependent ideology, and its manifestations vary enormously according to time, place and circumstance. Yet nationalism shows no sign of waning in the face of globalisation, as it continues to legitimate states and fuel independence movements. Consequently, this chapter explores the tension inherent in reconciling nationalism, regionalisation and globalisation. Its first section discusses region-building with reference to Southeast Asia, drawing a clear parallel with nation-building, before focusing on regionalism and globalisation in its second and third sections, respectively. At this point it is necessary to define some of the terms used.

In the same way as globalism can be defined as an ideology that 'makes normative claims about a set of social processes called "globalization"' (Hay & Rosamond 2002; Steger 2005, 6), so regionalism is understood here to operate at the analytical level of state ideology rather than the macro-level of regionalisation. Regionalism is therefore a political project, designed 'to accelerate, to modify or occasionally to reverse the direction of social change which processes like globalization and regionalization represent' (Gamble 2007, 27; see also Beeson 2007, 5; Palmujoki 2001, 6). Consequently, regionalism might present regionalisation as either 'rescuing' (Milward 1994) or undermining the nation-state. In sum, regionalism constitutes either a positive or a negative response to 'regional awareness and identity' and 'state-promoted regional integration' (Hurrell 1995, 41–3). Both governments supportive of European integration and so-called 'Eurosceptic' states thus represent forms of regionalism. With regard to nation-building, the question as to whether actual transfers of sovereignty take place is less important than the symbolic roles played by the likes of the EU and ASEAN. Regional organisations can conceivably be incorporated into the 'invention of tradition' (Hobsbawm & Ranger 1983) so central to nation-building. For example, constructs such as 'the ASEAN way' and assertions of regional identity can serve to underpin states' external sovereignty and, by extension, their domestic legitimacy (Sutherland 2006). This analysis suggests that if regionalism is as flexible as nationalism, then it is quite possible to reconcile this aspect of the cosmopolitan challenge with nation-building. The following section will show that regions are constructed in much the same way as nations and therefore subject to a wide variety of interpretations and uses.

Region-Building

The term Southeast Asia is a relatively recent label applied by outside forces to different parts of the land mass located between India and China. It has since been adopted by nation-states within the region to denote and organise their relations and activities, through the Association of Southeast Asian Nations (ASEAN), among other initiatives. This section traces how the idea of Southeast Asia as a region has developed and highlights its evolving historical and ideological usage in order to draw parallels with nation-building. A closer look at Southeast Asia as a concept will show that the region, like the nation, is malleable and contested. Consequently, region-alism can be interpreted either to complement or contradict nationalism as political ideology and expediency demand. It has been pointed out with reference to the European Union that studying something goes some way towards creating and maintaining it (Walters & Haahr 2005, 2). So too does the academic study of Southeast Asia go hand in hand with its politi-cal usefulness to ideologues and policy-makers. Like nations, regions are not natural but constructed, suggesting that they can be defined to chime with nationalist ideology and nation-building in particular. Vietnam, for instance, has invested in region-building through its membership of ASEAN since 1995, principally as a means of bolstering its own national legitimacy and international visibility (Sutherland 2009). The following discussion therefore examines different interpretations of Southeast Asia as both a subject of study and a political instrument.

Sandwiched between India and China, the Southeast Asian region has gained in strategic significance since the end of the Cold War, principally through ASEAN and linked ventures such as ASEAN+3 and the ASEAN Regional Forum. These regional initiatives are regarded as important vehicles for representing member states' interests on the world stage (Sutherland 2009). Together, their voices are less likely to be drowned out than alone. As such, ASEAN represents its ten members' aspiration to be greater than the sum of its parts. The organisation's very existence is also an important spur to a sense of regional identity, at least among its political and business elite, with the so-called 'ASEAN Way' going some way towards socialising participants into a pattern of shared behaviour. This process, more than any putative shared history or cultural identity, serves to make Southeast Asia meaningful as a political region today (Beeson 2007, 10–12). However, shared understandings among the region's elite must be distinguished from the perceptions of its population, which are more difficult to gauge but likely to be less strong. Any common characteristics must also be strongly qualified by major differences among member states' political regimes and outlooks, ranging from a military junta in Myanmar/Burma and an absolute monarchy in Brunei, through the communist systems of Vietnam and Laos, to the flawed democracies of Thailand, Indonesia, the Philippines, Malaysia, Singapore and Cambodia (Alden 2010, 1). As periodic border clashes between ASEAN members Cambodia and Thailand testify, Southeast Asia continues to be marked by conflicts to rival its commonalities.

Up to and including colonial times, a region very roughly corresponding to today's Southeast Asia was known under a variety of names by its larger neighbours, though each understood its contours differently (Reid 2004, 11). For instance, the Chinese name for the region located to its south included the Malay archipelago but not today's Burma or Laos (Anderson 1998, 3). From the tenth to fourteenth centuries, the empires of Pagan, Angkor, Dai Viet, Champa and many small-scale Tai polities controlled much of the mainland that stretches between the Irrawaddy basin and the South China Sea (Lieberman 2003, 24). Although the region may have seemed 'more coherent to outsiders' (Reid 2004, 11), period sources show that many of these rulers kept abreast of events on the fringes of their kingdoms and beyond, and so had a sense of the geographical space stretching from India as far as China, Korea and Japan (Wolters 1999, 28). However, Benedict Anderson highlights the lack of a hegemonic religion or imperial power across the region to compare with the Ottoman or Mughal realms. This fragmentation was compounded by six different countries' colonisation across several centuries (Anderson 1998, 4). Nevertheless, some historians have attempted to find economic and political patterns across pre-colonial Southeast Asia.

The historian O. W. Wolters used the Sanskrit term *mandala* to denote a 'circle of kings' (Wolters 1999, 27). According to this notion, the king at the centre of the *mandala* presided over lesser rulers, who were expected to pay tribute as vassals and provide military assistance in return for protection. Power was personalised and overlapped with that of other kings, each of whom claimed universal, divinely ordained sovereignty. In Angkor and Java, the *mandala* 'represented a particular and often unstable political situation in a vaguely definable geographical area without fixed boundaries and where smaller centers tended to look in all directions for security' (Wolters 1999, 28). The contrast with a bounded nation-state system is clear. Travelling officials functioned as symbols of the king's power by touring the kingdom bestowing patronage, collecting taxes and dispensing justice. This so-called 'solar system', whereby lesser planets felt the gravitational pull of the 'sun king' (Lieberman 2003, 33), shows that the cultural, territorial and political borders of Southeast Asia were once fluid and unfixed. Furthermore, its history has been marked by frequent migration as people took refuge from state encroachment: witness the southward movement of Hmong, Tai, Yao, Lahu and others from today's China into the northern highlands of Vietnam, Laos and Thailand (Scott 2009). Two-dimensional spatial representation through mapping was an unfamiliar process in cultures not predicated on bordered territorial power. Only with the introduction of European cartography did this innovation become more widespread (Thongchai 1994). Accordingly, the very idea of territorial borders, which are so central to nationalist ideology, should not be taken for granted. Southeast Asia, that 'primarily negatively-defined, geographically ambivalent, residual region' (King 2008, 25) somewhere between India and China, is particularly hard to pin down.

A vision of radiating *mandala* kingdoms in precolonial Southeast Asia, which were subsequently carved into bounded territories under imperialism and then consolidated into independent nation-states, is at once illuminating and potentially misleading. Any generalisation at the regional level is bound to involve approximation and exaggeration, highlighting a problem inherent in the regional frame of reference itself. Recent empirical research has shown that the equation of precolonial, colonial and postcolonial Southeast Asia with territorial fluidity followed by relative rigidity oversimplifies the nature of those respective borders (Gainsborough 2009). The pre-colonial kingdom of Champassak, for instance, which covered parts of today's southern Laos and eastern Thailand, reportedly had different types of borders existing concurrently; its southern border was clearly defined by a waterfall, whereas its western border merged into Bangkok's power radius and tended to be marked by tributary exchanges (High 2009, 83). In another corrective to the *mandala* model, case studies show that Vietnamese dynasties from the fifteenth to nineteenth centuries expended considerable energy in manning and policing their northern border with China, even recruiting local chiefs or bandit-hunters to help them do so (Gainsborough 2009, 7).

Anthony Reid's (1988) seminal survey of fifteenth- to seventeenth-century Southeast Asia attempted to sweep the whole region into what he called 'The Age of Commerce', principally characterised by extensive maritime trade. Subsequent work has criticised Reid's focus on island Southeast Asia and undertaken a wider-ranging survey of integrative trends across the mainland from 800–1830, but even this is premised on 'Southeast Asia's fragmentation' (Lieberman 2003, 18) into two broad sub-regions. In a radical departure from these historical surveys, James C. Scott (2009) offers a completely different perspective on Southeast Asia that is primarily concerned with the margins of *mandala* and subsequent polities. In this way, Scott wishes to redress the balance of histories that focus principally on political centres. These tend to chronicle royal courts and sedentary agricultural societies, because they have left behind better documentary sources and are thus easier to study. Scott, on the other hand, is interested in peoples who successfully spurned incorporation into the central state, often moving to remote geographical locations to escape military conscription, corvée labour and exploitative terms of trade. Indeed, Scott's provocative claim is that the inhabitants of the upland region he calls 'Zomia' consciously chose the lives of hunter-gatherers, slash-and-burn cultivation and even the lack of a written language in order to avoid state control of their labour and resources. In Scott's self-described 'anarchist history', the very notions of 'tribe' and 'ethnicity' are political creations to denote those outside state control: 'Ethnicity and tribe began, by definition, where sovereignty and taxes ended' (Scott 2009, 30).

Scott argues that the 'premise for calling a geographical area a region is typically that it shares important cultural features that mark it off from adjacent areas' (Scott 2009, 16). Others point to particularity, rather than homogeneity, as what characterises a region (Chou & Houben 2006, 13). That is, shared experience of specific developments, such as widespread colonisation, Japanese occupation, anti-colonial nationalism and (anti) communist struggle might serve to define Southeast Asia. Yet Scott's own analysis redirects the focus of Southeast Asian study towards 'Zomia', a very extensive and culturally diverse mountainous massif stretching from Sichuan in China across northern Vietnam, Laos, Thailand and Burma and south along Vietnam's central highlands into northern Cambodia (Scott 2009, 15). A key defining characteristic of Zomia according to Scott is that, but for the last few decades, it has rarely been incorporated into states. This highlights the fact that statehood has never been a given nor necessarily a widespread phenomenon, making the relatively recent emergence of the nation-state and its current pervasiveness appear quite extraordinary. It also shows that regions can be understood from many different perspectives, as precolonial Thai and Chinese maps indicate (Callahan 2006, 8; Thongchai 1994).

Histories of specific countries or royal courts penned in the colonial period tended to portray Southeast Asian polities in rather static, essentialising terms, as if they were incapable of their own cultural dynamism and non-derivative development. In so doing, they often emphasised Chinese and Indian, followed by colonial cultural influences, rather than indigenous particularities. This was a tendency that Vietnamese historians, among others, worked hard to reverse (Pelley 2002, 7). Scholars like Nguyen Van Hoang and nationalists like José Rizal in the Philippines took European orientalist interpretations as a point of departure in developing their own counter-perspectives (Reid 2004, 13). Following World War II, outside academics sympathetic to decolonisation also sought to emphasise Southeast Asia's autonomy and independent evolution. This was a trend evident in many analyses of Vietnamese history and culture produced during the Vietnam-American war, for instance (Vu 2007). All of these writings were deeply influenced by colonial and then Cold War agendas. The more recent scholarship discussed above has highlighted Southeast Asian societies' engagement with outside influence in selectively appropriating some elements, resisting others and all the while creating unique hybrid cultural forms. In itself, such scholarship does much to refute popular nation-building myths of *longue durée*, which maintain that today's nation-states are descended in a direct line from illustrious ancestors and noble civilisations (Taylor 1998). However, it is important to distinguish historical scholarship from political ideologies, which use historical episodes selectively and instrumentally to support their agenda.

Although Scott points out that the nation-state construct only dominates around the last 50 years in several millennia of Southeast Asian history, his thesis is still highly relevant to nation-builders' aim of fostering national unity and loyalty. In the newly decolonised Vietnamese state, for instance, the official categorisation of its people into 53 ethnic minorities and one *Kinh* majority was an important step towards controlling the population. Vietnamese government policies, such as those sponsoring internal migration from the overpopulated flatlands to so-called 'New Economic Zones' in Vietnam's central and northern highlands, encroached on these minorities' lands and lifestyles by opening up new areas for cultivation (Hardy 2003). By importing *Kinh* settlers to the borders of its territories, the government was asserting control over its farthest frontiers and attempting to bring the entire population under its purview, thereby 'transforming it [the nation-state] into a fully governed, fiscally fertile zone' (Scott 2009, 10). By contrast, the southern Vietnamese territories of Cochinchina, under the control of Nguyen lords in the seventeenth and eighteenth centuries, made no attempt to subjugate those living in the central highlands. Instead, theirs was a relationship of tribute and trade (Li 1998, 99). For the first time in Southeast Asian history, the concept of bounded, Westphalian sovereignty has left no lawless fringe where people can evade authority. The notion of the nation-state is, quite literally, all-encompassing (Ferguson & Gupta 2002). Those who, in Scott's view, may have deliberately rejected state-like organisation in favour of a peripheral lifestyle and habitat are now trapped within a state suspicious of their lack of conformity to its nation-building norms.

The idea of 'civilizing the margins' (Duncan 2004) is now inherent in many Southeast Asian states' policies towards their ethnic minorities. Often portrayed as 'backward' or 'primitive', they are encouraged to become more 'developed' and 'civilised' (Duncan 2004, 2–3) as a contribution to state stability and unity. Therefore, it may be in academics' own professional interest to promote the study of a particular regional perspective (Walters & Haahr 2005), but in the world of nation-building the stakes are clearly far higher.

In the US at the height of the Cold War, the dusty corners of academe came closer to the corridors of power than usual, not only due to the strongly polarising effects of the Vietnam war and campus protests, but also through military service and the staffing of government agencies, including the forerunner of the Central Intelligence Agency (CIA) (Berger 2003, 432). As a central theatre of the Cold War, Southeast Asia was key in establishing area studies as academic disciplines in the US (Chou & Houben 2006, 26). This was designed to improve the global superpower's understanding of foreign climes, and often went hand in hand with political scientists' expectation that democracy and capitalist modernity should and would spread across the world (Berger 2003, 422). Leading US scholars such as Samuel Huntington and Lucian Pye were influential in creating a universalising template for development, modelled on ideas of progress and nation-building. The resulting theory of modernisation included such variables as industrialisation and agrarian reform, but also order and stability. Linked to this, the nation-state was seen as particularly important in providing an alternative focus of loyalty to communist movements or ethnic ties, and a privileged means of leaving behind antiquated traditions in a forward march towards 'modernity'.

Before and during the Vietnam-American war, the US channelled economic and military aid as well as covert support for anti-communist movements into Southeast Asia to help build 'the bone structure of a modern nation' (Rostow, cited in Berger 2003, 437). This approach explicitly countered the Marxist development philosophies of communist states like China and the Soviet Union. Not only were theories of modernisation often developed with the help of Southeast Asian cases, then, but they also provided the rationale for targeting development aid to Southeast Asia in highly normative ways, the most egregious example of which was certainly the short-lived Republic of Vietnam (commonly know as South Vietnam). Unsurprisingly, therefore, the heyday of Southeast Asian studies in the US ended with the Vietnam War. By the close of the Cold War, not only the political but also the theoretical rationale behind this regional focus had fallen out of favour (Houben 2006, 148). Globalisation seemed set to break down cultural differences and to obviate the need for specific area studies (Chou & Houben 2006, 11). Against the backdrop of ASEAN's expanding membership, however, Asian political leaders had begun to use regionalist rhetoric to rail against what they considered paternalistic, even neo-colonial, interference. For instance, the so-called 'Asian values' debate conducted principally during the 1990s saw prominent regional leaders, including then prime ministers Mohamad Mahathir of Malaysia and Lee Kuan Yew of Singapore, advance an explicitly non-Western view of society and progress. This they identified as specifically Asian, thereby questioning supposedly universal values and human rights (Mahathir & Ishihara, 1995; for a critique, see Cheah 2003, 54). Notwithstanding its considerable intellectual baggage, then, local elites began to appropriate the concept of Southeast Asia for their own ends.

We can conclude from this survey of Southeast Asia as an idea that it is not an unproblematic label for a given landmass. Not only did its geographic borders fluctuate, but it was also imbued with different meanings according to the historical period and the political perspective in play. Latterly, statesmen within the region, who are only too mindful of the value of postcolonial national sovereignty, have adopted Southeast Asia as a term. This suggests that their interpretation of regionalism is not incompatible with their approach to nation-building. Indeed, it has often been argued that Southeast Asian states, all members of ASEAN bar recently independent East Timor, view regionalism as a means of bolstering domestic sovereignty and legitimacy (Narine 2004; Sutherland 2009). Attempts to transcend 'encapsulated' histories of a single country and trace Southeast Asian dynamics and similarities could potentially provide a basis for regionalist ideologies seeking to establish a sense of supranational identity, in order to link current cooperation to historical ties (Gainsborough 2009; Tran & Reid 2006). This might well be used to portray ASEAN integration as a 'natural' progression from centuries of shared history, or as a constructive partnership to replace past internecine conflict. However, a look at the intergovernmental nature of ASEAN, Southeast Asia's best established organisation, suggests that in practice nationalism trumps regionalism as a justification for action, even in response to globalisation and the scale of the cosmopolitan challenge as a whole (Sutherland 2009).

Regionalisation

Regional – in the sense of supranational – integration has taken place across all continents over recent decades, with the creation of the European Union (EU), Mercosur, North American Free Trade Agreement (NAFTA), African Union (AU), Southern African Development Community (SADC) and Association of Southeast Asian Nations (ASEAN) as just some examples. In particular, there has been a proliferation of regional bodies across Africa since the 1950s, many with overlapping memberships and objectives, but most with limited means at their disposal. Supporters of African regionalism evoke a range of potential benefits, aside from the functional advantages of economic integration. Here it is important to emphasise again the distinction between the macro-level phenomenon of regionalisation (of the same order as globalisation) and regionalism, defined here as member states' ideological response to integration. Those with a positive approach to regionalism regard integration as a means of reducing dependence on close economic, cultural and political ties to former colonisers by fostering co-operation with neighbouring states. Linked to this, they see it as a way of defusing regional tensions and taking concerted action against crises (Tordoff 2002, 240). In the wake of the Cold War and much like the rationale behind ASEAN, it also provides an opportunity to speak with a louder voice on the international stage. To gauge the relative success of African regionalisation in these terms, it is necessary to understand the context in which it evolves and the way its stated objectives can diverge from the capacity and commitment of member states.

A central aim of regional integration is to encourage free trade, but this is a highly contested concept in the African context. In postcolonial Africa, newly independent states often inherited colonial creations, which had been carved out principally with a view to maximising the exploitation of natural resources like mineral deposits, and were geared towards the production of one or two primary commodities such as cocoa or sugar. African states' over-dependence on exporting a limited range of raw materials contributed to worsening economic performance as prices dropped on world markets and debt levels soared. As a result, they were particularly vulnerable to the economic vagaries of trade globalisation. International assistance came in the form of much-maligned Structural Adjustment Programmes, or SAPs, championed by the likes of the World Bank and the International Monetary Fund. These followed a very specific economic model premised on privatisation, trade liberalisation and the assumption that prosperity would 'trickle down' from the moneyed elites to the masses. Stringent cuts in public spending and the civil service were required, in order to encourage optimum market conditions and promote 'good governance' in what were regarded as predominantly clientelistic, bloated and corrupt state institutions. This approach, often imposed on African states with little consultation as a condition of debt restructuring, mirrored the West's disenchantment with Keynesian economics after the oil shocks and recession of the 1970s (Olukoshi & Laakso 1996, 17). It is widely argued that the effect of SAPs were counter-productive, in that they undermined advances in areas like health and education, contributed to the flight of capable staff with a stake in state development, led to a drop in the relevance and legitimacy of institutions to people's daily lives, and thus weakened the very fabric of Africa's fledgling nation-states (Olukoshi & Laakso 1996). Regional integration has been presented as one possible means of addressing this enduring situation, although it has been suggested that the recent tendency to promote 'open regionalism', or trade outwith Africa through initiatives like the New Partnership for Africa's Development (NEPAD), merely perpetuates patterns of dependence on Western partners (Söderbaum 2007, 190).

As discussed in Chapter 4, the borders and institutions of African nation-states were often a legacy of colonialism, and were therefore as much a product as a repudiation of the past (Makinda & Okumu 2008, 15). In the Horn of Africa, for instance, 'the nationalist aim was to obtain and use the power of the state created by colonialism' (Markakis 1999, 66). Nationalism was a relatively narrow movement there, which flourished in economically developed and commercially active zones like northern Sudan, highland Kenya and southern Somalia, but not in these countries' predominantly pastoralist regions (Markakis 1999, 67). Africa's were so-called 'prestatized nationalisms' (Cheah 2003, 5), where state preceded nation. There were some newly independent states, like Ethiopia, which initially pursued legitimation through nation-building by asserting primordial links to ancient Abyssinia. In many parts of Africa, however, attempts at fostering national unity have given way to widespread fragmentation, strategic or otherwise. The state has been supplemented, but not replaced, by a wide range of transnational networks, ranging from sophisticated 'shadow' economies, which represent a majority share in the gross domestic product of Mozambique, Kenya and Angola (Nordstrom 2001, 220), to multinational companies that employ private security firms on a scale akin to small private armies (Ferguson & Gupta 2002, 989; Latham, Callaghy & Kassimir 2001). This has important implications for the nation-state construct; those leaders who have no ambition to control entire state territories (as opposed to merely the lucrative areas), or to represent the people as a whole, have no interest in nation-building. Conversely, the state loses legitimacy when it fails to deliver basic services or protection to its citizens, 'who thereby become citizens in name only' (Hylland Eriksen 1999, 57). It also has consequences for regionalisation, because prospects for the formal institutional integration of member states seem bleak if those member states do not have full control of their territories and resources. This contrasts with the dynamic brand of informal or 'shadow' transnationalism that has developed, in which small-scale traders, public servants and business cartels operate illegally across borders (Söderbaum 2007, 195).

Against this backdrop of skewed global trade, development and limited state structures further undermined by illegal trading networks, there are many public officials, warlords and international businesses nevertheless still coveting the protective mantle of state sovereignty for the international recognition, legal protection and business opportunities it provides. For example, Charles Taylor and Laurent Kabila sought to take over the capitals and governments of Liberia and Zaïre respectively, even though they already controlled much more lucrative territories elsewhere. African leaders of all stripes are therefore also interested in the 'regime-boosting' potential of regional integration. They are thus regionalists in that they seek 'to strengthen the status, legitimacy and the general interests of the political regime (rather than the nation state per se)' (Söderbaum 2007, 192). Here, the symbolism and prestige of diplomacy and summitry are key, rather than any commitment to implement policy or even to debate the issues on the agenda. Regionalisation's role here is interpreted as enhancing member states' visibility on the world stage, and even propping up weak state sovereignty itself. Attendance at a suitably magnificent international summit serves as ceremonial recognition of the member state – and its leader – as an international actor, while suspension from a regional body can be correspondingly humiliating. Finally, state leaders' support for 'regime-boosting' regionalism may also help explain the proliferation and overlap of African regional bodies, as these increase opportunities for representation and bidding for resources (Söderbaum 2007, 193).

This picture of limited resources and mixed motivations sheds some light on why the results of African regionalism have been relatively modest to date. For instance, the Economic Community of West African States (ECOWAS), founded in 1978, had difficulty promoting free trade within the area even before war broke out in Liberia and Sierra Leone in 1990. Although ECOWAS helped broker a peace deal in 1995, the organisation's monitoring force was not sufficiently large or well funded to police it, and a lack of resources has since continued to hamper progress on the economic front (Tordoff 2002, 245). ECOWAS members were also divided over how to respond to the tense and violent stand-off following Ivory Coast's disputed presidential election in 2010 (*Guardian* 2010c). Elsewhere, the Southern African Development Community (SADC) aimed to cooperate in promoting intra-regional trade and economic development, as well as reducing dependence on apartheid-era South Africa. On coming to power in 1994, however, the African National Congress (ANC) brought South Africa into SADC, thereby radically reconfiguring the balance of power within the group. Where once SADC had largely relied on Western aid to fund initiatives independent of South Africa, it now looked to its influential new member to help reduce that international dependence. Political co-operation was hampered by an unclear mandate to intervene in local conflicts, however, and the potential for trade integration was necessarily limited among economies producing similar goods, which were more likely to compete with than complement each other (Tordoff 2002, 249). More recently, SADC has been reluctant to condemn Robert Mugabe for overseeing the gradual economic collapse and political bankruptcy of Zimbabwe, one of its member states (Alden 2010, 5).

As in the case of ECOWAS, SADC has increasingly taken on a security role in addition to its primary economic objectives. This highlights the perennial tension between the principle of non-interference, which governs intergovernmental regional organisations, and the pursuit of common goals. Initial enthusiasm for creating regional bodies suggests that African leaders saw no basic incompatibility between nation-building and regional integration, and there has indeed been some progress in increasing intra-regional trade, customs and currency cooperation (Braveboy-Wagner 2009, 181). However, a lack of resources and political will has seen many regional organisations fail to advance their loftier principles, such as human rights protection, democracy and the rule of law (Braveboy-Wagner 2009, 169). As in the ASEAN case, integration remains resolutely intergovernmental and wedded to the principle of preserving state sovereignty. Unlike ASEAN member states, though, there is less of a tendency for African regionalism to be an adjunct to nation-building; nation-building is clearly no longer a major priority for some African leaders. Important exceptions do include South Africa, where both SADC membership and support for the AU can be inscribed within the ANC's policy of an 'African renaissance', designed to foster post-Apartheid nation-building within a pan-African discourse of unity (Tieku 2004). In sum, readiness to enjoy the strategic benefits of regional integration has not been matched by a willingness to accept internal censure from fellow member states or to make the financial commitment necessary for progress. These problems helped to scupper the now defunct Organisation of African Unity (OAU).

Despite paying lip service to the pan-African sentiment underlying the continent-wide OAU, member states fatally undermined its credibility by refusing to pay their dues, set achievable economic aims, seek public support or condemn even the most egregious human rights abuses (Tieku 2004, 252). It remains to be seen whether its successor, the AU, can live up to its aim of responding to globalisation and the cosmopolitan challenge more generally. Founded in 2001, the AU's institutions are consciously modelled on those of the EU and, similarly to the EU, its core aims include economic integration and the promotion of peace. Another AU objective is to meet the challenge of globalisation by encouraging African self-reliance through accelerated regional integration and economic development (Braveboy-Wagner 2009, 146). Since the collapse of Cold War funding prompted attempts to reconfigure security along regional lines, one further goal is to streamline and harmonise Africa's many regional bodies and their existing development agendas to encourage security and stability across the continent (Makinda & Okumu 2008, 53). Whereas the OAU had African decolonisation as its guiding mission, the AU's Constitutive Act lays down a wide range of principles in its Articles 3 and 4, covering gender mainstreaming, human rights, popular participation and the impact of globalisation, among other matters. At the same time, it seeks to qualify respect for the principle of non-interference and member states' 'sovereignty, territorial integrity and independence' (Article 3 (b)) by introducing a limited right to intervene in the event of 'war crimes, genocide and crimes against humanity' (Article 4(h)). Not only is the AU responding to the challenges of globalisation and regionalisation, then, but it is also addressing the limits of member state sovereignty; all of this has major implications for the nation-state. Indeed, it has been suggested that 'Africa and Asia, are the sites where new configurations of power shaping the world are most visible' (Nordstrom 2001, 239).

Countries of the global south tend to be enthusiastic about multilateralism in general and regional bodies in particular, seeing them as a means of countering their relative political and economic weakness on the world stage.

Ideally, regional integration enables 'states to share strategic information and ideas, to draw global attention to their particular concerns, to reduce the costs or penalties for noncooperation with dominant partners [...] and to facilitate adoption of alternative courses of action' (Braveboy-Wagner 2009, 7). ASEAN is one example of this trend, and the AU is another. The African case also demonstrates that a network of regional and sub-regional organisations can co-exist, though a huge part of the challenge is to make each one profitable and effective. This is unlikely to happen if institution-building remains weak and sluggish (Makinda & Okumu 2008, 121). Nevertheless, it is important to point out that the 'regime-boosting' aspects of regionalisation are not necessarily diminished by the lack of measurable progress. Similarly, globalisation is not inherently incompatible with either nationalism or regionalism: 'Like any construction, globalization has no preordained consequences' (Makinda & Okumu 2008, 115). Indeed, the AU's most urgent task is to make globalisation work in Africa's favour, and to shape national and regional projects accordingly, not least because Africa's share of world trade has dropped from 5.5 per cent in the 1970s to around 3 per cent in recent years (Braveboy-Wagner 2009, 91).

Globalisation

There is no generally accepted definition of globalisation, and yet the implications for nationalism clearly depend on how it is understood. Globalisation has variously been interpreted as an intensification of all forms of cultural and economic transfer and an increase in worldwide communication, characterised by the compression of distances and time delays. Theoretical approaches to the phenomenon can be divided into three very broad and much simplified trends (Guibernau 2001, 244). The so-called hyperglobalist thesis holds that globalisation heralds the end of the nation-state, which is increasingly being bypassed as a source of authority and legitimacy by ever accelerating flows of goods, capital, people and information (Ohmae 1996). More sceptical scholars, on the other hand, question whether globalisation is such a new phenomenon at all (Hirst & Thomson 1999), highlighting its uneven impact across the world and its manipulation by both left and right for ideological ends (Hay & Rosamond 2002). This suggests that some nation-states will be affected more than others and will have differing capacity to control the flows criss-crossing their borders. Still other theorists stress that globalisation is an unprecedented product of technological advances and imbue it with the potential to reconfigure global relations of power, including regional organisations like the ones discussed in the previous section.

How do we make sense of globalisation? Critics like the influential Marxian geographer David Harvey charge that global capitalism has paved the way 'for a postmodern version of imperialism, with its doctrine of universal human rights in the foreground' (Harvey 2009, 102). This view chimes with those who point to Western values, however defined, masquerading as universals, and condemn attempts to impose them on recalcitrant, generally postcolonial nation-states. Harvey (2009, 105) considers international organisations like the World Bank and the International Monetary Fund, along with former world leaders like US president George W. Bush and UK prime minister Tony Blair, to be key proponents of such projects. In other words, globalisation can be seen as a vehicle for neoliberal capitalism, reflecting the interests of those who are already rich and influential, rather than promising any prospect of a better deal for the billions who are not. However, globalisation is not a uniform, homogenising force, turning all that it touches into capitalist clones. Neither is it necessarily irreconcilable with regionalisation or, for that matter, nation-building. In the case of the ongoing war in Afghanistan, the events of 9/11 prompted a reaction to the internationally networked Al Qaeda in terms of conventional state warfare; NATO's terms triggered an international force to go to war with Afghanistan's Taliban regime, which was believed to be harbouring members of the terrorist organisation. Throughout a decade of conflict, the aims of the US and its allies have got bogged down in the fundamental incoherence of its initial position, which was to try and address a twenty-first-century phenomenon using twentieth-century tools. In this sense, the state-based approach to global threats like terrorism is anachronistic, but its continued prevalence is understandable. How else can we imagine and organise politics on a global scale, when every international organisation, from ASEAN to the UN, is built around the membership of nation-states? Again, some combination of globalism and nationalism seems necessary. As Stein Tønnesson (2004, 186) notes, 'the age of globalisation requires a certain degree of national cohesion within a state in order for it to be able to make the best out of its opportunities'. This is becoming more difficult, but no less necessary in response to the cosmopolitan challenge. Nation-states continue to need national solidarity as a basis for legitimacy and 'active support from their population of a kind that only people identifying with their state can provide' (Tønnesson 2004, 192).

Aihwa Ong (1999, 60) explores the role of ideological globalism in Southeast Asian nation-building, such as the Malaysian-led discourse of progressive, state-centred and business friendly 'New Islam' (Ong 1999, 227). Key icons of Malaysia's global reach are the twin Petronas towers in Kuala Lumpur. The tallest in the world when built, they incorporate elements of Islamic architecture into that archetype of modernity, the skyscraper. A look at the interplay of globalist and nationalist ideologies in Asia suggests that responses to globalisation are as diverse there as in Europe and elsewhere. Clearly, governments' capacity to intervene in financial markets, regulate multinational corporations, police the internet and create prosperity from global trade will affect their legitimacy and prestige in the eyes of citizens. However, none of these aspects of globalisation influences the nation in the way that migration and its attendant phenomenon – diaspora – have the capacity to do. Border management depends on current transnational relations, on the type of transfers (from contraband to capital flows) and the status of the people wishing to cross (from refugees and illegal workers to tourists with visas). It is therefore too sweeping to suggest that globalisation has brought with it a uniform breaking down of borders. Indeed, studies show that state regulation has become more stringent in places, not less. On the one hand, the management of some Southeast Asian industrial zones has been largely handed to the corporations based there, with limited state oversight (Ong 1999), while on the other, states have attempted to impose tougher controls on trade and population flows through closer border regulation. Even within the European Schengen area, the dismantling of physical border posts between member states has seen a concomitant increase in control by sharing information on illegal trafficking and other criminal activity, and in 2011 the principle of free movement itself was questioned (*Economist* 2011c). In any case, interstate cooperation is premised on the continued existence of borders that can be transgressed, for some crimes only become such in the act of crossing a border. Where borders are no longer a site of physical control signalled by guards, barriers and identity documents, they are still symbolic of state sovereignty. Borders are but one marker, however, among much more complex global networks.

With reference to West Africa and South America, Anthony Bebbington and Simon Batterbury (2001, 373) point out that people's livelihoods are affected not only by large-scale government programmes and non-governmental organisations, but also by transnational migrant worker networks, their remittances and the like. That is, globalisation not only has a top-down effect from the global to the local, but local actors can also influence its impact. As Mark Beeson puts it (2009, 10), 'local responses are important "intervening variables" that can influence the way in which both regional and global processes are realized'. With regard to nationalism, this perspective moves away from a state-centric analysis to one concerned with the relationships between a multitude of actors. This focus on individual relationships, as distinct from the wider-ranging international networks in which they are embedded, is transnational in that it both crosses and transcends nation-state borders. As discussed in Chapter 5, it attempts to trace specific connections, which have implications for the security and effectiveness of those borders, as well as the national communities that they profess to surround. This transnational perspective is therefore an important complement to analyses of nationalism and globalisation. Examples include studies of migration and refugee movements, ethnic communities or trading routes that straddle state frontiers, security regimes privileging individuals over states, trafficking, development flows, remittances and livelihoods shaped by a variety of local and global factors largely independent of the nation-state. All of these illustrate aspects of the cosmopolitan challenge to nations and nationalism. In many cases, 'careful comparative work (across families and places) is essential to tease out these effects' (Bebbington and Batterbury 2001, 374). For example, migrant flows returning (or not) from the US, Japan and the UK to the Dominican Republic, the Philippines or Poland can have a sizeable impact on the politics and economics of their home country.

While many analyses focus on the interrelationship between globalisation and the *state*, it is also important to underline the impact of globalisation on the *nation*. The focus is different, in that it is less concerned with the actual nature and extent of cross-border flows and their implications for state authority. Instead, it examines the potential conceptual crossover between nationalism and globalism as ideologies. In other words, the way in which the phenomenon of globalisation has been interpreted by nationalists and nation-builders. The likes of citizenship regimes, as discussed in Chapter 5, testify to how the nation-state construct is being maintained in official discourse. Globalisation, in turn, can be presented as a help or a hindrance to nation-building (Hay and Rosamond 2002). Similarly, minority nationalists variously ride the wave of globalist rhetoric or appear to draw strength from stemming its tide. We have seen that globalisation does not create a world without borders, but rather one where borders are more permeable to all sorts of flows. A major element of nation-building consists in maintaining these borders as meaningful ideological constructs, so as to distinguish citizen from foreigner and sovereign lands from neighbouring states, thereby delimiting belonging to a national community. Globalisation does not necessarily encourage homogeneity, however. Quite the opposite: it literally brings diversity home, as nationalists and nation-states are faced with increasingly heterogeneous communities due to migration and diaspora. Ironically, state borders are often being strengthened against precisely those aspects of the cosmopolitan challenge; 'in the much celebrated free circulation opened up by global capitalism, it is "things" (commodities) which freely circulate, while the circulation of "persons" is more and more controlled' (Zizek, cited in Jackson 2003, 34).

It is instructive to look at one of the world's least developed countries (LDCs) according to UN criteria, in order to gauge the impact of globalisation on nation-building. It has been argued that LDCs belong to a 'fourth world' largely untouched by the effects of globalisation, due to their very small share of global foreign direct investment flows and limited integration into world markets (Shatkin 1998, 381). The Southeast Asian state of Cambodia, however, one of around fifty LDCs, was already clearly being affected by globalisation throughout the 1990s, as evidenced by the impact of international tourism, donor aid flows, foreign entrepreneurs exploiting natural resources, increasing internet access in urban centres and the growth of organised crime, among other factors (Shatkin 1998, 382). Having endured the devastating effects of carpet bombing during the second Indochina war in the 1960s and '70s, immediately followed by the murderous rule of the Khmer Rouge and years of sporadic civil war after the regime was toppled by the Vietnamese, the former French colony finally reached a peace settlement in 1991. This paved the way for the largest ever UN operation to date. Designed to ensure Cambodia's transition to democracy, it also led to the rapid introduction of consumer goods, spiralling real estate prices in the capital Phnom Penh and a burgeoning service and leisure industry to cater for the 20,000 UN staff who descended on the country (Shatkin 1998). Elections in 1993 resulted in an uneasy government coalition, before the former Khmer Rouge cadre, Vietnamese protégé and consummate political survivor Hun Sen wrested sole control of the government from his partners in 1997, subsequently consolidating his own position as prime minister through a series of flawed elections. Meanwhile, Cambodia has only recently begun the process of coming to terms with its past. The trials of Khmer Rouge cadres only began in 2009. After years of negotiation between the UN and the Cambodian government over the composition, remit and role of the tribunal, it was agreed that it should be UN-funded but made up of both international and Cambodian judges (*BBC News* 2010). This shows that even Cambodia's engagement with its own recent history, which can be compared to the process of truth and reconciliation in South Africa or so-called *Vergangenheitsbewältigung* (coming to terms with the past) in Germany, is inscribed within the international community's understanding of appropriate values, norms and ways of meting out justice. This is one aspect of the cultural and ethical effects of globalisation that accompany globalisation's economic impact on Cambodian nation-building.

Cambodia's rapid insertion into the global textile trade and its 'neo-fordist' labour regime 'based on Western models' (Arnold & Han Shih 2010, 408) contrast sharply with its low per capita GDP, largely agricultural economy and limited urbanisation. Cambodia's expanding tourism sector and its established, though not always legal, logging and lumber industry have recently been joined by a growth in agribusiness ventures, amid claims that unscrupulous investors are grabbing the land of peasants who have no evidence of legal title due to the turmoil of the Khmer Rouge years (*BBC News* 2011a). Since the mid-1990s, preferential trade agreements with the US and the EU, together with the availability of cheap land and labour, have attracted foreign entrepreneurs to Cambodia and promoted rapid growth in the country's textile and garment industry. A hitherto unique trade initiative, put in place during Bill Clinton's administration, linked US market access to evidence of progressive improvements in Cambodian working conditions, as monitored by a donor-funded body led by the International Labour Organisation (ILO) and entitled 'Better Factories' (Arnold & Han Shih 2010, 406). This helped Cambodian exports benefit from an association with ethical, sweatshop-free consumption, although it is far from certain that this reputation will be sustainable now that the US trade agreement has come to an end. Having suffered from the global recession and exposure to direct market rivals in 2008 and 2009, Cambodia now finds itself urgently required to improve its garment industry's competitiveness and productivity, and there are indications that labour standards might deteriorate as a result. The need to support economic growth, at the expense of worker protection if need be, was underlined by the Cambodian Minister of Commerce, who argued that the country's labour linked trade policy might be watered down 'if the result of the support of ILO labour compliance means less purchasing orders and less business for Cambodia' (Arnold & Han Shih 2010, 420). This example shows how Cambodia's remarkably progressive Labour Law, including 90 days' maternity leave and paid breastfeeding breaks for the largely female workforce, was substantially shaped by the influence of external donors and trade partners on Cambodia's role in the 'global assembly line' (Derks 2006, 193). Again, this exemplifies the Cambodian government's double bind in the face of globalisation: how to balance the demands of foreign investors and donors with its own weak infrastructure, institutions, economic bargaining power and vulnerability to corruption and graft? From the domestic perspective, how to reconcile its attempts at nation-building with the status of returning exiles (Poethig 2006), restive workers ready to take strike action (Arnold & Han Shih 2010, 418) and a very young population yet to be integrated into the labour market? This dilemma is neatly encapsulated in official attitudes to the tourism sector.

A leading Cambodian political figure is quoted as saying; 'The Khmer will never perish because they built Angkor Wat, and Angkor Wat is their soul. The Ministry of Culture and Fine Arts [...] have to use these marvels as resources of our tourism industry' (Ranarridh cited in Winter & Chau-Pech Ollier 2006, 1). This illustrates how the extensive and spectacular twelfth-century temple complex of Angkor Wat, built at the apogee of the powerful Khmer empire and now a UNESCO world heritage site, is considered both an economic resource and a symbol of the distinctiveness and superiority of Cambodian culture. By the 1930s, 'Angkor had already solidified as the idealised apogee of a largely monolithic, mono-cultural nationalism' (Winter & Chau-Pech Ollier, 2006, 5), yet official Cambodian representations of the site for nation-building purposes continue to compete with colonial connotations. This competition for control over the meaning of Angkor has been ongoing ever since it was 'rediscovered' in the nineteenth century by the French explorer Henri Mouhot and became a subject of study for the *Ecole Française d'Extrême Orient* (French School of Asian Studies). It has only intensified in the era of globalisation. UNESCO has begun 'policing the "image" of Ankor' (Norindr 2006, 55) and the global tourist industry has marketed the temples, along with the Khmer Rouge legacy, as the two main 'attractions' of a visit to Cambodia (Winter 2006, 37). Significantly for the symbol of a country seeking to reconcile globalisation and nation-building, Angkor continues to be omnipresent within Cambodia itself, appearing on everything from banknotes to beer bottles from a state-founded brewery. Tellingly, it also features as the centrepiece on the national flag. As such, Angkor is used by Cambodian nation-builders to represent a national ideal of 'purity in the face of porous boundaries, cultural mobility and flux' (Winter & Chau-Pech Ollier, 2006, 10). To this extent, this official state 'branding' of Angkor largely chimes with the way in which the international tourism industry has marketed the country. There have also been government initiatives to turn key sites associated with the Khmer Rouge into tourist destinations, further illustrating the 'intersection of historical-cultural definition and political-economic circumstance' (Wood 2006, 181) in responding to the cosmopolitan challenge of globalisation. This commodification of national memory helps assert Cambodian state control over how the Khmer Rouge is to be interpreted by locals and foreigners alike, to the exclusion of competing narratives (Norindr 2006, 68). The government thereby sets out to establish its preferred reading 'of the past, while putting the country's history of suffering at the service of attracting revenue' (Wood 2006, 181), an approach that can also be observed in neighbouring Vietnam (Schwenkel 2008). This nation-building strategy promotes domestic unity while paying heed to international diplomacy, commerce and tourism, thereby incorporating aspects of globalisation into official nationalist ideology.

Conclusion

'Globalization is *not* a tide that lifts all boats', as former UN Secretary General Kofi Annan observed (cited in Makinda & Okumu 2008, 3; emphasis in original). Although it is widely accepted that 'developing' states of the southern hemisphere have been less well served by globalisation, this chapter's focus on Southeast Asia and Africa serves to show that their responses to globalisation are differentiated and context-dependent. Regionalist rhetoric is buoyant in both cases, but continues to be based on the preservation of Westphalian sovereignty. However, the pursuit of actual regional integration rings rather hollow in those cases where African leaders have largely abandoned nation-building as a means of pursuing popular legitimacy, instead prizing the state as a strategic tool for commercial gain. Most Southeast Asian states, by contrast, continue to see nation-building as a component of state legitimation, whether this is pursued by democratic means or not. Even Burma/Myanmar's military junta held a strongly manipulated election in late 2010 under the pretence of seeking state legitimation. Sovereignty may have become more 'fluid' (Braveboy-Wagner 2009, 88) since the end of the Cold War, but the meanings associated with it, and the linked concept of the nation-state, have been shown to differ widely across Africa and Southeast Asia. This illustrates the flexibility of ideologies linking nation, state and region.

In today's world, even though globalisation tends to be seen as the 'dominant metaphor [,] it has a very strong regional accent' (Beeson 2007, xvi). In other words, regional integration is often one state response to the pressures of globalisation. As such, the global and regional aspects of the cosmopolitan challenge are interconnected and, contrary to early predictions of its decline, have not eclipsed the nation-state. Instead, governments have had to incorporate some form of regionalism and globalism into their nation-building ideology. Some have opted to paint globalisation as a threat in order to encourage national solidarity and unity in facing it down, whereas others have portrayed it as an opportunity to enhance national prosperity (Brown 2000, 87: Hay & Rosamond 2002). Globalism, regionalism and nationalism thus emerge as eminently flexible ideologies that interpret events differently and draw on each other depending on the political context. This is an important response to the cosmopolitan challenge, which at first sight appears to be assaulting the nation-state construct and the *raison d'être* of nationalist movements on many fronts. Contrary to appearances, however, nationalism is able to meet that challenge by 'loving its enemy', so to speak, or incorporating the apparent threat posed by globalisation and regionalisation into its ideology. As such, globalisation and regionalisation should not be understood as alternatives to nations and states, which risk being rendered obsolete and replaced by regional organisations or a global world order. That is a highly unlikely scenario. Some nationalist variants will inevitably be more successful than others, however, in harnessing globalisation and regionalisation to maintaining nation-state legitimacy or securing greater sub-state autonomy.

Regionalisation and globalisation are aspects of the cosmopolitan challenge to nation-building that have led some states to construct regionalist and globalist ideologies compatible with their nationalist discourse in response (Sutherland 2009). The concept of regionalism thus provides a basis for comparing the way in which nation-builders have reconciled their ongoing pursuit of popular loyalty and legitimacy with very different forms of regional integration, as represented by organisations like the EU and ASEAN. However, it is at least as difficult to construct a convincing case for the existence of Southeast Asia as a large, sub-continental 'region' as it is to build a nation. As we have seen above, the very concept of Southeast Asia is something of an external imposition. The colonial-era cartographic demarcation of territories did not automatically signal a fundamental change in what was happening, literally, on the ground, but rather in the way that territory was perceived. Just as Cold War fears of communism

(Anderson 1998, 7) prompted a flurry of academic studies using the region as a frame of reference, some see anti-terrorism today as a new reason to study Southeast Asia. Again, the political rationale behind such endeavours looms large (Reid 2004, 5). In a sense, the current state of scholarship has come full circle in its approach to contemporary Southeast Asian nation-states, by questioning the view that globalisation would necessarily break down borders. Instead, the effects of globalisation have been mixed, with states allowing some things, like capital, to move more freely, while attempting to regulate increasing population flows more closely. As a result, there is a 'disjuncture between political and economic space: as a consequence of globalization, economic activity and political authority are no longer coterminous' (Beeson 2007, 23). Globalisation has prompted a re-examination of the nation-state's *raison d'être*, leading to a range of nationalist responses, but nationalists ignore the cosmopolitan challenge at their peril, for this would only make them outdated and unappealing. Rather, the aim of any ideology is to present a convincing world-view and a plan of action for realising its aims. Most nationalists have realised that they must address the cosmopolitan challenge, whether approvingly or critically, or else risk being rendered irrelevant. As we have seen, incorporating responses to globalisation and regionalisation into their brand of nationalism or nation-building is a key means of achieving this.

Conclusion

Nation-builders have long worked to maintain popular loyalty and legitimacy, but the combination of individuals' heightened mobility, global technologies and regional integration has put extra pressure on neatly bordered constructions of the nation-state. The cosmopolitan challenge has thus lent a new immediacy to the tension between globalisation and the 'modern conception' of the sovereign state, which has been described as 'fully, flatly, and evenly operative over each square centimetre of a legally demarcated territory' (Anderson 1991, 19). For instance, many post-communist states have found the transnational dimensions of twenty-first-century nation-building to be qualitatively different from the relative introspection of the Cold War (Duara 2009, 36). In other cases, postcolonial states relatively late in achieving independence were quickly confronted with the impact of global trade and other flows on their fledgling nation-building strategies. Still others, like India and China, have led the way in detaching nation-building from the strict confines of the territorial state by seeking to involve their national diaspora in the country's modernisation and development (Barabantseva & Sutherland 2011). Ironically, new conceptions of 'post-nationalism' and 'post-sovereignty' seem to echo pre-Westphalian polities, or 'the older imagining, where states were defined by centres [and] borders were porous and indistinct' (Anderson 1991, 19).

The tension between nation-building and the cosmopolitan challenge 'emanates from the nation-state's dual, and sometimes contradictory, role of both enabling participation in the global society and protecting national society – or select groups within the nation – from destructive competition' (Duara 2009, 7). The nation has also been frequently described as Janus-faced; looking backwards towards putative primordial origins as a means of securing the legitimacy necessary to move forwards. The cosmopolitan challenge has done little to undermine the time dimension of this linear sense of history, which can always construct globalisation, regionalism or transnationalism as the next stage in a nation's progress and modernisation. It has had a greater impact on nationalism's spatial dimension, however. While the territorial link to a 'homeland' remains a key element of national belonging, the nature of that link is changing. Be it through virtual communities, the unfulfilled nostalgia of a diaspora, or periodic returns by migrants

173

or their regular remittances, there are now many more ways of expressing belonging than simply residing in the 'homeland'. Emotional attachments to the place of birth can be extrapolated to a sense of national patriotism, for example. The return of a member of the Vietnamese diaspora to his or her childhood home often realises an intense longing that is intimately linked to their sense of national identity, one that the Vietnamese government is increasingly seeking to turn into concrete investments (Jellema 2007). In similar ways, transnational and diasporic belonging help contribute to nation-building across the world today. After all, if movement really is a fundamental component of contemporary identities (Kennedy 2001, 20), then diasporas are a key example of how national affiliations are increasingly likely to be fluid and deterritorialised.

The cosmopolitan challenge suggests that 'methodological nationalism', or the assumption that nation-states are the principal focus of social and political enquiry, is too narrow in its focus. Instead, greater attention to the interplay of transnationalism, regionalisation and globalisation with nationalist ideology encourages analysts to avoid essentialising either national or diaspora cultures; 'What is really being threatened by globalization, perhaps, is the need – both by citizens and some social scientists – to believe in the idea of bounded, coherent, distinctive, and separate societies, nations, cultures and communities, tied to familiar, concrete locations' (Kennedy 2001, 18). If, on the other hand, one accepts individuals' fluid identities and porous nation-state borders, then it is easier to suggest that cosmopolitanism is not inherently incompatible with nationalist ideology. The uneven impact of the cosmopolitan challenge has created a class of high-flying entrepreneurs and professionals – from corporate types, through development consultants, to celebrity DJs – who do not think twice about working across several continents. One essential travelling companion makes this cosmopolitan lifestyle possible: the passport. No-one, not even diplomats fast-tracking through customs and immigration, completely escapes a system premised on borders and nation-state citizenship. The docile queues of travellers waiting for entry stamps and enduring probing questions in the name of national security are very clear consequences of the nation-state system, which soon reveals itself to be complex and hierarchical. For example, visa arrangements depend on a web of bilateral and multilateral treaties that severely constrain the citizens of some states while allowing easy passage to others. Granting a visa in the first place is also often characterised by caution and mistrust, with innocent individuals sometimes the victim of misplaced suspicions (Dalrymple 2010, 15). Add to this the supplementary rights enjoyed by virtue of European Union citizenship, for instance, not to mention the divided loyalties and diverse obligations of migrants and diaspora communities, and it becomes very difficult to see a clear logic to the nation-state system itself, let alone construct any neat correspondence between an individual's citizenship and their sense of national belonging.

The hyphen linking nation and state may have 'loosened' as a result of the cosmopolitan challenge, but it has not 'led to the release of the nation from the state' as Gerard Delanty contends (2006, 358). On the contrary, it is a misguided conflation of concepts to equate 'post-sovereignty' with a 'post-national' political system. The former refers to a decline in states' domestically and externally recognised authority to act across the fields of politics, economics and finance, whereas the latter heralds an end to state legitimacy based on nation-building. This text has argued that whereas post-sovereignty may be envisaged in some sectors, such as those governed by a regional organisation, the same cannot be said for post-nationalism. The idea that 'the current situation points to a notion of the nation without nationalism' (Delanty 2006, 358) is an absurdity if one takes the nation to be a product of nationalist ideology, as this text has done from the outset. Instead, the issue at stake is how nationalism accommodates the cosmopolitan challenge (Chernilo 2006, 137). In other words, the question relates to how nation-building and sub-state nationalism respond to the cosmopolitan challenge, rather than the risk of them disappearing altogether, for that would leave the existing nation-state system bereft of its core legitimating ideology.

In the words of Andrew Vincent (2002, 221), the 'debate over cosmopolitanism and nationalism is central to the twenty-first century and marks out the domain of future political theory and practice'. At least two broad directions for future enquiry emerge; one is to explore the legitimating potential of 'rooted', 'contingent' or 'adjectival' cosmopolitanisms, of which liberal nationalism is but one, well-established example (Vincent 2002, 220). The other is to examine the consequences of rejecting the 'utopian politics of classical nationalism' (Chatterjee 2005, 940), which considers the 'imagined community' to be both a universal and unifying phenomenon. As Margaret Moore (2006, 101) points out, there is little doubt that it 'is no longer possible to create unity in the same way as nineteenth-century nationalists did'. Theorists like Partha Chatterjee argue that the legacy of colonialism is the demystification of capitalist modernity and its universalist ideals, thereby revealing asymmetries, heterogeneity and enduring inequality. Awareness of this means charting an analytical 'course that steers away from global cosmopolitanism on the one hand and ethnic chauvinism on the other' (Chatterjee 2005, 940). Whether this can be achieved using the vocabulary of nation-building and sub-state national-ism, with its inherent exclusionary bias, remains to be seen. Chatterjee, for one, apparently deems it possible to navigate between cosmopolitanism and nationalism in order to create hybrid ideologies. In response to the cosmopolitan challenge, then, 'the nation tries to reappropriate the state from authoritarian and global capitalist forces' (Cheah 2003, 11). That is, nation-builders seek to stop state legitimacy from being eroded by the likes of multinational companies and international organisations encroaching on their authority. At the same time, however, many postcolonial states are dependent on outside capital in the form of foreign direct investment and aid donations, in order to develop their economies and thereby retain popular legitimacy. This is a double bind; the challenge is to channel inter-national links towards supporting nation-building without letting them undermine that very edifice. For much of the postcolonial world, this is the crux of the cosmopolitan challenge.

We are left with a sense of transnational movement, both virtual and actual, that is influenced by myriad factors, from postcolonial legacies to trading tariffs, from internet firewalls to geographic inaccessibility, from worker contracts to warfare. All of these help shape contemporary nationalist ideologies and the various ways in which they permeate the nation-state system. In turn, the demands of sub-state nationalist move-ments must be seen in a new light, for what is the meaning of independence in an interdependent world? This reassessment prompts nationalists to adapt, redefining autonomy to fit in with globalising and regionalising forces. At first sight, then, there seems to be a tension inherent in those nation-states and sub-state movements that embrace global capital and concomitant cultural and technological flows. On the one hand, they look approvingly on cross-border trade and finance, while seeking to limit migration and demanding diplomatic recognition of national boundaries, state sovereignty and principles of non-interference on the other. However, this is hardly contradictory if we do not assume that national borders are necessarily breaking down. Instead, we should take a differentiated approach. The rapid rate of capital, trade and communication flows is not matched by labour mobility (Cheah 2003, 383), for example, but even though migration is less pervasive and flexible, and more uneven than the reach of global capital, it has a disproportionate influence on nation-building. Unsurprisingly, migration is also one of the key areas that border police seek to control.

Far from obviating the need for borders, migration is important in justifying their continued existence, because the movement of people goes to the heart of how communities are constituted and how they imagine themselves. Trading regimes and capital flows may have an impact on national legitimacy, which is what nation-building aims to achieve. Immigration, however, shapes the 'imagined community' of the nation itself, which nation-building cannot do without. Emigrants also make meaning in the national context by blurring the boundaries of national community which nation-states purport to represent. Nation and state are no longer co-extensive when the national diaspora is scattered all over the world, providing a range of headaches for governments. By moving away from methodological nationalism, we can focus on the specifics of why and how borders are becoming more porous in order to show the ways in which this is changing, but not destroying, the nation-state within. In other words, immigration and diaspora can fundamentally alter people's self-understanding as a member of a nation, while other aspects of the cosmopolitan challenge can have a less direct effect on the nation's relationship to the state. In sum, it still matters where you belong, but how you belong now matters just as much. Analysis built on the concept of ideology helps unpick the principle and practice of nationalism's response to the cosmopolitan challenge.

References

Alam, J. (2009) 'Democracy in India and the Quest for Equality', *Community Development Journal* 44:3, 291–304.

Alden, C. (2010) '"A Pariah in Our Midst" – regional organisations and the problematic of western-designated pariah regimes – the cases of SADC/Zimbabwe and ASEAN/Myanmar', Crisis States Research Centre, working paper 73, London School of Economics.

Alter, P. (1985) *Nationalismus* (Frankfurt am Main: Suhrkamp).

Anand, D. (2002) 'A Guide to Little Lhasa in India: the role of symbolic geography of Dharamsala in constituting Tibetan diasporic identity', in, P. C. Klieger (ed.) *Tibet, Self and the Tibetan Diaspora* (Leiden: Boston, Cologne: Brill).

Anderson, B. (1991) *Imagined Communities*, 2nd edn. (London: Verso).

Anderson, B. (1998) *The Spectre of Comparisons* (New York: Verso).

Appadurai, A. (1990) 'Disjuncture and Difference in the Global Cultural Economy', in *Theory, Culture and Society* 7, 295–310.

Appiah, K. A. (1998) 'Cosmopolitan Patriots', in P. Cheah & B. Robbins (eds) *Cosmopolitics* (Minneapolis & London: University of Minnesota Press).

Appiah, K. A. (2006) *Cosmopolitanism* (New York & London: Norton & Co.).

Archibugi, D. (2003) 'Cosmopolitical Democracy', in D. Archibugi & M. Koenig-Archibugi (eds) *Debating Cosmopolitics* (London: Verso).

Ardley, J. (2002) *The Tibetan Independence Movement* (London & New York: Routledge Curzon).

Armakolas, I. (2001) 'Identity and Conflict in Globalizing Times: experiencing the global in areas ravaged by conflict and the case of the Bosnian Serbs', in P. Kennedy & C. Danks (eds) *Globalization and National Identities* (Basingstoke: Palgrave Macmillan).

Armstrong, J. (1982) *Nations before Nationalism* (Chapel Hill: University of North Carolina Press).

Arnold, D. & Han Shih, T. (2010) 'A Fair Model of Globalisation? Labour and global production in Cambodia', *Journal of Contemporary Asia* 40:3, 401–24.

Axtmann, R. (2011) 'Cosmopolitanism and Globality: Kant, Arendt and Beck on the global condition', *German Politics and Society* 29:3, 20–37.

Balasubramaniam, V. (2007) 'A Divided Nation: Malay political dominance, Bumiputera material advancement and national identity in Malaysia', *National Identities* 9:1, 35–48.

Barabantseva, E. (2009) 'Change vs. Order: *Shijie* meets *Tianxia* in China's interactions with the world', *Alternatives* 34, 129–55.

Barabantseva, E. & Sutherland, C. (2011) 'Introduction; Diaspora and Citizenship', *Journal of Nationalism and Ethnic Politics* 17:1, 1–13.

Baubock, R. (1994) *Transnational Citizenship – membership and rights in international migration* (London: Edward Elgar).

BBC News (2010) 'Long Haul for Cambodia's Genocide Court', 25 July 2010, Guy Delauney, http://www.bbc.co.uk/news/world-asia-pacific-10739518. Accessed 26 January 2011.

BBC News (2011a) 'Has Cambodia Become a Country for Sale?' 13 January 2011, Mukul Devichand, http://www.bbc.co.uk/news/world-asia-pacific-12152759. Accessed 26 January 2011.

BBC News (2011b) 'Scottish Election: SNP wins election', 6 May 2001, http://www.bbc.co.uk/news/uk-scotland-13305522. Accessed 12 May 2011.

Bebbington, A. & Batterbury, S. (2001) 'Transnational Livelihoods and Landscapes: political ecologies of globalization', *Ecumene: A Journal of Cultural Geography* 8:4, 369–80.

Bebbington, A. & Kothari, U. (2006) 'Transnational Development Networks', *Environment and Planning* 38, 849–66.

Beck, U. & Sznaider, N. (2010 [2006]) 'Unpacking Cosmopolitanism for the Social Sciences: a research agenda', *British Journal of Sociology* 60, 381–403.

Beeson, M. (2007) *Regionalism and Globalization in East Asia* (Basingstoke: Palgrave Macmillan).

Beeson, M. (2009) 'Introduction', in M. Beeson (ed.) *Contemporary Southeast Asia* (Basingstoke: Palgrave Macmillan).

Berger, M. (2003) 'Decolonisation, Modernisation and Nation-Building: political development theory and the appeal of communism in South-East Asia, 1945–1975', *Journal of Southeast Asian Studies* 34:3, 421–48.

Bhabha, H. (1990a) 'Introduction', in H. Bhabha (ed.) *Nation and Narration* (London: Routledge).

Bhabha, H. (1990b) 'DissemiNation: time, narrative, and the margins of the modern nation', in H. Bhabha (ed.) *Nation and Narration* (London: Routledge).

Bhabha, H. & Comaroff, J. (2002) 'Speaking of Postcoloniality in the Continuous Present: a conversation', in D. Goldberg & A. Quayson (eds) *Relocating Postcolonialism* (Oxford: Blackwell).

Bhatt, C. (2004). 'Democracy and Hindu Nationalism', *Democratization* 11:4, 133–54.

Bhatt, C. & Mukta, P. (2000) 'Hindutva in the West: mapping the antinomies of diaspora nationalism', *Ethnic and Racial Studies* 23:3, 407–41.

Billig, M. (1995) *Banal Nationalism* (London: Sage).

Binnie, J. (2003) 'Locating Transnationalism: agency and method', *Sociology* 37:3, 599–604.

BJP (n.d.) 'BJP History: its birth and early growth', http://www.bjp.org/content/view/432/284/. Accessed 14 November 2009.

Blad, C. and Couton, P. (2009). 'The Rise of an Intercultural Nation: immigration, diversity and nationhood in Quebec', *Journal of Ethnic and Migration Studies* 35:4, 645–67.

Boone, C. (2003). *Political Topographies of the African State* (Cambridge: Cambridge University Press).

Bradley, M. (2000) *Imagining Vietnam and America* (Chapel Hill: University of North Carolina Press).

Brass, P. (1991) *Ethnicity and Nationalism: Theory and Comparison* (New Delhi & London: Sage).

Braveboy-Wagner, J. (2009) *Institutions of the Global South* (London & New York: Routledge).

Brennan, T. (2003) 'Cosmopolitanism and Internationalism', in D. Archibugi & M. Koenig-Archibugi (eds) *Debating Cosmopolitics* (London: Verso).

Breuilly, J. (1993) *Nationalism and the State* (Manchester: Manchester University Press).

Brown, A., McCrone, D. and Paterson, L. (1996) *Politics and Society in Scotland* (Basingstoke: Macmillan).

Brown, D. (1999) 'Are There Good and Bad Nationalisms?', *Nations and Nationalism* 5:2, 281–302.

Brown, D. (2000) *Contemporary Nationalism* (London & New York: Routledge).

Brubaker, R. & Cooper, F. (2000) 'Beyond Identity', *Theory and Society* 29:1, 1–47.

Brun, C. (2008) 'Birds of Freedom: young people, the LTTE, and representations of gender, nationalism, and governance in northern Sri Lanka', *Critical Asian Studies* 40:3, 399–422.

Burke, A. & McDonald, M. (2007) *Critical Security in the Asia-Pacific* (Manchester: Manchester University Press).

Burlet, S. (1999) 'Gender Relations, "Hindu" Nationalism, and NGO Responses in India', *Gender and Development* 7:1, 40–7.

Byman (1998) 'The Logic of Ethnic Terrorism', *Studies in Conflict and Terrorism* 21, 149–69.

Calhoun, C. (2007) *Nations Matter: Culture, History and the Cosmopolitan Dream* (London & New York: Routledge).

Calhoun, C. (2008) 'Cosmopolitanism and Nationalism', *Nations and Nationalism* 14:3, 427–48.

Callahan, W. (2006) *Cultural Governance and Resistance in Pacific-Asia* (London & New York: Routledge).

Canovan, M. (1996) *Nationhood and Political Theory* (Cheltenham: Edward Elgar).

Case, W. (2009) 'Low-Quality Democracy and Varied Authoritarianism: elites and regimes in Southeast Asia today', *The Pacific Review* 22:3, 255–69.

Castles, S. (1999) 'Citizenship and the Other in the Age of Migration', in A. Davidson & K. Weekley (eds) *Globalisation and Citizenship in the Asia-Pacific* (New York: St. Martin's Press).

Castles, S. & Miller, M. (2003) *The Age of Migration* (Basingstoke: Palgrave Macmillan).

Chatterjee, P. (1993) *Nationalist Thought and the Colonial World: a derivative discourse* (Minneapolis: University of Minnesota Press).

Chatterjee, P. (1996) 'Whose Imagined Community?' in G. Balakrishnan (ed.) *Mapping the Nation* (London & New York: Verso).

Chatterjee, P. (2005) 'The Nation in Heterogeneous Time', *Futures* 37, 925–42.

Chazan, N., Lewis, P., Mortimer, R., Rothchild, D. and Stedman, S. (1999) *Politics and Society in Contemporary Africa* (Boulder, CO: Lynne Rienner).

Cheah, P. (2003) *Spectral Nationality* (New York: Columbia University Press).

Chernilo, D. (2006) 'Methodological Nationalism and its Critique', in G. Delanty & K. Kumar (eds) *The Sage Handbook of Nations and Nationalism* (London: Sage).

Chou, C. & Houben, V. (2006) 'Introduction', in C. Chou & V. Houben (eds) *Southeast Asian Studies: debates and new directions* (Singapore: Institute for Southeast Asian Studies).

Chryssochoou, D. (2007) 'Democracy and the European Polity', in M. Cini (ed.) *European Union Politics* (Oxford: Oxford University Press).

Clifford, J. (1997) *Routes: Travel and Translation in the Late Twentieth Century* (Cambridge, MA: Harvard University Press).

Closs Stephens, A. (2010) 'Citizenship without Community: time, design and the city', *Citizenship Studies* 14:1, 31–46.

Cohen, A. (1996) 'Personal Nationalism: A Scottish view of some rites, rights and wrongs', *American Ethnologist* 23:4, 802–15.

Cohen, R. (1997) *Global Diasporas: an introduction* (London: UCL Press).

Connor, W. (1978) 'A Nation is a Nation, is a State, is an Ethnic Group, is a ...', *Ethnic and Racial Studies* 1:4, 377–400.

Connor, W. (1984) *The National Question in Marxist-Leninist Theory and Strategy* (Princeton, NJ: Princeton University Press).

Connor, W. (1994) *Ethnonationalism; the Quest for Understanding* (Princeton, NJ: Princeton University Press).

Cruise O'Brien, D. (1996) 'A Lost Generation? youth identity and state decay in West Africa', in R. Werbner & T. Ranger (eds) *Postcolonial Identities in Africa* (London & New Jersey: Zed).

Dalrymple, W. (2010) 'Author, Author', *Guardian Review*, 19 June, p. 15.

Danks, C. (2001) 'Russia in Search of itself', in P. Kennedy & C. Danks (eds) *Globalization and National Identities* (Basingstoke: Palgrave Macmillan).

Davidson, A. (1999) 'Never the Twain Shall Meet? Europe, Asia and the citizen', in A. Davidson & K. Weekley *Globalisation and Citizenship in the Asia-Pacific* (New York: St. Martin's Press).

Day, G. & Thompson, A. (2004) *Theorizing Nationalism* (Basingstoke: Palgrave Macmillan).

De Boeck, F. (1996) 'Postcolonialism, Power and Identity: local and global perspectives from Zaire', in R. Werbner & T. Ranger (eds) *Postcolonial Identities in Africa* (London & New Jersey: Zed).

Delanty, G. (2006) 'Nationalism and Cosmopolitanism: the paradox of modernity', in G. Delanty & K. Kumar (eds) *The Sage Handbook of Nations and Nationalism* (London: Sage).

Delanty, G. (2009) *The Cosmopolitan Imagination* (Cambridge: Cambridge University Press).

Delanty, G. & Kumar, K. (2006) 'Introduction', in G. Delanty & K. Kumar (eds) *The Sage Handbook of Nations and Nationalism* (London: Sage).

Derges, J. (2009). 'Eloquent Bodies: conflict and ritual in northern Sri Lanka', in *Anthropology & Medicine* 16:1, 27–36.

Derks, A. (2006) 'Khmer women and global factories', in L. Chau-Pech Ollier & T. Winter (eds) *Expressions of Cambodia: the politics of tradition, identity and change* (London: Routledge).

Deutsche Bundesregierung (2008). *Nationaler Integrationsplan: Erster Fortschrittsbericht, Presse- und Informationsamt der Bundesregierung*; Berlin.

Drummond, L. & Thomas, M. (2003) 'Introduction', in L. Drummond & M. Thomas (eds) *Consuming Urban Culture in Contemporary Vietnam* (London & New York: Routledge Curzon).

Duara, P. (2009) *The Global and Regional in China's Nation-Formation* (London & New York: Routledge).

Duiker, W. (1981) *The Communist Road to Power in Vietnam* (Boulder, CO: Westview).

Duncan, C. (ed.) (2004) *Civilizing the Margins: Southeast Asian government policies for the development of minorities* (Ithaca, NY & London: Cornell University Press).

Economist (2010a) 'Lexington: the perils of hero worship', 23 September 2010, p. 64.

Economist (2010b) 'Charlemagne: the treat of treaties', 23 October 2010, p. 48.

Economist (2010c) 'Brussels Beckons: Serbia comes a step closer to EU membership', 28 October 2010, http://www.economist.com/node/17363537?story_id=17363537. Accessed 29 December 2010.

Economist (2011a) 'Banyan: truth and consequences', 30 April 2011, p. 60.

Economist (2011b) 'Independence by Stealth', 12 May 2011, p. 37.

Economist (2011c) 'Charlemagne: another project in trouble', 28 April 2011, http://www.economist.com/node/18618525. Accessed 18 May 2011.

Emirbayer, M. (1997) 'Manifesto for a Relational Sociology', *American Journal of Sociology* 103:2, 281–317.

Endicott, K. & Knox Dentan, R. (2004) 'Into the Mainstream or into the Backwater? Malaysian assimilation of Orang Asli', in C. Duncan (ed.) *Civilizing the Margins* (Ithaca, NY: Cornell University Press).

Englund, H. (1996) 'Between God and Kamuzu: the transition to multi-party politics in central Malawi', in R. Werbner & T. Ranger (eds) *Postcolonial Identities in Africa* (London: Zed).

Etzioni, A. (2007) 'Citizenship Tests: a comparative, communitarian perspective', *Political Quarterly* 78:3, 353–63.

Evans, G. (1998) 'Ethnic Schism and the Consolidation of Post-Communist Democracies: the case of Estonia', *Communist and Post-Communist Studies* 31:1, 57–74.

Ewing, W. (1969) *Scotland v. Whitehall; Winifred Ewing's black book* (Edinburgh: Scottish National Party).

Ferguson, J. & Gupta, A. (2002) 'Spatializing States: toward an ethnography of neoliberal governmentality', *American Ethnologist* 29:4, 981–1002.

Flynn, M. (2000) *Ideology, Mobilization and the Nation* (London: Macmillan).

Forrest, J. (2004) *Subnationalism in Africa: ethnicity, alliances and politics* (Boulder, CO: Lynne Rienner).

Fox, J. & Miller-Idriss, C. (2008) 'Everyday Nationhood', *Ethnicities* 8, 536–63.

Frechette, A. (2007) 'Democracy and Democratization among Tibetans in Exile', *The Journal of Asian Studies* 66:1, 97–127.

Freeden, M. (1998) 'Is Nationalism a Distinct Ideology?' *Political Studies* 46:4, 748–65.

Freeden, M. (2000) 'Practising Ideology and Ideological Practices', *Political Studies* 48:2, 302–22.

Fukuyama, F. (1992) *The End of History and the Last Man* (Harmondsworth: Penguin).

Gainsborough, M. (2007) 'Globalisation and the State Revisited: a view from provincial Vietnam', *Journal of Contemporary Asia* 37:1, 1–18.

Gainsborough, M. (ed.) (2009) *On the Borders of State Power* (Abingdon & New York: Routledge).

Gallie, W. (1962) 'Essentially Contested Concepts', in M. Black (ed.) *The Importance of Language* (Englewood Cliffs: Prentice-Hall).

Gamble, A. (2007) 'Regional Blocs, World Order and the New Medievalism', in M. Telò (ed.) *European Union and the New Regionalism* (Aldershot: Ashgate).

Ganguly, R (2004) 'Sri Lanka's Ethnic Conflict: at a crossroad between peace and war', *Third World Quarterly* 25:5, 903–18.

García Canclini, N. (2001) *Consumers and Citizens* (Minneapolis: University of Minnesota Press).

Gasper, D. (2006) 'Cosmopolitan Presumptions? On Martha Nussbaum and her critics', *Development and Change* 37:6, 1227–46.

Gellner, E. (1964) *Thought and Change* (London: Weidenfeld & Nicholson).

Gellner, E. (1983) *Nations and Nationalism* (Oxford: Blackwell).

Gellner, E. (1994) *Encounters with Nationalism* (Oxford: Blackwell).

Gellner, E. (1996) 'Do Nations have Navels?' *Nations and Nationalism* 2:3, 366–70.

Ghosh, D. (2004) 'Re-Crossing a Different Water: colonialism and Third Worldism in Fiji', *Third World Quarterly* 25:1, 111–30.

Giesen, B. (2001) 'National Identity and Citizenship: the cases of Germany and France', in G. Eder & B. Giesen (eds) *European Citizenship* (Oxford: Oxford University Press).

Gilberg, T. (2000) '"Yugoslav" Nationalism at the End of the Twentieth Century', in L. Suryadinata (ed.) *Nationalism and Globalization: east and west* (Singapore: Institute for Southeast Asian Studies).

Glick-Schiller, N. (2010) 'Old Baggage and Missing Luggage: a commentary on Beck and Sznaider's "Unpacking cosmopolitanism for the social sciences: a research agenda"', *British Journal of Sociology* 60, 413–20.

Goscha, C. (1995) *Vietnam or Indochina? contesting concepts of space in Vietnamese nationalism 1887–1954* (Copenhagen: Nordic Institute of Asian Studies).

Gould, R. (2000) 'Integration, Solidarität and the Discourses of National Identity in the 1998 Bundestag Election Manifestos', *German Life and Letters* 53:4, 529–51.

Gowan, P. (2003) 'The New Liberal Cosmopolitan', in D. Archibugi & M. Koenig-Archibugi (eds) *Debating Cosmopolitics* (London: Verso).

Green, S. (2004) *The Politics of Exclusion: institutions and immigration policy in contemporary Germany* (Manchester: Manchester University Press).

Greenfeld, L. (1993) *Nationalism: five roads to modernity* (Cambridge, Mass. & London: Harvard University Press).

Gregory, D. (2004) *The Colonial Present* (Oxford: Blackwell).

Guardian (2010a) 'Alex Salmond Postpones Plans for Scottish Independence Referendum', Severin Carrell, *Guardian Online*, Monday, 6 September 2010, http://www.guardian.co.uk/politics/2010/sep/06/salmond-postpones-scottish-independence-referendum?INTCMP=SRCH. Accessed 1 January 2011.

Guardian (2010b) 'Angela Merkel: German multiculturalism has "utterly failed"', 17 October, http://www.guardian.co.uk/world/2010/oct/17/angela-merkel-german-multiculturalism-failed. Accessed 22 November 2010.

Guardian (2010c) 'Ivory Coast Leader Accuses Rival of Plotting Coup as Civil War Looms', 2 January, http://www.guardian.co.uk/world/2011/jan/02/ivory-coast-civil-war-fears. Accessed 2 January 2011.

Guibernau, M. (1996) *Nationalisms* (Cambridge: Polity).

Guibernau, M. (1999) *Nations without States: political communities in a global age* (Cambridge: Polity).

Guibernau, M. (2001) 'Globalization and the Nation-State', in M. Guibernau & J. Hutchinson (eds) *Understanding Nationalism* (Cambridge: Blackwell).

Guibernau, M. (2004) 'Anthony D. Smith on Nations and National Identity: a critical assessment', *Nations and Nationalism* 10:1/2, 125–41.

Guibernau, M. (2007) *The Identity of Nations* (Cambridge & Malden, MA: Polity).

Gunlicks, A. (2007) 'German Federalism Reform: part 1' *German Law Journal* 8:1, 111–32.

Habermas, J. (2003) 'On Law and Disagreement: some comments on "interpretative pluralism"', *Ratio Juris* 16:2, 187–94.

Hall, S. (1997) 'Old and New Identities, Old and New Ethnicities', in A. King (ed.) *Culture, Globalization and the World-System* (Minneapolis & London: University of Minnesota Press).

Hardy, A. (2003) *Red Hills: migrants and the state in the highlands of Vietnam* (Copenhagen: Nordic Institute of Asian Studies Press).

Harvey, D. (2009) *Cosmopolitanism and the Geographies of Freedom* (New York & Chichester: Columbia University Press).

Hassall, G. (1999) 'Citizenship in the Asia-Pacific: a survey of contemporary issues', in A. Davidson & K. Weekley (eds) *Globalisation and Citizenship in the Asia-Pacific* (New York: St. Martin's Press).

Hay, C. & Rosamond, B. (2002) 'Globalization, European integration and the Discursive Construction of Economic Imperatives', *Journal of European Public Policy* 9:2, 147–67.

Hearn, J. (2006) *Rethinking Nationalism; a critical introduction* (Basingstoke: Palgrave Macmillan).

Held, D. (1995) *Democracy and the Global Order: from the modern state to cosmopolitan governance* (Cambridge: Polity).

Held, D. (2010) 'Cosmopolitanism after 9/11', *International Politics* 47:1, 52–61.

Hepburn, E. (2008) 'The Neglected Nation: The CSU and the territorial cleavage in Bavarian party politics', *German Politics* 17:2, 184–202.

Hepburn, E. (2009) 'Regionalist Party Mobilisation on Immigration', *West European Politics* 32:3, 514–35.

High, H. (2009) 'Dreaming beyond Borders: the Thai/Lao borderlands and the mobility of the marginal', in M. Gainsborough (ed.) *On the Borders of State Power* (Abingdon & New York: Routledge).

Hirschman, A. (1970) *Exit, Voice and Loyalty: responses to decline in firms, organisations and states* (Cambridge, MA & London: Harvard University Press).

Hirst, P. & Thompson, G. (1999) *Globalisation in Question: the international economy and the possibilities of governance*, 2nd edn (Cambridge: Polity).

Hobsbawm, E. & Ranger, T. (eds) (1983) *The Invention of Tradition* (Cambridge: Cambridge University Press).

Hodson, J. (2000) 'Globalization and Nationalism in the United States', in L. Suryadinata (ed.) *Nationalism and Globalization: east and west* (Singapore: Institute for Southeast Asian Studies).

Holmes Cooper, A. (2002) 'Party-Sponsored Protest and the Movement Society: the CDU/CSU mobilises against citizenship law reform', *German Politics* 11:2, 88–104.

Houben, V. (2006) 'Southeast Asian history: the search for new perspectives', in C. Chou & V. Houben (eds) *Southeast Asian Studies: debates and new directions* (Singapore: Institute for Southeast Asian Studies).

Houston, S. and Wright, R. (2003) 'Making and Remaking Tibetan Diasporic Identities', *Social & Cultural Geography* 4:2, 217–32.

Hroch, M. (1985) *Social Preconditions of National Revival in Europe* (Cambridge: Cambridge University Press).

Hurrell, A (1995) 'Regionalism in Theoretical Perspective', in L. Fawcett & A. Hurrell (eds) *Regionalism in World Politics* (Oxford: Oxford University Press).

Hutchinson, J. (1994) *Modern Nationalism* (London: Fontana).

Hutchinson, J. & Smith, A. D. (eds) (1996) *Ethnicity* (Oxford: Oxford University Press).

Huynh K. K. (1982) *Vietnamese Communism 1925–45* (Ithaca, NY: Cornell University Press).

Hylland Eriksen, T. (1999) 'A Non-Ethnic State for Africa', in P. Yeros (ed.) *Ethnicity and Nationalism in Africa* (Basingstoke: Macmillan).

Ichijo, A. & Uzelac, G. (2005) 'Introduction', in A. Ichijo & G. Uzelac (eds) *When is the Nation?* (Abingdon & New York: Routledge).

Jackson, P. A. (2003) 'Space, Theory, and Hegemony: the dual crises of Asian area studies and cultural studies', *SOJOURN: Journal of Social Issues in Southeast Asia* 18:1, 1–41.

James, P. (1996) *The Politics of Bavaria* (Aldershot: Avebury).

Jary, D. (1999) 'Citizenship and Human Rights – particular and universal worlds and the prospects for European citizenship', in D. Smith &

S. Wright (eds) *Whose Europe? the turn towards democracy* (Oxford: Blackwell).

Jazeel, T. (2009) 'Reading the Geography of Sri Lankan Island-ness: colonial repetitions, postcolonial possibilities', *Contemporary South Asia* 17:4, 399–414.

Jellema, K. (2007) 'Returning Home: ancestor veneration and the nationalism of doi moi Vietnam', in P. Taylor (ed.) *Modernity and Re-enchantment: religion in post-revolutionary Vietnam* (Singapore: Institute of Southeast Asian Studies).

Jenkins, B. & Sofos, S. (1996) *Nation and Identity in Contemporary Europe* (London & New York: Routledge).

Kahn, J. (1998) 'Introduction', in J. Kahn (ed.) *Southeast Asian Identities* (London: Tauris & Co).

Kaiser, R. & Nikiforova, E. (2006) 'Borderland Spaces of Identification and Dis/location: multiscalar narratives and enactments of Seto identity and place in the Estonian-Russian borderlands', *Ethnic and Racial Studies* 29:5, 928–58.

Kaldor, M. (2004) 'Nationalism and Globalisation', *Nations and Nationalism* 10:1/2, 161–77.

Kasian, T. (1997) 'The *Lookjin* Middle Class and Thai Official Nationalism', in A. Reid & D. Chirot (eds) *Essential Outsiders* (Seattle and London: University of Washington Press).

Keating, M. (2001) *Nations against the State: the new politics of nationalism in Quebec, Catalonia and Scotland*, 2nd edn (Basingstoke: Palgrave Macmillan).

Kedourie, E. (1966) *Nationalism* (London: Hutchinson).

Kellas, J. (1991) *The Politics of Nationalism and Ethnicity* (Basingstoke: Macmillan).

Kelly, J. (1998) 'Time and the Global: against the homogeneous, empty communities in contemporary social theory', *Development and Change* 29, 839–71.

Kelly, J. D. & Kaplan, M. (2001) *Represented Communities: Fiji and world decolonization* (Chicago, IL: University of Chicago Press).

Kennedy, P. (2001) 'Introduction', in P. Kennedy & C. Danks (eds) *Globalization and National Identities* (Basingstoke: Palgrave Macmillan).

Kennedy, P. & Roudometov, V. (2003) *Communities across Borders: new immigrants and transnational cultures* (London & New York: Routledge).

Kerkvliet, B., Heng, R. & Koh, D. (eds) (2003) *Getting Organised in Vietnam: moving in and around the socialist state* (Singapore: Institute of South East Asian Studies).

King, D. (2005) *The Liberty of Strangers* (Oxford: Oxford University Press).

King, V. (2008) *The Sociology of Southeast Asia* (Copenhagen: Nordic Institute of Asian Studies).

Kleinfeld, M. (2003) 'Strategic Troping in Sri Lanka: September eleventh and the consolidation of political position', *Geopolitics* 8:3, 105–26.

Klieger, P. C. (2002) 'Introduction', in P. C. Klieger (ed.) *Tibet, Self and the Tibetan Diaspora* (Boston, Cologne & Leiden: Brill).

Klopp, B. (2002) *German Multiculturalism: immigrant integration and the transformation of citizenship* (Westport, Conn.: Praeger).

Kohn, H. (1961) *American Nationalism: an interpretive essay* (New York: Collier).

Kolakowski, L. (1980) 'Why an Ideology is always Right' in M. Cranston & P. Mair (eds) *Ideology and Politics* (Alphen aan den Rijn: Sijthoff).

Kostakopoulou, D. (2006) 'Thick, Thin and Thinner Patriotisms: is this all there is?' *Oxford Journal of Legal Studies* 26:1, 73–106.

Kostakopoulou, D. (2008) *The Future Governance of Citizenship* (Cambridge: Cambridge University Press).

Kothari, U. (2006) 'Spatial Imaginaries and Practices: experiences of colonial officers and development professionals', *Singapore Journal of Tropical Geography* 27:3, 235–53.

Kruse, I., Orren, H. & Angenendt, S. (2003) 'The Failure of Immigration Reform in Germany', *German Politics* 12:3, 129–45.

Laclau, E. & Mouffe, C. (1985) *Hegemony and Socialist Strategy* (London: Verso).

Laitin, D. (1998) *Identity in Formation: the Russian-speaking populations in the near abroad* (Ithaca, NY: Cornell University Press).

Lal, B. (2007) '"Anxiety, Uncertainty, and Fear in Our Land": Fiji's road to military coup, 2006', http://www.fijilive.com/archive/showpdf. php?pdf=2007/06/Dr_Brij_Lal.pdf. Accessed 31 December 2010.

Laqueur, W. (2003) *No End to War; terrorism in the twenty-first century* (New York: Continuum).

Larson, E. & Aminzade, R. (2008) 'Nation-Building in Post-Colonial Nation-States: the cases of Tanzania and Fiji', *International Social Science Journal* 59:192, 169–82.

Latham, R., Callaghy, T. & Kassimir, R. (eds) (2001) *Intervention and Transnationalism in Africa* (Cambridge: Cambridge University Press).

Lawrence, P. (2005) *Nationalism: History and Theory* (Pearson: Harlow).

Lawson, S. (1996) *Tradition versus Democracy in the South Pacific* (Cambridge: Cambridge University Press).

Lawson, S. (2004) 'Nationalism versus Constitutionalism in Fiji', *Nations and Nationalism* 10:4, 519–38.

Leonard, P. (2005) *Nationality between Poststructuralism and Postcolonial Theory* (Basingstoke: Palgrave Macmillan).

Levy, R. (1986) 'The Search for a Rational Strategy: the Scottish National Party and devolution 1974–79', *Political Studies* 34:2, 236–48.

Levy, R. (1995) 'Finding a Place in the World Economy. Party strategy and party vote; the regionalisation of SNP and Plaid Cymru support 1979–92', *Political Geography* 14:3, 295–308.

Li, B. & Wu, Y. (1999) 'The Concept of Citizenship in the People's Republic of China', in A. Davidson & K. Weekley (eds) *Globalisation and Citizenship in the Asia-Pacific* (New York: St. Martin's Press).

Li, T. (1998) *Nguyễn Cochinchina* (Ithaca, NY: Cornell University Press).

Lieberman, V. (2003) *Strange Parallels: Southeast Asia in global context c. 800–1830* (Cambridge: Cambridge University Press).

Lieven, A. (2004) *America Right or Wrong* (London: Harper Collins).

Llobera, J. (1994) *The God of Modernity* (Oxford: Berg).

LMU (2008) 'Landtagswahl Bayern 2008: Ein politisches Erdbeben und seineUrsachen',Ludwig-Maximilians-Universität,Munich.http://www.landtagswahl-bayern.uni-muenchen.de/cms/index.php?page=ein-politisches-erdbeben-und-seine-ursachen. Accessed 21 October 2009.

Loomba, A. (1998) *Colonialism/Postcolonialism* (London & New York: Routledge).

Loughran, T. (2007) *The Republic in Print: print culture in the age of U.S. nation building* (New York & Chichester: Columbia University Press).

Lynch, P. (1996) *Minority Nationalism and European Integration* (Cardiff: University of Wales Press).

Lynch, P. (2001) *Scottish Government and Politics* (Edinburgh: Edinburgh University Press).

MacLean, K. (2008) 'The Rehabilitation of an Uncomfortable Past: everyday life in Vietnam during the subsidy period (1975–1986)', *History and Anthropology* 19:3, 281–303.

Magnusson, J. (2002) 'A Myth of Tibet: reverse orientalism and soft power', in P. C. Klieger (ed.) *Tibet, Self and the Tibetan Diaspora* (Boston, Cologne & Leiden: Brill).

Mahathir, M. & Ishihara, S. (1995) *The Voice of Asia* (Tokyo, New York & London: Kodansha International).

Makinda, S & Okumu, F. (2008) *The African Union* (London & New York: Routledge).

Malešević, S. (2006) *Identity as Ideology* (Basingstoke: Palgrave Macmillan).

Mann, M. (1993) *The Sources of Social Power: the rise of classes and nation states, 1760–1914* (Cambridge: Cambridge University Press).

Mann, M. (2001) 'Explaining Murderous Ethnic Cleansing: the macro-level', in M. Guibernau & J. Hutchinson (eds) *Understanding Nationalism* (Cambridge: Blackwell).

Marinelli, M. (2009) 'Making Concessions in Tianjin: Heterotopia and Italian colonialism in Mainland China (1860–1945)', *Urban History* 36:3, 399–425.

Marinetto, M. (2003) 'Who Wants to be an Active Citizen?' *Sociology* 37:1, 103–20.

Markakis, J. (1999) 'Nationalism and Ethnicity in the Horn of Africa', in P. Yeros (ed.) *Ethnicity and Nationalism in Africa* (Basingstoke: Macmillan).

Marr, D. (1971) *Vietnamese Anticolonialism 1885–1925* (Berkeley: University of California Press).

Marr, D. (1981) *Vietnamese Tradition on Trial 1920–1945* (Berkeley: University of California Press).

Marshall, T. H. (2006 [1950]) 'Citizenship and Social Class', in C. Pierson & F. Castles (eds) *The Welfare State Reader* (Cambridge & Malden, MA: Polity).

McCrone, D. (1998) *The Sociology of Nationalism* (London: Routledge).

McHale, S. (2004) *Print and Power : Confucianism, communism, and Buddhism in the making of modern Vietnam* (Honolulu: University of Hawai'i Press).

McKenna, G. (2007) *The Puritan Origins of American Patriotism* (New Haven: Yale University Press).

McMillan, A. (2008) 'Deviant Democratization in India', *Democratization* 15:4, 733–49.

Millar, D. (1995) *On Nationality* (Oxford: Oxford University Press).

Milward, A. (1994) *The European Rescue of the Nation State* (London: Routledge).

Minogue, K. (1967) *Nationalism* (London: Methuen).

Mintzel, A. (1995) '*Bayern und die CSU – Regionale politische Traditionen und Aufstieg zur dominierenden Kraft*', in B. Haneke and R. Höpfinger (eds) *Gechichte einer Volkspartei – 50 Jahre CSU* (München: Hanns-Seidel-Stiftung).

Mintzel, A. (1999) *Die CSU-Hegemonie in Bayern* (Passau: Rothe).

Miščević, N. (2001) *Nationalism and Beyond* (Budapest: Central European University).

Modood, T. (2007) *Multiculturalism* (Cambridge & Malden, MA: Polity).

Mohapatra, B. (2002) 'Democratic Citizenship and Minority Rights', in C. Kinnvall & K. Jönsson (eds) *Globalization and Democratization in Asia* (Abingdon: Routledge).

Moore, M. (2006) 'Nationalism and Political Philosophy', in G. Delanty & K. Kumar (eds) *The Sage Handbook of Nations and Nationalism* (London: Sage).

Mukta, P. (2000) 'The Public Face of Hindu Nationalism', *Ethnic and Racial Studies* 23:3, 442–66.

Nadarajah, S. and Sriskandarajah, D. (2005) 'Liberation Struggle or Terrorism? the politics of naming the LTTE', *Third World Quarterly* 26:1, 87–100.

Nadkarni, M. (2003) 'The Death of Socialism and the Afterlife of its Monuments', in K. Hodgkin & S. Radstone (eds) *Contested Pasts: the politics of memory* (London & New York: Routledge).

Nairn, T. (1981) *The Break-up of Britain* (London: Verso).

Narine, S. (2004) 'State Sovereignty, Political Legitimacy and Regional Institutionalism in the Asia-Pacific', *The Pacific Review* 17:3, 423–50.

Neuliep, J. (2003) *Intercultural Communication: a contextual approach* (New York: Houghton Mifflin).

Newman, S. (1996) *Ethnoregional Conflict in Democracies* (Westport & London: Greenwood).

Ninh, K. (2002) *A World Transformed: the politics of culture in revolutionary Vietnam 1945–65* (Ann Arbor: University of Michigan Press).

Nordstrom, C. (2001) 'Out of the Shadows', in T. Callaghy, R. Kassimir & R. Latham (eds) *Intervention and Transnationalism in Africa* (Cambridge: Cambridge University Press).

Norindr, P. (2006) 'The Fascination for Angkor Wat and the Ideology of the Visible', in L. Chau-Pech Ollier & T. Winter (eds) *Expressions of Cambodia: the politics of tradition, identity and change* (London: Routledge).

Norval, A. (2000) 'The Things We Do with Words: contemporary approaches to the analysis of ideology', *British Journal of Political Science* 30:2, 313–46.

Nothnagle, A. (1993) 'From Buchenwald to Bismarck: historical myth-building in the German democratic republic, 1945–1989', *Central European History* 26:1, 91–113.

Nussbaum, M. (1996) 'Patriotism and Cosmopolitanism', in J. Cohen (ed.) *For Love of Country: debating the limits of patriotism* (Boston: Beacon Press).

Ohmae, K. (1996) *The End of the Nation-State* (New York: Free Press).

O'Leary, B. (1996) 'On the Nature of Nationalism: an appraisal of Ernest Gellner's writings on nationalism', in J. Hall & I. Jarvie (eds) *The Social Philosophy of Ernest Gellner* (Amsterdam: Rodopi).

Olukoshi, A. & Laakso, L. (1996) 'Introduction', in A. Olukoshi & L. Laakso (eds) *Challenges to the Nation-State in Africa* (Uppsala: Nordiska Afrikainstitutet).

Ong, A. (1999) *Flexible Citizenship* (Durham NC & London: Duke University Press).

Oommen, T. K. (1997) 'Introduction', in T. K. Oommen (ed.) *Citizenship and National Identity* (New Delhi: Sage; London: Thousand Oaks).

Özkirimli, U. (2000) *Theories of Nationalism* (London: Macmillan).

Özkirimli, U. (2005) *Contemporary Debates on Nationalism* (London: Macmillan).

Pääbo, H. (2008) 'War of Memories: explaining "memorials war" in Estonia', *Baltic Security and Defence Review* 10, 5–28.

Painter, M. (2005) 'The Politics of State Sector Reforms in Vietnam: contested agendas and uncertain trajectories', *Journal of Development Studies* 41:2, 261–83.

Palmujoki, E. (2001) *Regionalism and Globalism in South-East Asia* (Basingstoke: Palgrave Macmillan).

Parekh, B. (2002) *Rethinking Multiculturalism* (Basingstoke: Palgrave Macmillan).

Paterson, L. (1994) *The Autonomy of Modern Scotland* (Edinburgh: Edinburgh University Press).

Paterson, L., Brown, A., Curtice, J., Hinds, K., McCrone, D., Park, A., Sproston, K. & Surridge, P. (2001) *New Scotland, New Politics?* (Edinburgh: Polygon).

Pattie, C., Seyd, P. & Whitely, P. (2003) 'Citizenship and Civic Engagement: attitudes and behaviour in Britain', *Political Studies* 51, 443–68.

Pelley, P. (2002) *Postcolonial Vietnam: visions of the present and past* (Durham: Duke University Press).

Pettai, V. & Hallik, K. (2002) 'Understanding Processes of Ethnic Control: segmentation, dependency and co-optation in post-communist Estonia', *Nations and Nationalism* 8:4, 505–29.

Pettai, V. & Molder, M. (2009) 'Estonia', in *Nations in Transit 2009*, http://www.freedomhouse.org/uploads/nit/2009/Estonia-final.pdf. Accessed 18 July 2011.

Piller, I. (2001) 'Naturalization Language Testing and its Basis in Ideologies of National Identity and Citizenship', *International Journal of Bilingualism* 5:3, 259–77.

Poethig, K. (2006) 'Sitting between Two Chairs: Cambodia's dual citizenship debate', in L. Chau-Pech Ollier & T. Winter (eds) *Expressions of Cambodia: the politics of tradition, identity and change* (London: Routledge).

Porter, H. (2011) 'Can We Ever Condone the Notion of State-Sponsored Assassination?', T*he Observer*, 8 May 2011, http://www.guardian.co.uk/commentisfree/2011/may/08/osama-bin-laden-death-morality. Accessed 9 May 2011.

Prasad, A. (2008) 'Moving Beyond "Ethnic" Conflict in Fiji: from colonization to the coup of 2006', *International Journal of Social Economics* 35:12, 951–62.

Puri, S. (2004) *The Caribbean Postcolonial* (Basingstoke: Palgrave Macmillan).

PuruShotam, N. (1998) 'Disciplining Difference: "race" in Singapore', in J. Kahn (ed.) *Southeast Asian Identities* (London: Tauris & Co.).

Ramachandran, S. (1999) 'Of Boundaries and Border Crossings', *Interventions* 1:2, 235–53.

Raphael, R. (2006) *Founding Myths: stories that hide our patriotic past* (New York: New Press).

Ray, A. (2002) 'Globalization and Democratic Governance: the Indian experience', in C. Kinnvall & K. Jönsson (eds) *Globalization and Democratization in Asia* (Abingdon: Routledge).

Reicher, S. & Hopkins, N. (2001) *Self and Nation* (London: Sage).

Reid, A. (1988) *Southeast Asia in the Age of Commerce 1450–1680* (London & New Haven: Yale University Press).

Reid, A. (1997) 'Entrepreneurial Minorities, Nationalism and the State', in A. Reid & D. Chirot (eds) *Essential Outsiders* (Seattle & London: University of Washington Press).

Reid, A. (2004) 'Studying Southeast Asia in a Globalised World', *Taiwan Journal of Southeast Asian Studies* 1:2, 3–18.

Renan, E. (1994 [1882]) 'Qu'est-ce qu'une nation?' in J. Hutchinson & A. D. Smith (eds) *Nationalism: a reader* (Oxford: Oxford University Press).

Robbins, B. (1998) 'Introduction Part I: actually existing cosmopolitanism' in P. Cheah & B. Robbins *Cosmopolitics* (Minneapolis & London: University of Minnesota Press).

Robertson, R. & Sutherland, W. (2001) *Government by the Gun; the unfinished business of Fiji's 2001 coup* (Annandale, NSW: Pluto).

Robinson, F. (1994) 'Islam and Nationalism', in J. Hutchinson & A. D. Smith (eds) *Nationalism* (Oxford: Oxford University Press).

Rodan, G. & Jayasuriya, K. (2007) 'The Technocratic Politics of Administrative Participation: case studies of Singapore and Vietnam', *Democratization* 14:5, 795–815.

Rosaldo, R. (2003) 'Introduction: the borders of belonging' in R. Rosaldo (ed.) *Cultural Citizenship in Island Southeast Asia: nation and belonging in the hinterlands* (Berkeley: University of California Press).

Roy, S. (2001) 'Nation and Institution: commemorating the fiftieth anniversary of Indian independence', *Interventions* 3:2, 251–65.

Sarkar, S. (2005) 'Inclusive Democracy and its Enemies', *Interventions* 7:3, 304–9.

Sautman, B. (2006) 'Colonialism, Genocide, and Tibet', *Asian Ethnicity* 7:3, 243–65.

Schlemmer, T. (1999) '*Die aufsässige Schwester: Forschungen und Quellen zur Geschichte der Christlich-Sozialen Union 1945–1976*', in Konrad-Adenauer-Stiftung (ed.) *Historisch-politische Mitteilungen* (Cologne: Konrad-Adenauer-Stiftung).

Schwarzmantel, J. (2003) *Citizenship and Identity* (London & New York: Routledge).

Schwenkel, C. (2008) 'Exhibiting War, Reconciling Pasts: photographic representation and transnational commemoration in contemporary Vietnam', *Journal of Vietnamese Studies* 3:1, 36–77.

Scott, J. (2001) 'You and Me Against the World': Christian fundamentalists and white poverty in the USA', in P. Kennedy & C. Danks (eds) *Globalization and National Identities* (Basingstoke: Palgrave Macmillan).

Scott, J. (2009) *The Art of Not being Governed* (London & New Haven: Yale University Press).

Shain, Y. (2005) *The Frontier of Loyalty* (Ann Arbor: University of Michigan Press).

Shatkin, G. (1998) 'Fourth World Cities in the Global Economy: the case of Phnom Penh, Cambodia', *International Journal of Urban and Regional Research* 22:3, 378–93.

Shiladitya Bose, P. (2008) 'Home and Away: diasporas, developments and displacements in a globalising world', *Journal of Intercultural Studies* 29:1, 111–31.

Sillars, J. (1986) *Scotland; the case for optimism* (Edinburgh: Polygon).

Smith, A. D. (1981) *The Ethnic Revival* (Cambridge: Cambridge University Press).

Smith, A. D. (1986) *The Ethnic Origins of Nations* (Oxford: Blackwell).

Smith, A. D. (1991) *National Identity* (London: Penguin).

Smith, A. D. (1995) *Nations and Nationalism in a Global Era* (Cambridge: Polity & Blackwell).

Smith, A. D. (1996) 'Nations and their Pasts', *Nations and Nationalism* 2:3, 358–65.

Smith, A. D. (2002) 'When is a Nation?', *Geopolitics* 7:2, 5–32.

Smith, A. D. (2004) 'History and National Destiny: responses and clarifications', *Nations and Nationalism* 10:1/2, 195–209.

Smith, A. D. (2005) 'The Genealogy of Nations', in A. Ichijo & G. Uzelac (eds) *When is the Nation?* (Abingdon & New York: Routledge).

Smith, A. M. (1998) *Laclau and Mouffe: the radical democratic imaginary* (London: Routledge).

SNP (2008) 'New Immigration Rules Announced', Scottish National Party Website, 5/6/08, http://www.snp.org/node/13782. Accessed 30 September 2010.

SNP (2010) 'Immigration Cap "Doesn't Fit", says SNP MP', Scottish National Party Website, 28/6/10, http://www.snp.org/node/17126. Accessed 30 September 2010.

SNP (2011) *SNP Manifesto 2011* (Edinburgh: Scottish National Party).

Söderbaum, F. (2007) 'African Regionalism and EU-African Inter-regionalism', in M. Telò (ed.) *European Union and New Regionalism* (Ashgate: Farnham).

Sørensen, N. & Olwig, K. (2002) *Work and Migration: life and livelihoods in a globalizing world* (London: Routledge).

Soucy, A. (2003) 'Pilgrims and Pleasure Seekers', in L. Drummond & M. Thomas (eds) *Consuming Urban Culture in Contemporary Vietnam* (London & New York: Routledge Curzon).

Soysal, Y. (1994) *Limits of Citizenship: migrants and postnational membership in Europe* (Chicago & London: University of Chicago Press).

Soysal, Y. (2010) 'Unpacking Cosmopolitanism: an insider-outsider's reading', *British Journal of Sociology* 60, 405–11.

Spencer, P. & Wollman, H. (2002) *Nationalism; a critical introduction* (London: Sage).

Spivak, G. (2008) *Other Asias* (London: Blackwell).

Sridharan, K. (2000) 'Grasping the Nettle; Indian nationalism and globalization', in L. Suryadinata (ed.) *Nationalism and Globalization: east and west* (Singapore: Institute for Southeast Asian Studies).

Stalin, J. (1994 [1913]) 'Marxism and the National Question', in J. Hutchinson & A. D. Smith (eds) *Nationalism* (Oxford & New York: Oxford University Press).

Steen, A. (2010) 'National Elites and the Russian Minority Issue. Does EU-NATO integration matter?', *Journal of European Integration* 32:2, pp. 193–212.

Steger, M. (2005) *Globalism*, 2nd edn (Lanham: Rowman & Littlefield).

Stewart Leith, M. (2008) 'Scottish National Party Representations of Scottishness and Scotland', *Politics* 28:2, 83–92.

Stokke, K. (2006) 'Building the Tamil Eelam State: emerging state institutions and forms of governance in LTTE-controlled areas in Sri Lanka', *Third World Quarterly* 27:6, 1021–40.

Stoler, A (1997) 'Sexual Affronts and Racial Frontiers: European identities and the cultural politics of exclusion in colonial Southeast Asia', in F. Cooper & A. Stoler (eds) *Tensions of Empire: colonial cultures in a bourgeois world* (Berkeley & Los Angeles: University of California Press).

Stratton, J. & Ang, I. (1994) 'Critical Multiculturalism', *Continuum* 8:2, http://www.mcc.murdoch.edu.au/ReadingRoom/8.2/Stratton.html. Accessed 23 February 2011.

Süddeutsche Zeitung (2008) '*Der Nimbus ist Weg*', Interview with Prof. Alf Mintzel, 28/9/08, http://www.sueddeutsche.de/bayern/136/312053/text. Accessed 21 October 2009.

Sutherland, C. (2001) 'Nation, Heimat, Vaterland; the reinvention of concepts by the Bavarian CSU', *German Politics* 10:3, 13–36.

Sutherland, C. (2005a) 'Nation-Building through Discourse Theory', *Nations and Nationalism* 11:2, 185–202.

Sutherland, C. (2005b) 'Another Nation-Building Bloc? Integrating nationalist ideology into the EU and ASEAN', *Asia-Europe Journal* 3:2, 1–17.

Sutherland, C. (2006) 'ASEAN Discourse: the rhetoric of human rights and Asian values', *Borderlands* 5:2, no page.

Sutherland, C. (2009) 'Reconciling Nation and Region: Vietnamese nation building and ASEAN regionalism', *Political Studies* 57:2, 316–36.

Sutherland, C. (2010) *Soldered States: nation-building in Germany and Vietnam* (Manchester: Manchester University Press).

Sutherland, C. (2011) 'Introduction: nation-building in China and Vietnam', *East Asia: an international quarterly* 28:4, 1–13.

Szporluk, R. (1988) *Communism and Nationalism* (Oxford, Toronto & New York: Oxford University Press).

Tai, H.-T. (1992) *Radicalism and the Origins of the Vietnamese Revolution* (Cambridge, MA: Harvard University Press).

Tamir, Y. (1993) *Liberal Nationalism* (Princeton & Chichester: Princeton University Press).

Taylor, B & Botea, R. (2008) 'Tilly Tally: war-making and state-making in the contemporary third world', *International Studies Review* 10:1, 27–56.

Taylor, K. (1998) 'Surface Orientations in Vietnam: beyond histories of nation and region', *Journal of Asian Studies* 57:4, 949–78.

Thomas, B. (2007): *Civic Myths; a law-and-literature approach to citizenship* (Chapel Hill: University of North Carolina Press).

Thongchai, W. (1994) *Siam Mapped; a history of the geo-body of a nation* (Chiang Mai: Silkworm).

Tieku, T. (2004) 'Explaining the Clash and Accommodation of Interests of Major Actors in the Creation of the African Union', *African Affairs* 103, 249–67.

Tønnesson, S. (2004) 'Globalising National States', *Nations and Nationalism* 10:1/2, 179–94.

Tordoff, W. (2002) *Government and Politics in Africa* (Basingstoke: Palgrave Macmillan).

Tran, N. T. & Reid, A. (eds) (2006) *Vietnam: borderless histories* (Madison: University of Wisconsin Press).

Treml, M. (1994) *Geschichte des Modernen Bayern* (Munich; Bayerische Landeszentrale für Politische Bildungsarbeit).

Vasavakul, T. (1995) 'Vietnam: the changing models of legitimation', in M. Alagappa (ed.) *Political Legitimacy in Southeast Asia* (Stanford: Stanford University Press).

Vetik, R., Nimmerfelft, G. & Taru, M. (2006) 'Reactive Identity versus EU Integration', *Journal of Common Market Studies* 44:5, 1079–1102.

Vertovec. S. (2009) *Transnationalism* (London & New York: Routledge).

Vincent, A. (2002) *Nationalism and Particularity* (Cambridge: Cambridge University Press).

Viroli, M. (1995) *For Love of Country: an essay on patriotism and nationalism* (Oxford: Oxford University Press).

Vu, T. (2007) 'Vietnamese Political Studies and Debates on Vietnamese Nationalism', *Journal of Vietnamese Studies* 2:2, 175–230.

Walters, W. & Haahr, J. (2005) *Governing Europe: discourse, governmentality and European integration* (London & New York: Routledge).

Weekley, K. (1999) 'Introduction', in A. Davidson & K. Weekley *Globalisation and Citizenship in the Asia-Pacific* (New York: St. Martin's Press).

Welch, S. & Wittlinger, R. (2011) 'The Resilience of the Nation State: cosmopolitanism, Holocaust memory and German identity', *German Politics and Society* 29:3, 38–54.

Welt-Online (2009) '*Wirbel um Becksteins Äußerung über Wähler*', 3/8/09, http://www.welt.de/muenchen/article2333391/Wirbel-um-Becksteins-Aeusserung-ueber-Waehler.html. Accessed 15 November 2010.

Werbner, P. (1999) 'Global Pathways. working-class cosmopolitans and the creation of transnational ethnic worlds', *Social Anthropology* 7:1, 17–35.

Werbner, R. (1996) 'Introduction', in R. Werbner & T. Ranger (eds) *Postcolonial Identities in Africa* (London & New Jersey: Zed).

Wertsch, J. (2008) 'Collective Memory and Narrative Templates', *Social Research* 75:1, 133–56.

Wesley, M. (2000) 'Nationalism and Globalization in Australia', in L. Suryadinata (ed.) *Nationalism and Globalization: east and west* (Singapore: Institute for Southeast Asian Studies).

Wiebe, R. (2002) *Who we are; a history of popular nationalism* (New Jersey & Woodstock: Princeton University Press).

Wiener, A. (1998) *'European' Citizenship Practice: building institutions of a non-state* (Boulder, CO & Oxford: Westview).

Wilder, G. (2005) *The French Imperial Nation-State* (Chicago: University of Chicago Press).

Wilson, W. (1984) *The Papers of Woodrow Wilson Vol. 45* (Princeton, NJ: Princeton University Press).

Winter, T. (2006) 'When Ancient Glory Meets Modern Tragedy', in L. Chau-Pech Ollier & T. Winter (eds) *Expressions of Cambodia: the politics of tradition, identity and change* (London: Routledge).

Winter, T. & Chau-Pech Ollier, L. (2006) 'Introduction', in L. Chau-Pech Ollier & T. Winter (eds) *Expressions of Cambodia: the politics of tradition, identity and change* (London: Routledge).

Wolters, O. W. (1999) *History, Culture and Region in Southeast Asian Perspectives* (Ithaca, NY: Cornell University Press).

Wood, T. D. (2006) 'Touring Memories of the Khmer Rouge', in L. Chau-Pech Ollier & T. Winter (eds) *Expressions of Cambodia: the politics of tradition, identity and change* (London: Routledge).

Wright, S. (2008) 'Citizenship Tests in Europe: editorial introduction', *International Journal on Multicultural Societies* 10:1, 1–9.

Yeh, E. (2002) 'Will the Real Tibetan Please Stand Up! Identity politics in the Tibetan Diaspora', in P. C. Klieger (ed.) *Tibet, Self and the Tibetan Diaspora* (Boston, Cologne & Leiden: Brill).

Yoshino, K (1999) *Consuming Ethnicity and Nationalism* (Honolulu: University of Hawai'i Press).

Index